MY FIRST 80 YEARS

MY FIRST
80 YEARS

by CLARENCE POE

CHAPEL HILL

The University of North Carolina Press

Library of Congress Catalog Card Number
63-21079

A Dedication

To these fourteen men and women, one from each Southern state, who helped me in my efforts to make the South "A Land of Plenty, a Land of Rural Comradeship" and win nation-wide "Equality for Agriculture," this book is dedicated.

TEXAS: Eugene Butler, the son of Dr. Tait Butler and my able successor as president and editor-in-chief of *The Progressive Farmer*

LOUISIANA: Seaman A. Knapp, whose farm demonstration idea led to world-wide "agricultural extension"

OKLAHOMA: George Miller, who was a gracious host in 1905 on his 110,000-acre "101 Ranch"

MISSISSIPPI: Stephen D. Lee, Confederate general and later beloved A. & M. College president

ARKANSAS: W. C. Lassetter, my comrade in editorial work who could "disagree without being disagreeable"

TENNESSEE: Dr. Edwin Mims, who shared my enthusiasm for great books and poets—and Southern progress

KENTUCKY: Jesse Stuart, the "bull tongue plow" novelist of our mountain people

ALABAMA: Alexander Nunn, courageous fighter for farmers' rights—and anybody else's

GEORGIA: Martha Berry, whose Berry School is a perpetual memorial to her love for all underprivileged youth

FLORIDA: Dr. C. W. Burkett, charter director of our company and co-founder of Alpha Zeta fraternity

SOUTH CAROLINA: Mrs. David R. Coker, who popularized camellias and worked to make Dixie "A Land of Beauty"

NORTH CAROLINA: Susan Dismukes Poe, my gifted teacher-mother who loved me, taught me, and inspired me

VIRGINIA: Virginius Dabney, one of many fellow editors who cheered me on

MARYLAND: W. F. Massey, who preached the moral duty of soil-saving and proclaimed "We are tenants of the Almighty"

Preface:
80 Years of Fights,
Fun, and Friendships

MY TITLE SUGGESTS CHANGES, MANY CHANGES.

"Farmers," my friend Dean Colvard of Mississippi said to me, "now do only one thing the way they did when you were born. They still put on their pants one leg at a time!"

In both town and country other changes have been legion. In the 1880's it was said, "To become President a man better be born in a log cabin." Now there are no log cabins to be born in. Then it was said, "The hand that rocks the cradle rules the world." Now there are few cradles for anyone to rock. Then a mule, one-horse wagon, and one-horse plow were often thought equipment enough to be called "a farm." Now, "in order to farm," as someone recently said, "you need enough money to start a bank—and enough nerve to rob one!"

How great have been other major changes in my lifetime is suggested by the fact that I first thought of calling this book *I Have Lived 7,000 Years*—meaning that in my lifetime changes have occurred as dynamic and far-reaching as all others since Homer and Abraham. When I was born, all around me were men who had been slaves and other men who had owned slaves. It was a time when men who had fought in or lived through four years of one of history's blood-

iest and most decisive wars were comrades of my father and
my kin; a time when all over the South more people were
engaged in farming than in all other occupations combined;
a time when the kingship of cotton was virtually absolute
and usurious "time prices" credit based on cheap cotton represented practically the South's second form of slavery; a
time when more than one-fourth of the white people in my
state could not read and write, and a far greater proportion
of our colored people; a time when farmers believed that to
get ahead one must simply trust signs of the moon and zodiac
plus five rules concisely summarized in Josh Billings' lines:

> He who by farmin wood git rich
> Must rake and hoe and dig and sich,
> Work hard all day, sleep hard all nite,
> Save every cent and not git tite.

Another title I considered for this book was *A Happy
Warrior in the Changing South.* For I am glad that in the
revolutionary changes that have taken place since the 1880's
my constant aim has been to be not merely an onlooker but a
fighter. "Fight for all underdogs" has been almost a lifetime
motto. But along with my fighting, this book is also a story of
multi-varied friendships—from field hands to White House
occupants—that went with the fighting and of the fun that
went with both.

As an elderly friend said to me when I began writing, "We
who have lived through this period owe it to all future Southerners (and others) to report life exactly as we have seen it.
If we fail to do this, the picture of the South in this era, as it
will exist in the minds of future Americans, will be either too
romantic or too distorted to be either accurate or cred-
ible." To recount the too-little-publicized heroism of men and
women in these years has seemed to me a high privilege.

What then is the greatest value of these chapters of personal experience? It is not that they report in part, and only in part, my own life story from the 1880's into the 1960's. Rather it is that they reflect with almost uncanny duality my story and the story of the South and its people in this eighty-year period, their varying victories and defeats, their triumphs and disasters.

At the very beginning we find my struggle in the first month of my life with a disease science has now conquered but which threatened to inter me in one of the numberless "short graves" that still bear pathetic testimony to the ancient ravages of the diseases of infancy. Next were years of happy rural comfort, followed by years of crushing poverty caused by poor farming, crop failures, and the indifference of a government that held out no helping hand to "the needy when he crieth, the poor also, and him that hath no helper." Wretchedly poor were most public schools, but this situation was partly remedied in my own case by the love and persistence of a teacher-mother. There was my own early determination to become an editor, with seemingly no chance to do so, followed by my becoming editor of *The Progressive Farmer* at age eighteen. Bitter partisanship had hurt the magazine so greatly that many predicted defeat for me when, on a shoestring, I organized a company to own and operate it —but its circulation grew from 5,000 in 1903 to 1,000,000 in 1930. Then, however, there followed almost immediately the near-universal bankruptcy of the Hoover Era, which threatened financial destruction for both me and my business.

My life? Is it not rather All Men's Life—or nearly so? For all the men and women whose generous friendships have enriched my fourscore years and to the God who has prospered me beyond my deserving I am forever grateful.

CLARENCE POE

Raleigh, N.C.

Acknowledgments

FOR HELP IN PREPARING THIS BOOK MY ESPECIAL THANKS GO TO Betsy Seymour, who also assisted me with *True Tales of the South at War: How Soldiers Fought and Families Lived, 1861-1865;* to librarians and archivists in Raleigh, Chapel Hill, and elsewhere; to members of our *Progressive Farmer* staff and my own family; and to those included in my formal dedication. Miss Clyde Smith, Mrs. James W. Reid, and Charles Poe rendered valuable assistance. In addition to leaders in our company already mentioned, I wish to thank warmly for their interest and encouragement Miss Oris Cantrell, Romaine Smith, and editors of our five localized editions as follows: Texas, C. G. Scruggs; Mississippi-Arkansas-Louisiana, Ed Wilborn; Kentucky-Tennessee, Pete Head; Georgia-Alabama-Florida, Otis Copeland; Carolinas-Virginia, Joe Elliott.

The sketch of my Uncle Stephen Moore included in this book is taken from a chapter I wrote for *Culture in the South* many years ago.

Contents

Preface   vii

1. The Country I Was Born In   1

   *Old home charming with flowers, trees, antiques /
   Happy social life / Love-hallowed labor / Negro playmates and Black Bob / Rural schools, a steamboat, arrowheads, stars / Webster's Blueback stupid / Rural wit and
   wisdom*

2. Country Kin   25

   *Sketches of father and uncles—self-reliant, individualistic,
   live-at-home small farmers / Aunt Alice, courageous
   widow / Mother won gold medal / Any kin to Edgar Allan
   or football Poes? (A run was "poetry in motion") / Julia
   Tutwiler, Alabama educator*

3. Doctors and Preachers   43

   *Epidemics: typhoid, diphtheria, measles, yellow fever /
   Seven children in one family died of typhoid / Rare and
   racy stories of Dr. Budd / Revivals, shouting sisters /
   Eternal punishment vs. God is love / Tribute to pioneer
   preachers*

4. "Here Once the Embattled Farmers Stood"   56

Disastrous crop failure worsens hard time / Farmers turn to Farmers' Alliance and Colonel Polk in "Agrarian Rebellion" / "Raise less corn and more hell" / Alliance becomes nation-wide political power and boosts "Polk for President" / Gardner and Allan Nevins praise Alliance revolt

5. A Country Boy Makes City Friends   68

My heartfelt appeal for better schools brings invitation to serve as assistant editor / Raleigh's old families, often war-ruined, received me cordially / A foolish mistake / Pretty girls, stars, and summer vacations

6. Building *The Progressive Farmer*   87

I became editor, 1899 / Organized company to buy it, 1903 / Became president / "A leader, not a boss" / Dr. Butler becomes vice president and co-editor / Raleigh, Birmingham, Dallas, Memphis regional offices / Reliability of advertising guaranteed / Circulation grew from 5,000 in 1903 to 1,000,000 in 1930

7. "To Be Young Was Very Heaven"   107

Peele, Daniels, McIver organized Watauga Club to promote education and industry / Page denounces reactionary leaders as "Mummies" / Says state needed "a few first-class funerals" / His "Forgotton Man" speech historic

8. We Fought the Man in the Moon   128

Costly superstitions about moon and zodiac signs exposed / Too little livestock / I preach "Two-Armed Farming" / Dr. Knapp's farm demonstration idea sweeps the South

9. The Ananias Club—and Other Causes   145

Child labor in factories shocking / Temperance legislation / I support World War I and offer service / Later with Nelson Rockefeller in Point Four Program

10. Governor Aycock As I Knew Him   160

He risked his political life to turn the furies of a bitter political campaign into constructive channels of education, progress, and racial good will / Equally famous as a lawyer, stories of his eloquence and humor gleaned from courthouses and United States Supreme Court

11. The Worlds Across the Seas   175

Studies I made and experiences I encountered / First in Europe / Then in Japan, Korea, China, India / Again in Ireland, England, Germany, Denmark / Surprising comparisons and contrasts with world today

12. A Lifelong Crusade for Better Health   196

Old-time epidemics / My part in historic campaign against hookworm / Served on Hospital and Medical Care Commission, American Commission on Hospital Care, and Committee on Health Needs of the Nation / Presented creed on equal health rights for all

13. Poe for Governor   210

But for outbreak of World War II South-wide "Campaign for Balanced Prosperity in the South, 1940-1950" might have proved my life's supreme achievement

14. When the Great Depression Came   223

Foreclosures, banks, businesses failed everywhere / Un-employed men wept / 1932 was "Suicide Year" / But to stronger men a fierce, primal, masculine response to a

CONTENTS

cyclonic challenge / Only Negroes happy / "My bank will keep open till Hell freezes over" but it waited for no freeze / "You can't escape bankruptcy" I was told. "No, I shall fight it out." I did. / Groucho Marx's comment

15. Presidents I Knew   232

"What qualities does one need to achieve success as an individual and as a leader of men? What difficulties have you had to conquer?" / The remarkably frank, intimate, face-to-face answers Eisenhower and Truman gave me will surprise and delight, as should my lively contacts and friendships with Theodore Roosevelt, Wilson, Franklin Roosevelt, Hoover

16. About Myself   253

Life at my country home: farm activities, many guests, games and sports for children / "Sunny Jim" for myself / "Seaside University" in the summer / William Poe / Cherished ideals from Confucius, Bryce, and Kipling / My personal "Ideals for a Working Day"

MY FIRST 80 YEARS

CHAPTER ONE

The County I Was Born In

I WAS "ORIGINALLY BORN," AS AN OLD NEGRO USED TO PUT IT, in Chatham County, North Carolina, January 10, 1881. And I still maintain I could hardly have chosen a better place to be born or a better time.

Why was it a good time? First, because farm yields and prices seemed relatively good and secure. Secondly, the Civil War was fifteen years behind us and the long overdue withdrawal of Federal troops and carpetbag rule in 1877 had given both sections new friendship for each other. Furthermore, Americans not only enjoyed peace at home but never expected to become embroiled in any "entangling alliances" or foreign wars. Finally, there was then a truly profound belief in an oncoming world-wide triumph of Christian missions and the Christian religion in Asia and Africa. (Europe, including Russia, was already Christian.)

So it was that in 1881 not only my native community and county but our whole country looked happily forward to a long-time continuation of Peace, Progress, and Prosperity. And with this background for our thinking we may next consider why Chatham was a good place in which to begin my earliest occupation of this planet.

My birthplace was within about two miles of what geog-

1

raphers say is the exact center of North Carolina. The home
my father inherited was on the main highway from the Salem-
Greensboro area to Fayetteville, long the head of navigation
on the Cape Fear River. Not far away, at the junction of Haw
and Deep Rivers, was the now-vanished town of Haywood
which tradition (and I think ample records) says lacked only
one vote of being selected as the capital of North Carolina—
and Haywood folks claimed that a too-liberal use of wine by
Wake's representatives explained the victory for the present
site of Raleigh!

Chatham had long been a county of more than average intelligence and literacy, resulting in part from the influence of
two or three notable academies, one for girls at Rock Rest
and the long-famous Bingham School for boys which my
Grandfather Dismukes attended when it was located in Pittsboro. The fact that the University at Chapel Hill was only a
few miles from the Chatham line also attracted Chatham
students who might not otherwise have attended any college.
There had also been a better than usual distribution of wealth
in Chatham, a fairly large number of slaves, but few very
large slaveholders.

All over Chatham relatives of my father's family and my
mother's were scattered—the Poes, Hackneys, and Moores,
having come from England via Virginia; the Dismukes (originally spelled Desmeaux) branch from France via Virginia;
and the Pattersons from Scotland. (Ambassador James Bryce
once told me that in England the name Poe was pronounced
in two syllables—Po-e—and an English lady I met in India
always insisted on calling me Mr. Po-e.) Other families to
which my mother was related, the Shepperds and Strudwicks,
lived in adjoining Orange County.

My father, his two brothers, and four sisters, all settling
within three miles of the old homes of their parents and
grandparents, formed a rare intimacy of contacts and affec-

tion such as modern conditions almost universally prohibit. I have never forgotten what an intelligent old man said about my home neighborhood long afterward: "I used to visit at your grandfather's place. In those days all the Chatham folks loved everybody and loved one another. They loved to have dinners and invite their parents, their brothers and sisters, and uncles and aunts." Several families of friendly neighbors including my Grandfather Dismukes lived on the high hills around Pittsboro. When one family wanted to have a party— then always called a "sociable"—they would simply build a heavily smoldering "brush heap" fire at nightfall. Its ascending smoke was a "Come one, come all" welcome to friends.

It was such people in our little country community who provided the cultural and moral atmosphere in which I grew up. These were such people as James Whitcomb Riley sang of in this period—

> The good old-fashioned people—
> The hale, hard-working people—
> The kindly country people
> 'At Uncle used to know.

To modern economists they would be considered barely middle-class people. But to the humanely discerning they were nothing but first-class people. Nobody was looked up to because he was rich or down upon because he was poor. They were never satiated with life but accepted its daily difficulties as challenges to meet and overcome. When necessity justified it they could look any unprincipled man in the eye and tell him where to go—but their great preference was to take some yearning youth by the hand and help him to heights he should aspire to. They prized honor more than honors and valued their own self-respect and the freedom to speak their own sincere thought more than any riches that might be won by those who "bend the pregnant hinges of the knee that thrift may follow fawning."

The old country home where I was born, a sturdy six-room one-and-a-half-story frame house with a tall rock chimney at each end, a separate kitchen and dining room, smokehouse, barns, carriage house, and screw cotton gin, had been built long before the Civil War. A wide porch ran the entire length of the house on the sunny south side with inviting benches along the wall. On them in summer my father took a midday rest while his work team enjoyed a similar respite from labor in field or forest. My grandfather had long before planted sycamores whose gleaming white bodies, now grown quite large, bordered the picket fence that enclosed the yard. A large "horse apple" tree was nearby, also a vegetable garden, a grape arbor, and apple, peach, and pear trees.

In the house were such now extinct objects as a flint-lock musket, powder horn, a spinning wheel, a flax wheel, a four-poster bed with accompanying trundle bed, an old-fashioned Seth Thomas clock adorned by the face of Martha Washington, candle molds and candle snuffers, the saddle-bags my grandfather had used as deputy sheriff, a carefully-kept parlor, a Confederate bayonet, and chinaware of a beautiful blue, probably Spode. There was also silverware that my mother had inherited from her great-grandparents, Jacob and Pamela Shepperd, whose son Augustine was for thirty years a North Carolina Whig Congressman.

My mother was a great lover of flowers and I still recall some lines from a poem she had me memorize—

> Then wherefore had they birth?
> To minister delight to man,
> To beautify the earth.

So I never think of our front yard without thinking of the deep fragrance of hyacinths, the early gold of jonquils, the later beauty of lilies, the early flowering of japonica, and the fragrance of syringa.

At least two objects of historic significance added interest to my old home farm. Directly in front of our house was "Schoolhouse Hill." On it had been built in ante-bellum days one of the first "free school" buildings in whose construction the state of North Carolina and the counties co-operated and pioneered around 1840. This "Poe School" my father, his brothers, and sisters had attended in the 1850's. And ever after they remembered a red-letter day in 1856 when the whole school had been dismissed to go to Egypt, a village two miles away on Deep River, to join in a county-wide jubilee celebration welcoming the first steamboat to anchor there. With the aid of great stone locks at intervals on the river, it had sailed from Fayetteville, about fifty miles away, and the Egypt locks were still visible when I left Chatham.

The other objects of historic significance on our farm were, strangely enough, some of the old steel cannon mounts and axles which had once heard the shouts of John Brown's raiders at Harper's Ferry. Later the Confederates transported the material to Fort Fisher. Still later it was shipped up the Cape Fear to Fayetteville. To escape capture by the Yankeees the Confederate authorities then had had the equipment transported by steamboat to Egypt, and after Appomattox it belonged to "anybody who wants it." So my father had hauled home some of the former Harper's Ferry cannon axles and they were rusting in our cornfield when I was born!

In and around my home were also many seemingly unimportant places that it may nevertheless be interesting to mention because we now see nothing like them—the bit of saline marsh known as "the salt lick" because deer frequently used to come there and from which my kinsfolk secured much welcome venison; the cotton and cornfields in which my father and grandfather had worked and the meadow strip from which we hauled loads of hay more fragrant (to me) than any perfume Milady can now import from Paris; the log cabin with the mud-daubed chimney where Black Bob and his family lived; our front yard from which we could hear the occasional music of hounds trailing a fox in daytime and the more frequent nocturnal music of men and boys with well-trained dogs in hot pursuit of coons and 'possums; the bee tree we once robbed of honey; the place where Captain Sorrell of the Revolutionary War had lived; an old, old graveyard, probably dating back to 1750, with an oak that in its encircling growth had left visible only a fraction of an ancient headstone; the sassafras trees from whose roots we made tea in springtime and the lowgrounds where pungent wild cresses were then found; the chinquapin bushes, then a common source of edible nuts and now seemingly extinct.

What kind of cavalcades traveled the ancient road in front of my house? There were covered wagons often drawn by over-burdened mules or horses; uncovered wagons and buggies, carriages or "rockaways" as they were sometimes called; occasionally an oxcart; and of course many people traveling afoot, including Negroes with heavy loads on their heads. For example, in carrying water from a spring a Negro woman sometimes carried one bucket on her head and one in each hand. Just before Christmas came wagons loaded with tempting red apples from the mountain country to fill Christmas stockings. Occasionally came some music lover, carrying a banjo or fiddle with him; I still recall the beautiful notes of a violin I once heard at a long distance from some countryman on the highway. About Christmas, too, peddlers carried remarkably heavy loads on their backs with an astonishing variety of articles then not usually found in country stores and designed especially to appeal to feminine interests.

Of especial charm for me was the old covered bridge across Deep River two miles from home—and the never-to-be-forgotten rhythm of the horses' hooves echoing against roof and rafter as men and women crossed the bridge on horseback or in carriage, buggy, or wagon. Long afterward in distant Florence, Italy, I was to hear at duskfall the incalculably more thunderous music made by a seemingly mile-long regiment of Italian cavalry crossing the Arno and to recall at that time with hardly less delight the music made by horses and horsemen on a long-vanished bridge of my boyhood.

The countryfolk of Chatham were a hardy breed. Of Old Man Jehu Hart, the only Mexican War veteran in our community, it was said that he could bite a tenpenny nail in two with his teeth! When my doughty Uncle Jordan Tysor got a severe case of religion and couldn't wait for warm weather to be immersed, they had to break the ice in Rocky River for him and the preacher to perform the ceremony! Uncle Jordan survived it to die at age ninety-eight. He was the only man I ever saw who was born in the 1700's and could conceivably have seen George Washington!

Everybody, of course, rode horseback, and my grandfather and Aunt Rachel even made the trip from Georgia to North Carolina and back on horses. "My horse broke his all-time speed record one night when a panther screamed behind me," Grandfather Poe used to say.

Physical prowess was much admired. Nearly every man liked to boast of his skill as a wrestler, how much weight he could lift or tote, how many rails he could split in a day, how much cotton he could pick. Especially important was that combination of strength, judgment, and courage needed to break and manage unruly colts, stubborn oxen, and unpredictable mules. "Folks talk about horse sense," as thoughtful observers would say, "but mule sense beats horse sense any day!"

At that time many people still believed in ghosts. An old man named Oldham whose doorway was loosely fastened by a chain on a nail used to tell how he would hear a lost and loved daughter come and rattle the chain night after night. Most superstitions were fairly harmless, such as a woman turning her apron wrongside out to avert bad luck when a rabbit crossed her path. But one superstition certainly brought bad luck to every friend who came within smelling distance; this was the belief that the malodorous asafetida, worn around a child's neck, would ward off certain children's diseases.

That countryfolks have long memories has become proverbial and was proved by the observance of "Old Christmas" by many people when I was a boy. In the change to the Gregorian calendar in 1752 eleven days were dropped out and many devout old-timers insisted that in order to correct this loss in days, January 6 was the true Christian date everybody should observe as Christmas.

Of course men were supposed to be the dominant partners in a marriage, although the wiles of women no doubt prevented this from actually happening in many circumstances. At any rate one of my old friends, Oran Johnson, tried to take no chances. On waking up the morning after his marriage, he pointed to his trousers hanging on the chair and said, "Mary, if you are going to wear the breeches, get up *now* and put them on. Otherwise I'll put them on and we'll live accordingly!"

Often nowadays I hear people speak of expensive weddings, all of which reminds me of my boyhood friend, Eli Dowdy. He was an old bachelor who had long been courting his "Miss Emily." But when she finally accepted him he lost no time. He put her in his new one-horse wagon and drove with her to Egypt. There he called a store clerk who was a magistrate to come to the wagon along with a friend as a witness. The ceremony was over in about as little time as it has taken me to report the romance, and they lived happily ever after. Countryfolks have a reputation for being reserved in demonstrations of affection, but at least I never heard of any Chathamite approaching the reserve Dr. Ralph W. Sockman attributes to a silent Vermont farmer who, on his golden wedding anniversary, said to his wife, "Martha, I've always loved you and several times I've been almost tempted to tell you!"

Back in those days there was a great deal of nonconformity in politics, religion, and everything else, along with a frankness and sincerity that are sometimes suppressed nowadays. For example, Great-aunt Rachel said, "Parents tell their children, 'God made you.' Well, God made Adam and Eve, but *folks* have made all the others." Another such original character, a lively old lady in her seventies, once said, "They say men are so bad that they can't get to heaven. Well, if there are no men there, I don't want to go myself."

My rural kin in old Chatham did not merely live in a rural atmosphere physically speaking; they lived also in an atmosphere in which a genuinely rural philosophy prevailed. From the activities of farm life they gathered most of their proverbs, some of which have been continuously useful to me. Always in any movement I have entered into I have remembered the importance of trying to get every individual to take some active part, recalling a wise observation made by some countryman long ago, "No dog ever enjoyed a hunt unless he did some of the barking!" About the need for setting a definite time for getting things done I could quote my Uncle Stephen: "It's all right to plant some corn on June 20, but June 21 is entirely too late." About disagree-

able zealots in any cause who keep on making trouble even
after the issue has been finally decided: "A chicken will
flop around awhile after its head is cut off." About people
who even though other people are ready to help them will
not help themselves, my father used to tell this folk tale,
probably handed down through generations: "A man who
pertinaciously refused to do any kind of work and was starving was being carried for burial when a benevolent onlooker
said, 'Don't do that; I'll give the man a bushel of corn.' The
sluggard raised his head and asked, 'Is it shelled?' 'No,' came
the reply, whereupon the sluggard ordered, 'Then drive on!'"
About the certainty of some unfavorable weather I like to
quote an old Negro who said, "Always we're bound to have
some kind of drouth. If it ain't a dry drouth, it's a wet
drouth." Of a notoriously stingy man my people would say,
"He would skin a flea for its hide and tallow." About a
mule: "When you go to his funeral always do your weeping at the front end." A husband's remark about a hypochondriac wife: "Sally's been complaining and grunting for
nigh onto five years; I do wish she would get well—or
somep'n!" About a very ugly man: "The Lord made him as
ugly as He could and then jumped at him and scared him."
About a very selfish man: "He doesn't lack anything of being a hog except bristles."

It was not just the independence of the individual
countryman but also the interdependence of individuals in
group actions that gave my country community a special
beauty, dignity, and charm. When a child was born, neighbor women attended the mother and one often served as
midwife. Later on, through all life's vicissitudes, through
church and school and community activities, when weddings
occurred, when wheat was to be threshed, corn shucked, or
hogs killed, when a "new ground" clearing called for a log
rolling, or a "house raising" was required to house a newly

married couple, when a sick man got behind with his plowing or a woman became incapacitated by long illness—all these crises merely afforded opportunities to express a neighborliness that was not merely a duty but to a great degree a joy. And when a final illness came, there were always neighbors ready to sit up all night and (with no help from any hired mortician) conduct the funeral, dig the grave with their own hands, and later visit the widow and the fatherless.

Such love hallowed the hard work of men and women I knew. What mother could mind the seeming drudgery of the day's work—the cooking, darning, weaving, washing, sewing—since all of it was done, not for some uncaring boss in a shop or factory, but for "her man" and for the boys and girls they both had nurtured and cherished? What father did not find his long hours at the plowhandles lightened by the knowledge that he was not merely earning a few pieces of silver but producing actual bread and meat for those he loved?

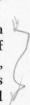

As a child I very much enjoyed and learned something not only from people but from all animals on the farm, the lambs, colts, pups, pigs. And, of course, I learned from my dogs. God pity the town boy who has to grow up without a dog. All I have ever owned have given me pleasure—collie, beagle, bulldog, and pointer. My first dog Ring, a feist, could catch and kill snakes faster than any other dog I have ever seen.

While still toddlingsize I had a lesson in the value of caution. An old gander as big as I was became infuriated at my interfering with his children, and with powerful wings he gave me the worst flogging I ever had. Few people today know that a gander's wings are as powerful for weapons of defense as for flight. Country boys also learned something

from roosters that helped them evaluate loud-talking politicians later on. As humorist Josh Billings said, "What I like
about a rooster is not just the crow that is in him, but the
spurrers he has to back the crow up with!"

Among my earliest playmates were two young Negro
boys, Mose and Rufe, who daily worked in the fields but
played with me in their leisure. I remember that Mose, who
must have been about fourteen when I was five, ran a race
with me, exclaiming trumphantly at the end, "I beat!" My
response was, "Well, I beat last!" I do not know the psychological significance of my answer, but I think it means that
I had put everything I had into my little feet and felt that
that was triumph enough. All my life I have had admiration
for those who come out second or "beat last" but yet deserve praise for doing their utmost. Mose used to say about
me, "Clarence is going to be a book man."

The other young Negro, Rufe, used to delight me by
dancing and singing—

> Ranktum-a-tanktum I'se gwine to de fair
> To see dem ladies' curly hair!

Rufe was almost a genius in wood carving, especially toys,
and of course I considered it a real treat to watch him. He
also charmed me by telling me stories about Uncle Remus
characters that I have never seen in print—a significant loss
to Southern literature since probably no one now alive remembers any of them. And who can say how many such
stories have now been lost forever?

But the Negro who made the deepest impression on me
as a youngster was Bob Wilson or "Black Bob" as we called
him. Bob grew up as the slave of my great-grandfather,
later became a friend and tenant of my father, and was a
real friend of my own boyhood. In an estate inventory of
my great-grandfather's Negroes in 1859 (it doesn't call them

"slaves" but simply "Negroes"), Black Bob, age sixteen, was valued at $941. Still earlier, as small boys, he and my father had played together. I have heard my father laugh and say, "At such times when a stranger drove up to the house, the little Negroes had been taught by their parents to run away and hide [on the chance that such a visitor might sometimes be a slave trader]—and I would run away and hide with them!"

Black Bob was one of twenty-six Negroes owned by my great-grandfather, and on his farm the Negroes seem to have regarded their master more as their friend and provider than as any selfish exploiter of their labors. Not only in life but in death itself this relationship continued, as one unforgotten incident illustrates. Jesse Poe buried his slaves in the family burying ground along with his wife Charity Patterson who had died in 1848, and once when it was proposed to accord to a strange Negro who had died a place in this select burying ground, the slaves rose up in unanimous opposition! As definitely as soldiers in an army they felt themselves bound together in an exclusive, family-like comradeship of service. If they labored to keep their master in moderate comfort, they also worked to support themselves and their families, their very young and their very old—a fact all too often overlooked by historians. Hence no outsider should share with "the Poe Negroes" the privilege of a final resting place alongside that of the master and mistress for whom they had toiled. As a boy of five or six in the 1880's I remember giving Bob a full-page picture of Lincoln that I had found in *The Century Magazine,* saying to him, "Bob, here's a picture of the man who freed you!"

Bob not only had a full fund of common sense but often expressed himself with picturesque vividness. For example, when a neighbor's dog had raided Bob's henhouse, he told my father next day, "I'se got a mighty sharp axe an' if dat dog comes a-nigh my henhouse again, I'se gwine to make two dogs out'n him!"

As a freed man, Bob continued his deep respect and affection for my father, while my father respected Bob's individual rights as a citizen in the new order into which both had come. I well remember how respectfully but definitely Bob made known his support of "Duckery," meaning Colonel Dockery, the Republican candidate for governor—and my father made no effort to prevent him from exercising his franchise as he chose.

When both men had grown old, one of my father's last visitors was Black Bob who did not mind walking any distance to show his undiminished affection for "Marse Bill." Nor did the friendly relationship between this black man and the white family he had served end with the death of my father and his brothers. After I left the old home area for service in new fields, whenever word went back home of anything worthwhile I had done or was supposed to have done, Bob was quick to say to anybody who mentioned me, "Clarence is some of my folks!"

I still remember vividly the last day I ever saw Black Bob, a day when I carried my younger son on a visit to our old home place. I introduced Black Bob to him and afterward said to my son: "This is an occasion you must remember as long as you live. For centuries long past no doubt there have been men in your ancestry whom someone called 'Master.' But possibly never again will you or any of your descendants ever see another man who to them will be what Bob called my father—'Marse Bill.'"

All over the South in this period of transition, incidents like these were occurring—the last exchange of acquaintance and understanding between someone who had been a slave

and a younger son or daughter of the former master. Each
such instance was indeed a day of historic symbolism—truly
the end of an era.

Of my childhood neighbors and kin, I remember gratefully that they not only had faith in my future but rein-
forced that faith with continuing inspiration designed to
spur wholesome ambition. Today are not too many boys
and girls turned over entirely to teachers who may not have
the time or inclination to furnish inspiration as well as information? In my youth a great deal was done by both
parents and teachers to make boys believe the truth President Eisenhower once told me his mother had instilled in
him and his brothers, namely, "In America there are no
limits to what a boy may aspire to!" Certainly we were then
very near the time of Lincoln's long leap from log cabin to
White House and similar climbs from poverty to greatness
made by Andrew Jackson, Andrew Johnson, and others.
Pilgrim's Progress, The Autobiography of Benjamin Frank-
lin, John Ploughman's Talks, the heroic counsel of Emerson,
the well-loved poems of Longfellow, Whittier, and numerous passages in our textbooks—all these provided an incentive to achievement that seems somehow lacking in
the more sophisticated curricula of present-day schools. As
Henry Thoreau once wrote, "It is always a recommendation
to me to know that a man has ever been poor. . . . I require
to be assured of certain philosophers that they have once
been barefooted, footsore, have eaten a crust because they
had nothing better, and know what sweetness resides in it."
The mothers and fathers of my day did not deride Longfellow's "Psalm of Life" as being "too moralistic." Thus
when my mother had me "learn by heart" (which was the
common phrase for memorizing) Longfellow's lines, "Lives

of great men all remind us, we can make our lives sublime," it was not strange that I included the phrase in one of my original compositions for Friday evening recitation, adding, "I want to make my life sublime; don't you?"

At four I learned the ABC's from a colorfully decorated box of supposedly superior seed wheat my father had ordered. Then my mother, who had been a teacher, regularly continued to teach me at home and I was nearly seven before starting to school. At that time the "spelling match" (we never said spelling bee) was the highlight of each week's teaching. Like many other youngsters I had somewhat dreaded going to school, but this quickly disappeared after my mother's preparation enabled me to "cut down seven"—that is to say, I moved up seven points from my newcomer-place at the foot of the class by knowing how to spell "horseback."

Just what were the country schools like in physical appearance and teacher personnel seventy years ago? The first one I attended was a small one-room schoolhouse—so small, in fact, that as I look at a picture of it now I hardly see how thirty or forty students squeezed into it each day, plus a teacher with more courage and versatility than formal education. Mostly we were taught spelling and the Three R's. By teachers, pupils, and parents Noah Webster's *Blueback Speller* was regarded as an almost sacred institution. Actually, it was the most illogical piece of educational material I have ever seen. The words it gave for spelling were chosen entirely on the number of syllables in each word and the position of the syllable to be accented. The result was that the child of six, seven, or eight was called on to spell words he might never use, while his *Blueback* ignored many words he would constantly hear in daily conversation.

There was also much emphasis on good penmanship. In

fact, one of the top priority qualifications for a teacher was the ability to write very legibly and neatly at the top of a page some sentence for the pupil to copy several times over as precisely as he could. About one teacher it was a half-whispered scandal that she never could write "a good hand" and that all the "copies" she brought for pupils to emulate had been written at home by her sister!

The teacher was, above everything else, one who merely asked questions about the lesson and tried to correct wrong answers. There were no "grades" and the same pupil might be studying at the same time subjects that would now be taught in the third, fifth, and eighth grades. As there were no required lists of textbooks, some children studied Sanford's *Arithmetic* and some Robinson's *Arithmetic;* the teacher was simply expected to use whatever textbook the child brought. Of course classes were large, and since many people said, "Compulsory attendance is a damnable meddling with control by parents," many children of school age did not attend at all, and many others attended very irregularly. I never remember any child bringing an excuse for nonattendance.

School benches were hard so that we looked forward to "big recess" at the noon hour when all could go outside and play. Often our teachers were so young they joined in and enjoyed the games as much as the pupils did. Occasionally Merritt Burns and I became so engrossed in studying that we stayed indoors in order to learn more about some subject in which we had especial interest. Usually, however, I enjoyed the indoor and outdoor sports and had my share of fistfights with "Fat Lemons" and other boys my size.

But real excitement came at commencement time, or "school closing" as we then called it. The most gifted pupils were put on the program for declamations, and parents of all the children were invited to attend the exercises. Pupils of all ages recited favorite poems or orations, all the way from the youngest participant beginning—

> You'd scarce expect one of my age
> To speak in public on the stage

to poems inciting to life's highest duties—

> For the cause that lacks assistance,
> For the wrong that needs resistance,
> For the future in the distance,
>   And the good that I can do.

More cheerful were the Negro dialect poems, such as a favorite recitation of mine beginning—

> I'se gwine ter preach a sermon
> And dis here am de text—
> Dat half-way doin's ain't no count
> For dis world nor de next.

Frequently some amateur play was presented. Everybody dressed up in his very best clothes, parents came, and we had a grand time.

My education in those days came from many different sources: my mother regularly taught me at home; I went to public school during the four-month term; I attended the extended subscription school terms financed by tuition payments of the more interested parents; and I boarded with an uncle some distance away to take advantage of an extra school term in his district while my school was not in session.

One year when I was nine years old I attended the graded schools in Greensboro (population 3,000) where we moved in order for my father to get extra income to help pay off the mortgage on his farm and also to get better school advantages for my sister and myself. Upon applying for school entrance and being asked what textbooks I had studied, the sophisticated town students almost laughed out loud when I presented, among others, my Webster's *Blueback Speller*. But I must pay these town boys and girls the tribute of saying that they later cheered me on as I kept up with the best of them and made the highest grade in my class. Maybe my teacher, Miss Lizzie M. Lindsay, had been country-bred herself; anyhow she appeared to take all the more interest in me because I was a country boy in a class of town boys and girls. To this day I remember my pride when she read one of my compositions aloud to the class. All my teachers, in fact, were more than generous in their interest in me.

My life-long interest in better schools was no doubt increased also by the fact that the job my father had secured in Greensboro required a greater degree of education than the state had provided for the youth of his day, and we soon returned to our old home farm.

A generation ago a great many distinguished men and women all over America would have joined me in saying that one of the greatest friends and most powerful educational influences of their childhood was the incalculably delightful and inspiring weekly, *The Youth's Companion*. Founded in Boston about 1827, it was for a hundred years one of the foremost cultural influences in American life. It contained entertaining articles, stories, and poems. But it also had discussions of highly important subjects by the foremost men and women of America and abroad, for example, Prime Minister William E. Gladstone of England. Always there was one article at a special place of a definitely spiritual but not "preachy" or denominational quality—a series that unquestionably had great character-building influence on the devoted followers of this weekly magazine. For me the day *The Youth's Companion* came was by all odds the red letter day of the week. I do not believe any other publication in American history has been loved by so many people. Now in the hectic competition of commercially minded publishers will any other publication ever again be so much loved? In my case appreciation was heightened by the fact that its editors could take time to write an encouraging note to a fifteen-year-old farm boy for stories he sent them, saying they were "most promising" to have been written by one of my age.

Books and magazines were an important part of my education. My mother had grown up reading *Harper's Magazine;* I also enjoyed *Harper's Round Table* for young people and *McClure's Magazine* when it was carrying Ida M. Tarbell's life of Lincoln as a farm boy. But there was no public library within fifty miles. Not many years later I especially rejoiced to help get a special state appropriation (on a matching basis) to provide libraries for small rural schools. In my home community a book was then a precious possession and some then owned and kept had been printed in the 1700's when the old-fashioned f-like *s* was standard usage. Most of the books were of solid character, such as *Pilgrim's Progress* and *John Ploughman's Talks*. America was so young that a great part of the history people read was European history, with especial attention to noted heroes of England and the Continent. In fact, the influence of English life still so colored American country life when I was a boy that a dime was called a shilling and a nickel, a sixpence. But one popular book gave me and my kinfolks a comprehensive glimpse of world history such as most young people do not even now possess. This was Peter Parley's *History of the World*. Written in simple and entertaining style, it summarized the most interesting facts and colorful anecdotes about the great civilizations and governments, and the foremost figures in Oriental and European as well as American history.

The duty of reading the Bible was universally emphasized and every word in it was supposed to be taken literally. It almost seemed that people believed everything in it except perhaps the phrase "male and female created He them." From an almost complete ignoring of sex at that time we have now gone to its intensely commercialized ultra-glorification with, I think, serious results to the national character. Just how far we have come may be indicated by the fact that when I was a boy I heard it said, "There are parts of Shakespeare no lady ought to read." *The Scarlet Letter* was almost alone among American novels dealing with sex and then only against a definitely religious background. When a demand came for books such as *What a Boy Ought to Know* and *What a Young Man Ought to Know* or their feminine counterparts, such discussions gained acceptance only because the books were written by a minister—the Reverend Sylvanus Stall, D.D. About the only sentence referring to unlawful sex that I recall in any magazine in my teens was in a *Scribner's* article in which Walter Wycoff was permitted to refer to a woman on the street as "giving the look that takes the surest hold on hell." Much later Edward W. Bok startled America when he printed in the *Ladies' Home Journal* a bold article about the menace of syphilis and started a frank facing up to the problem in which *The Progressive Farmer* later joined.

It should not be thought, however, that humor did not have an important place in books and publications of the time. In the only copy I have of a publication, *The Communicator*, edited by my Grandfather Dismukes in 1847, most of the front page is taken up by a humorous dialect story he wrote—humorous even though it was written to advance the temperance cause by reporting the fantastic adventures of two drunks crossing the same fence several times one night in their blunderingly erratic efforts to get home! The standard columnist of the time was Bill Arp who was a sort of combination Walter Lippmann and Will Rogers. Especially enjoyed was the dialect humor of Josh Billings. I do not know just when the first Mark Twain book reached our community but I know I was quite a small boy when the whole neighborhood laughed over "The Celebrated Jumping Frog of Calaveras County."

One of my chief boyhood interests was collecting Indian arrowheads. At that time we were not so far removed from Indian occupation of the land, and arrowheads could be found in much greater numbers and variety than now. By the time I left home for Raleigh I had acquired such an extensive and varied collection that when I later saw the arrowhead collection in the Smithsonian Institution I sincerely felt that I had several types that equaled or surpassed theirs. About them I felt as did Henry Thoreau, "Why make so great ado about the Roman and Greek and neglect the Indian? This arrow-headed character is probably more ancient than any other."

But of my boyhood hobbies one gave me far more delight than any other—astronomy. Of all the books I have ever owned, I doubt that any one has given me more pleasure than an old battered astronomy book published in 1833 and given me by my Aunt Martha. The author was Elihu Burritt known as "The Learned Blacksmith." At that time some men who could not go to college would develop an absorbing interest in some branch of science, history, or literature and win genuine distinction in that field. Burritt took up astronomy and became so enthusiastic that he wrote and published the book I have referred to. Somehow the maps had been

torn out of my copy. But it was a constant joy to me to identify the principal stars and constellations by his listing of
those which year after year appeared on the meridian at
8 P.M. each month and fascinating to learn all the stories
from ancient mythology relating to them. Eagerly each summer evening I watched for Vega with its twin attendants
nearing the zenith and red Antares low in the southern sky;
then in autumn I watched Arcturus until it disappeared to
return the next spring. Especially did I enjoy the winter
skies made glorious by the Belt of Orion, the Pleiades, and
Hyades; and I had a year-round interest in the North Star
and the encircling Great Bear as perpetually visible friends.
Without ever really ceasing to practice his trade as a blacksmith, Burritt became one of America's best-known cham-
pions of the only sound rule for solving the slave problem,
namely, compensated emancipation. It almost broke his heart
that neither North nor South would heartily endorse a cause
for which he fought with genuinely religious zeal. A final
postscript to the Burritt story is this: among the future total
eclipses of the sun he reported was one scheduled to occur
May 28, 1900. And sure enough, about one hour before the
predicted event, I climbed to the top of our state capitol
building (I was by that time living in Raleigh) and saw
the world darken precisely at the hour predicted by "The
Learned Blacksmith" in 1833!

Today when Telstar and other scientific discoveries are
opening up new worlds and galaxies to our vision, probably
the most remarkable of all the paragraphs in this old astronomy is the one that reminds the reader that we should
not think of our earth as God's greatest achievement but
only an insignificant atom among His illimitable works—
"only one of the many mansions He has created for His
worshippers; and He may now be at work in regions more

distant than geometry ever measured, creating worlds more manifold than numbers ever reckoned."

What a staggering new vision of the universe did Elihu Burritt thus prepare for me and others as he worked between his jobs as a blacksmith to reveal to us the deepest thoughts he had gleaned from his study of the heavens!

CHAPTER TWO

Country Kin

SOME OF MY HAPPIEST CHILDHOOD MEMORIES ARE OF TIMES
my family went to visit relatives. I remember with especial
happiness a Christmas day visit to my Uncle John Lea's. As
he lived four miles away and the days were short at Christmas time, we got up long before daylight to start on the
trip. He and Aunt Celia had five children, most of them older
than my sister and I, but not enough older to keep them
from enjoying with us all the usual games and sports of the
time along with an exchange of Christmas gifts and of course
a wonderful Christmas dinner. I especially remember recit-
ing Longfellow's poem beginning—

> I heard the bells on Christmas day
> Their old familiar carols play,
> And wild and sweet the words repeat
> Of peace on earth, good will to men.
>
> I thought how, as the day had come,
> The belfries of all Christendom
> Had roll'd along th' unbroken song
> Of peace on earth, good will to men.

What a day of world-wide peace it truly seemed to all of
us when "the belfries of all Christendom" included America

and every nation in Europe, even Russia! Also we felt it a time of "peace and plenty." Not that any of us were rich, but everybody in our community had the basic necessities of life and no consuming eagerness for riches beyond that.

Uncle John proudly showed us his new barn, told us of some banner corn yields he had made, and eagerly discussed the new forward movements in the South as voiced by Henry W. Grady in the *Atlanta Constitution* and Walter H. Page in the *State Chronicle*. Both my mother and her sister, Aunt Celia, had been teachers and could exchange reminiscences of teaching, my mother in North Carolina and Aunt Celia in Mississippi. Aunt Celia had studied art at Greensboro Female College and some of her paintings were hanging in her "parlor"—a room such as every well-to-do family was supposed to maintain and to use only when guests came. Like many other farm boys, my cousin Peyt had a pet squirrel whose tricks amused all of us. He also had goats, kids, and colorful strutting peacocks. Both Uncle John and my father, having served in the Confederate army, had stories to exchange about the war years and preceding years in the Old South. Altogether this was a rarely pleasant day for old and young—typical of many such gatherings friends and kinsfolk enjoyed in a time in many respects happier than our own.

Now when unhappy marriages and divorces are so common as to be typified by the report that in Hollywood "people are marrying more but enjoying it less," it interests me to recall that in my ten years from six to sixteen I do not remember, among all the persons I either knew or heard of, a single case of divorce or a case where someone ended his own life. Even the Negroes, secure in their new found freedom from slavery, revealed contentment in their easy laughter, their good will, and the rich melody of the songs with which they accompanied their daily tasks.

At this point it might be well to consider a typical small farmer of that period and the difficulties he had to overcome after returning from the Civil War and in the agricultural depression of the latter 1880's lasting through the Panic of 1893. The character and record of my own farmer-father should furnish an excellent example. So modest in thought and word was he that I never heard a boast from his lips. A week before his death, when the Confederate cross of honor was pinned on his coat with the words, "I am proud to give this to a brave soldier," he remonstrated good naturedly, declaring that he fought no more than compelled to—preferring to ignore the fact that it was as an early volunteer that he had joined the army.

But it was greater courage than a soldier must have that he displayed in times of trial in later life. It was the time of greatest disappointment that yet seems to me his greatest triumph. He was never rich, but at his old homestead on which his father and his father's father and their slaves had worked, he lived in simple comfort until 1890 when an unfortunate business venture, coupled with an attack of fever at a critical period, swept away all his hard-earned savings and left him resourceless with a mortgaged home. I like to think that then, instead of murmuring, he turned to his old neighbors, rented a smaller farm of more fertile land, and working under other men with as much dignity as he had shown when other men worked for him, he struggled through the terrible years of five- and six-cent cotton until he won back the homestead of his fathers free of debt. Through it all he kept his splendid courage and his merry blue eyes were always ready to laugh at all clean humor. Even when, after sixty years and more of robust health, a trying and painful disease gripped him, his cheerfulness was the envy of many whom fortune favored. A humble Christian, he lived a godly life without cant or show. Firm in his own convictions, but tolerant of other men's views, his spirit happily combined the elements of strength and gentleness. The heritage of such a character is worth more to a son than a golden fortune—and for him who lives it, too, we know that such a life has its reward.

That he was always ready to help the needy and distressed one characteristic incident illustrates. An old sick Negro, bound for some goal of which we did not know, grew too weak and ill to go farther on his pilgrimage when he reached our door. So my family looked after him until the end, after which my father made a rude board coffin with his own hands and interred him in what Judge Bennett calls "the all-embracing democracy of the grave" to await whatever resurrection may come alike to those who once wore "purple and fine linen" or the rags of a pauper Negro.

My father had not only set for me a high example in character but he had been a pioneer in the community in more than one effort to improve farming conditions. He was quick to order a supposedly improved quantity of seed wheat when most farmers used grain from their own crops. He was one of the first Chatham farmers to sow red clover. He subscribed to farm journals and obtained many ideas from them. He had been especially successful in managing the much tangled estate of his father who died in 1868 and who, like so many other man of his period, had "stood security" for friends who later could not or would not pay.

Both of my grandfathers had serious financial losses because of having accommodated friends by "going security" for them on loans. As a matter of fact, this situation was so common throughout the South that a word of explanation should be helpful. I have never heard of a bank existing in my county before the Civil War. Some of the wealthiest men would make loans and, since there were no laws to prevent it, might charge high interest rates and ask for double security. Acceptable collateral at that time consisted mainly of slaves and land. And while the Civil War continued, collateral of varying estimated values was found in the uncounted millions which had been invested in Confederate and state bonds. If we consider that such bonds, slaves, and Confederate money—all three—were absolutely and simultaneously extinguished as sources of wealth and credit in 1865, it is easy to see that the best-intentioned men were often unable to pay the merest fraction of their debts.

Around the middle 1880's my father, his brother Alvis, and my Uncle Stephen found a good millsite on George's Creek which ran through their land. There they built an extensive dam from native stones, with an additional earth dike, and for some years operated a grain mill and saw mill. Of course the relationship of mosquitoes to malaria was not then known. But the mill was abandoned about 1886 for some cause, possibly because the mosquitoes made living uncomfortable regardless of any effects on health.

Maybe because he was the oldest of all my uncles, my Uncle Stephen Moore, who farmed alongside my father on a 150-acre tract, furnished the best illustration of completely self-contained "live-at-home" farming I have ever seen. He "raised his bread and meat," as the country phrase has it. For him the wheat-and-oats threshing was a happy festival of midsummer as was corn shucking in the fall. Strong men tanned by the sun, glowing with health, helped one another at the work, enjoyed meals such as no modern hotel can surpass, and laughed and joked in rare good fellowship. Hog killing also brought neighbors together in the first severe weather of winter.

In those days, I think it should be explained that cattle and hogs ran at large in the woods, while rail fences surrounded and protected the area in which crops were grown.

Each neighbor marked his livestock in the ear with his own special brand. For example, my father's was "a crop and underbit in the right ear, a slit in the left." Hogs grew almost fat on the vast quantities of acorns grown by four or five different types of oaks but were then penned up for final fattening on corn.

Uncle Stephen's and our family made their own bread—"cornbread and biscuit and lightbread" as its three usual forms were called—and also prepared their own meat. Hogs were converted into delicious sausage and souse meat, hams and shoulders; but we also had home-raised beef and mutton at frequent intervals. There were all kinds of vegetables and old-fashioned herbs in a never-neglected garden, an abundance of milk and cream, poultry and eggs, and home-produced honey. One of my earliest memories is that of seeing Uncle Stephen making sorghum cane syrup, a substitute for store-bought syrup or molasses. Nor shall I ever forget the old cider-press that provided him (and many friends) with sweet cider every summer. (A faithful deacon, he never let it get too hard, except for an amount he wished changed into farm-produced vinegar!) He even grew his own tobacco. This he mixed with dried fig leaves (to furnish an added aroma) for smoking in a long-stem reed pipe.

From wool he had sheared from the backs of his own sheep his wife, my Aunt Samantha, wove the homespun of which his clothes were made. His socks, too, whether of cotton or wool, were home-carded, spun, and knitted. Blankets were obtained in exchange for wool from his sheep; beds and pillows were stuffed with feathers from geese raised on his farm. An old-fashioned "lye hopper" (in which he made lye from wood ashes) mixed its product with thriftily-conserved "soap grease" to provide home-made soap for all laundry work. He was his own carpenter and had his own blacksmith shop of the type so memorably described in

Longfellow's poem beginning "Under the spreading chest-
nut tree." The only tar kiln I remember seeing was his. Even
light for night reading or work was largely from home-produced "lightwood knots" such as lighted Lincoln's books for
him as a boy. One gallon of kerosene lasted Uncle Stephen
quite a while. Chickens, eggs, and butter were exchanged at
the local store for small necessities such as coffee, pepper,
and salt; as a rule no money was offered for such things. A
few bales of cotton each year paid taxes, the preacher, doctors' bills, and other unavoidable expenses. He did not make
his own coffin. But George Burns, a neighbor of ours, did
make his long before his death, and kept it under his bed.
In no other respect do I recall anyone who surpassed Uncle
Stephen as a "live-at-home farmer."

With such independence he lived and worked and yet
never seemed overworked or overly hurried. He always
found time for his church meetings, the Farmers' Alliance
and Masonic meetings, public speakings, and the like, and
no home that I have ever known dispensed a more delightful and unaffected hospitality.

After he had passed his threescore years and ten and was
no longer able to work, he said to me: "I sometimes think
it is not quite fair that I did not know the things they know
today about how to save the soil, enrich the land, improve
the seed and manage crops, and save the wastes. With this
knowledge thirty years ago my whole life would have
been different!"

All through life a strong religious faith was the major
influence in his character and conduct. No matter who his
guests might be or how many strangers were included, the
old family Bible was brought out for reading at bedtime by
a lightwood fire or a kerosene lamp, after which all kneeled
for a prayer in which my uncle led. Most of his phrases I
have forgotten. But one that did not then seem significant I

have always remembered: "We thank Thee that we live in a land where every man may worship Thee according to the dictates of his own conscience with no one to molest us or make us afraid." Unquestionably this was a phrase inherited from the earliest days in America when his and my Huguenot ancestors had escaped from religious tyranny in France and my Baptist and Methodist ancestors from the limitations imposed on them in old England and New England. Thus a priceless treasure we now take for granted and almost never mention—freedom of worship—was something to mention with daily gratitude in the days of my Uncle Stephen and our forefathers.

A love of learning and even of teaching seems to have been in the blood of both my mother's and father's families. My grandfather Joseph M. Poe once set out to develop a "subscription school" before the days of public schools. In trying to get a sufficient number of families to "subscribe" the slight tuition fee, he encountered one man whose response my father often mentioned as representing the attitude of more than a few people around 1830. "No, not one child of mine shall go to your school or any other," the old man said. "Education and speculation are the ruination of this country!" My other grandfather, Alexander Hamilton Dismukes, evidently had more success during the relatively few years he was engaged in teaching. Perhaps one reason was that his unfailing sense of humor kept cropping out even in handling the daily lessons. For example, pointing to a geography-book picture of two men looking up at a tall tree in California, he would say to his class, "You can see why they put two men in this picture. The tree is so high it takes two men to see to the top!"

My mother attended one of the state's rather noted academies conducted at Cary (eight miles from Raleigh) by

Professor A. H. Merritt, a school which was also attended by Walter Hines Page. My mother's record there brought her a distinction she seldom or never mentioned but of which she was justifiably proud. In those days of the South's poverty Principal Merritt did not feel able to offer a specially designed gold medal for the student making the finest record but instead offered a gold medal he himself had won at college. This my mother won and later exchanged it at some jeweler's for a beautiful breastpin.

My cousin Tom Poe had a winning personality and I can still see him back home on vacation from Chapel Hill as he sat with my mother on the long porch facing the road by our house and repeated a verse she later had me memorize:

> Live for something; have a purpose
> And that purpose keep in view.
> Half the wrecks that strew life's ocean
> If some star had been their guide
> Might e'en now be riding safely
> But they drifted with the tide.

On one of his vacation trips home when I was eight years old, Tom brought his Greek grammar. Its strange characters fascinated and challenged me, and I soon learned the Greek alphabet and how to write my name in Greek, using the Greek "Kappa" to begin "Clarence," since the Greek alphabet has no C or H. Later I found it not too difficult and quite challenging to get elementary lessons in Greek by studying this book at home.

None of my cousins who attended college found life there made easy for them. They helped themselves and found numerous ways of doing so. Tom Poe, for example, somehow convinced the elders of Gulf Presbyterian Church that he knew enough about painting or could find out enough to justify their giving him the job of painting the church building during his vacation. This involved painting all the way from the ground to the top of the highest steeple I had ever seen. When he finally finished that steeple, he had acquired from me a respect fully equal to that he had won when he convinced me of his mastery of Greek. In other vacation periods he taught school. So did my other cousin, likable Charlie Riddle, while attending Chapel Hill. After Charlie had taught school two or more years during the vacation season in a little rural community in Camden County, so winning was his personality that the people named their postoffice and community for him—a remarkable tribute to a young man who had been only in his early twenties. The name "Riddle" continued to appear on state highway maps until a decade ago. Since my cousin Peyton Fearrington lived a little farther away from me I am not sure by just what means of self-help he managed to get through Trinity College (now Duke) and later take a medical course. But I am sure it required no less industry and resourcefulness than was displayed by my cousins at Chapel Hill and Wake Forest. They did whatever came to hand—as did Governor Hodges, who once told me that in getting through Chapel Hill he won the reputation of being "the most expert dishwasher ever known at that institution."

One of my favorite cousins was also a boyhood comrade and schoolmate, Rom Moore. Rom never thought he had made a success in life. Several of our cousins from nearby farms had gone off and made good in law, medicine, the ministry, or business. Rom had elected to live in and serve his old home community. He took up the work his father left off in the old home church, in the Masonic lodge, and other community organizations; he was everybody's friend and a worker in all good causes. The outpouring of friends when the end came and the sincere and simple tributes of those who loved him indicated rewards worth more than all the money others had accumulated. As someone has well said, "It is better to live a great life than to be a great man," and I have always applauded Carlyle's fine saying, "Oh, it is great and there is no other greatness—to make some nook of God's creation a little better, fairer, more fruitful, and more worthy of God."

My Uncle John Quincy Poe, who was named for the leader of the great Whig party to which my grandfather belonged, was about the jolliest man I have ever known. As my Aunt Alice wrote long ago: "Quincy loved outdoor life. He began to plow by the time he could reach the plow handles and was never happier than when he became big enough to hitch his two mules to a two-horse plow in the spring and begin turning over the soil, whistling and singing as he worked." His brothers and sisters liked school but he didn't. They engaged in church work but he never did. He went to the Civil War but he didn't want to go. After the war was over my Uncle Dan went to every Confederate reunion he could hear of, but Uncle Quince never went at all. Later when he was old and poor he even refused a Confederate pension. If it was charity, he was too proud to receive it. If it was for heroism, he said he hadn't displayed any. He liked to keep away from towns and to patronize the old craftsmen of the community; he was over sixty before he ever wore a store-bought suit or store-bought shoes. Operating a rather small farm he made it provide almost his entire living and rarely left it. He enjoyed visits from friends but would seldom repay them. He made little money but had little use for it; like Thoreau's friend Minott he "was not poor for he did not want riches." He lived so close to nature that his nephews called him "one of Nature's noblemen." Living a generation later than our pioneers he nevertheless liked to live as they did.

Though they differed in many ways he and my father had

a great affection for each other, but neither ever sentimentalized about it. One of the unforgettable experiences of my boyhood occurred when my father became seriously ill and Uncle Quince visited him. After dusk I was for some reason riding horseback and encountered Uncle Quince riding homeward on his horse, weeping like a child. In his last days when the resources of the church were suggested for him he was not interested. "I have tried to do right by everybody," he said, "and I think that is enough." As much as any other man, Uncle Quince reminded me of an unidentified poem, "Hill Farm," published in *Vermont Life:*

> A man, to be a man, must live his life
>   The way he sees it ... not as others see it ...
>   On the lost hill farms beyond the signboards
> Beyond the metal silos and macadam,
>   Now and again you come upon a man
> Who lives his life as men before him lived it,
>   Trusting the past the way he trusts the winter
>   To end in spring—spring when the April promise
>   Of one small blade of grass coming alive
> Assures him all dark meadows will survive.

Although she had three brothers who served the Confederate cause not one of them was more truly a hero than my Aunt Alice (1850-1934). She married young Nat Brown who was industrious and enterprising and they started farming together, expecting eventually to own a farm of their own. But after three years of married life typhoid fever, that arch enemy especially of young people from eighteen to thirty, carried off her husband, leaving her with an infant daughter barely two and another born a few months after Uncle Nat's death. To most women the outlook would have seemed appalling if not hopeless. But she faced it with unflagging courage. Three of her nephews who had left for

Georgia let her have their old home to live in and she set out to make a living for herself and her children almost unaided. Besides a garden and poultry flock to help provide food she fortunately had excellent taste and skill as a dressmaker and hat designer. She enjoyed wearing good clothes herself and I remember as a boy hearing reports of her rash extravagance (before marriage) in paying $4.00—indeed a great deal at that time—for a bonnet. She later moved to Georgia where my mother and sister later joined her in maintaining a comfortable home in Vidalia. When some years past her "threescore and ten" she wrote the following beautiful expression of her faith in the future life and her feeling that, all in all, she had lived in a happy age on earth:

"I am the only one left of our family; no brother or sister. But I know it won't be long before we meet to part no more.

> I will soon be at home over there,
> For the end of my journey I can see
> Many dear to my heart over there
> Who are waiting and watching for me.

"I am now seventy-five years old; my brothers and sisters all gone. Not one left to talk to about old times. But my childhood is so fresh in my mind that I am now living in the past. I am enjoying it with no regrets that I was born away back in what the people now call the dark ages. But I think of it as happy ages."

I visited my mother, sister, and Aunt Alice just before starting on my long trip around the world, at which time my mother talked happily of old times she remembered and her almost limitless hopes for my future career. Her last letter reached me in Peking a few months later. But her health then declined and she died on March 6, 1911, just as my boat, delayed by a heavy mid-winter storm, arrived in

New York—too late for me to have a final meeting with her. We had her body brought back to North Carolina immediately and buried in the old Poe family burying ground alongside my father (who had died in 1907) and many other kinsfolk who had loved her as she had loved them.

To judge by the question most often asked me in America and in almost every country I have visited, the most interesting possible inquiry about my ancestry is, "Are you any kin to Edgar Allan Poe?" or sometimes, "Are you any kin to the famous football Poes?" To this I might answer that when I write "Poe" in my signature it is a reminder of my father's family. But when I write "Clarence" it is a reminder of my mother's family—who are descendants of another group of Poes who claim kinship with Edgar Allan. I was named for a "Clarence Poe" of that group. He was a brilliant and charming young kinsman who often visited at my mother's home. In 1861 he and a few other impetuous volunteers, excited by the Southern victory at Bull Run, were afraid another Southern victory would end the war before they could get into any real battle fighting. Accordingly they got permission to go on ahead of the regiment in quest of danger. And danger indeed they did find—but alas! not of the kind they sought. One of the many camp diseases resulted in his being the first soldier from our county to die in the Confederate cause.

If any spark of Edgar Allan's poetic gift descended to the family it would seem to have reached a sister of this Clarence on my mother's side whose poems appeared in some leading periodicals in the state; my mother, herself an ardent lover of poetry, used to repeat some of her verses for me.

But now when we have a generation more concerned with sports than poems, more people are interested in the family's claim to a relationship with the six Poe brothers whose fabulous football victories gave Princeton its greatest glory in the sports world. As a contemporary wrote: "They were poets in action, with all the grace and finish and éclat their famous relative won for literature. To see a Poe make a run was to see poetry in motion." Some Yale Episcopal students were reported to have added to their litany, "And from ye race of Poes, Good Lord deliver us!" One of the six, halfback John Prentiss Poe, went on to add a later career so astonishingly varied and colorful as to justify summarizing here in one kaleidoscopic sentence: "He volunteered in the Spanish American War, saw service in the Philippino insurrection, next was a cow-puncher in New Mexico, joined the Kentucky militia to suppress disorders, hurried to Nevada in the 1907 gold rush, fought in Nicaragua and Honduras, and then volunteered in World War I, meeting his death with the Black Watch."

About my great-grandparents a few incidents are I think significant. To what was then almost a wilderness my Scotch Great-grandmother Poe brought a life-long love of beauty. Because the blossoming peach trees gratified this love of beauty more than anything else she saw, she was buried by her request under a peach tree. My Great-grandfather Poe, always kind to his slaves, disinherited a son-in-law because of reports that he sometimes treated some of his slaves cruelly. About my Grandfather Dismukes, my historian kinsman, Samuel A. Ashe, said, "Four things about him impressed me—his charm as a host, his remarkable fund of information, his impeccable dress, and his affection for his daughters." My mother said of him, "He was the neatest man I've ever seen."

Always on the look-out for kinfolks in other states I found an especially charming and gifted kinswoman who was a leading figure in Alabama life and progress. She was Miss Julia Strudwick Tutwiler. Few women of the South have ever had such a varied career of really distinguished activities. Educated at Vassar, in Berlin, and in Paris, she chose education as her life's work and early became president of Alabama Normal College. As a result of her efforts, the University of Alabama was opened to girls and the trustees named the Women's Annex for her. It was said that she never turned away one of the hundreds of girls in straitened circumstances who came to her for an education. If her own pocket happened to be empty at the moment, she always discovered someone with means to help these ambitious girls. She died in 1916 but her name has been perpetuated in that of a leading Birmingham hotel.

Finally, the oldest kinsmen I knew were my Great-uncle Jesse Poe and his wife, my Great-aunt Rachel. I think they had married while Thomas Jefferson and John Adams were still living. Aunt Rachel used to tell me, "I remember seeing the soldiers come home from the Norfolk War," which is what she called the War of 1812. Uncle Jesse, until his death in 1895, continued to have his homespun suits made with trousers in the sailor-style we find in portraits of Henry Clay and Daniel Webster. A ruddy-faced, large-framed, and outspoken pioneer, he has always seemed to me a virtual incarnation of the "Great-Granddad" in a poem written many years ago by an author I have never been able to identify. At any rate in a few lines it gives a more vivid picture of the early pioneer settlers and fathers than many people would get from volumes on the subject. Hence both as a picture of Great-uncle Jesse and the era in which he grew up a part is inserted here:

> Great-granddad when the land was young
> Barred his door with a wagon tongue.
> The times were rough and the wilderness mocked
> And he said his prayers with his shotgun cocked;

He was a citizen tough and grim;
Danger was like duck soup to him.
Freud was a mystery, so was jazz,
Or giving their parents a scornful razz.
If they got fresh with great-granddad
He tanned their hides with a hickory gad.
He raised them rough but he raised them well,
And if they took hold of the ways of hell,
He filled them full of the fear of God,
And flailed their pants with an old ramrod. . . .
They grew strong of heart, and strong of hand,
The firm foundation of our land.

Similarly, I have never read the poem "Lucinda Matlock"
in Edgar Lee Masters' *Spoon River Anthology* (published
by Macmillan in 1914, 1915, 1942, and printed herewith by
permission of Mrs. Edgar Lee Masters) without thinking
what an almost perfect picture it presents of my Great-
aunt Rachel:

I went to the dances at Chandlerville,
And played snap-out at Winchester.
One time we changed partners,
Driving home in the moonlight of middle June,
And then I found Davis.
We were married and lived together for seventy years,
Enjoying, working, raising the twelve children,
Eight of whom we lost
Ere I had reached the age of sixty.
I spun, I wove, I kept the house, I nursed the sick,
I made the garden, and for holiday
Rambled over the fields where sang the larks,

❖   ❖   ❖   ❖   ❖   ❖

At ninety-six I had lived enough, that is all,
And passed to a sweet repose.
What is this I hear of sorrow and weariness,
Anger, discontent and drooping hopes?
Degenerate sons and daughters,
Life is too strong for you—
It takes life to love Life.

CHAPTER THREE

Doctors and Preachers

I AM NOW PAST EIGHTY-TWO YEARS OLD. BUT THERE WAS A time when everybody around gave me little chance of living even eighty-two days. And I really did have extremely little chance.

All my life I have been fighting for one cause or another. But the only one which was truly a life-or-death struggle began with this incident when I was only nine days old. Or perhaps I might more accurately say that it began when I was only one day old! For on that day I contracted a germ which took eight days of incubation before developing into the full-fledged enemy that almost destroyed me—whooping cough. I fought my battle against such heavy odds that two or three times I was thought dead. But my mother continued working with untiring fingers to expel the choking phlegm from my little throat and help my heart overcome the constantly recurring spasms of coughing that each time left me gasping for breath. Did I have some innate "will to live" that helped me win the final victory? I do not know. But that I recovered at all still seems almost a miracle to the expert doctors to whom I have reported the incident as it was repeatedly told me in my childhood. As a matter of fact my survival brought me the first honorary degree I ever received. Our discerning old neighbor, Oran Johnson, officially dubbed me "Light'ood Knot"—a lightwood knot being the toughest of all known forms of tree or fiber—and never after called me anything but "Light'ood Knot."

This experience, as reported to me later, was one of the real factors influencing me in the struggles I made in later years to help improve health conditions and to eradicate or combat such scourges as children's diseases, diphtheria, typhoid, and scarlet fever. "To one who visits old graveyards of that time," as a friend remarked recently, "there is no more nearly heart-rending feature than the vastly greater proportion of 'short graves' as compared with full-length graves than we ever find in cemeteries today—signifying the tragic ravages of children's diseases."

My Aunt Alice made this report that I copied verbatim because of its vividness: "A man named Malone lost seven grown children the same fall from typhoid fever. And Joe Elkins had four children; all died of diphtheria. Hath Gilmore lost four boys in two weeks from diphtheria." There was still some smallpox and I remember one old friend whose face was permanently pock-marked.

Tuberculosis also frequently carried off most members of a family. Walter Hines Page told me on a transcontinental trip he would not ride on a Pullman for fear of contact with tuberculosis germs. Malaria was so extensive that the Reverend Dr. H. M. Edmonds of Birmingham, Alabama, once said it was almost "an anti-social act" for a young person not to have malarial chills and fever for six or eight years between the ages of ten and twenty-five. Life insurance companies were reported as not taking policies in widely infected malarial areas. "What are the causes of malaria?" was for years a hotly debated medical question. So many regarded it as "bad air" that this belief gave it its permanent Latin name. "Stay in out of night air" was recommended for years before the true cause was discovered, and then house screening and swamp drainage were introduced, along with quinine, to reduce its ravages.

Nearly everybody has heard of the old-time ravages of yellow fever, especially the wholesale epidemics in Southern seaports such as Wilmington and New Bern, North Carolina, during the Civil War. One of my great-uncles, who had begun practicing medicine in Mississippi, treated victims of the disease until he himself contracted it and died. While most people now think of yellow fever as a scourge of very, very long ago, I am reminded that in 1898 Memphis was suffering from a yellow fever scare and quarantine when I went through the city. The railroad cars of the train in which I was riding were locked at both back and front to keep anyone from getting either off or on the train. One Mississippi-born member of our editorial staff, G. H. Alford, had once contracted the disease but made a successful recovery.

Now let's talk about the doctors I knew. It was quite natural that one of the most important and universally loved members of our community family was our country doctor, Dr. Abram van Wyck Budd. The Methodists might love their preachers, the Baptists their preachers, and the Presbyterians theirs, but all of them loved our country doctor. Dr. Budd was a giant of a man who added obesity to what nature had already given him and weighed about 300 pounds. I remember the groaning two-wheeled sulky in which he rode to see his patients.

Dr. Budd was a native of New Jersey who came South before the Civil War but gave his support to the Confederate cause after secession and remained a loyal Southerner forever after. Without any of the equipment that modern surgeons would think necessary, he saved the lives of many

people by daring operations whenever daring seemed the
only alternative to death. One of my cousins was the bene-
ficiary of such an operation. He had an unusual intestinal
obstruction and without quick surgery by Dr. Budd he
would surely have died.

Dr. Budd, without the aid of modern psychiatry, also
chalked up some successful experiences in this field. With
women patients he seemed to have been especially successful. One woman who insisted that she could not walk a step,
was induced to take a buggy ride with Dr. Budd. He drove
the lady about half a mile, then forcibly put her out and
said, "Now walk home!" And she walked. Again he is said
to have threatened to build a fire under another bedrid-
den hypochondriac and even brought in the lightwood and
matches. She then suddenly discovered she had excellent
facilities for walking! Even more daring was another case in
which he said to the woman patient, "If you don't get out
of this bed, I'm going to get in there with you." When he
proceeded to start action to match the words, her recovery
was both immediate and complete!

In a medical journal after Dr. Budd's death, Dr. P. E.
Hines told this characteristic story about him: "On one occasion he was called to see a large and very poor family,
all ill with typhoid fever. Not only did he give them medical
treatment but he had the house and whole premises thoroughly cleansed and well whitewashed and bought beds,
bed-clothes, clothes, and food for the whole family. Eventually he had the pleasure of seeing all get well. Years after-
wards one of these boys, having gone out into the world
and made money, offered to pay Dr. Budd but he refused to
receive a cent."

Dr. Hubert Royster, a noted surgeon, has said that Budd's
successes in surgery were largely due to going into cases

early and the fact that he did not leave them until they were either well or beyond his aid.

Visits from a doctor in my immediate family were rare. My father said that from 1865 to 1890 he never had a doctor's bill for himself. I never slept on a hospital bed until I was sixty-seven and then only because of appendicitis. But when I served on the National Committee on Health Needs of the Nation, one of the doctor members said that until the coming of penicillin the greatest benefit from the average doctor's visit was psychological!

The doctors in my youth first greeted a patient with two inquiries and one admonition, none of which I ever find repeated today. "First of all," the doctor would say, "let me see your tongue." Next, "Let me feel your pulse." One part of his prescription was, "Be sure to get plenty of fresh air."

And almost sure to be prescribed was calomel. Calomel was so generally used that for a generation afterward people repeated the statement, "North Carolinians believe in Hell, Calomel, and Democracy"—and which of the first two was worse it was sometimes hard to say! To take cold baths in unheated rooms in winter was another health rule I heroically endured.

Because doctors had to travel such long distances in slow buggies and carts, it was impossible for them to reach everybody needing treatment. I remember how bitter one of my older friends was whose wife died after childbirth and he felt that his doctor should have saved her.

Nobody had ever heard of vitamins. To be fat was not considered discreditable, but the hard work in which both men and women engaged usually prevented its becoming a major health problem.

Doctors forbade giving a typhoid patient anything more than the barest minimum of food and many people now believe not a few deaths were actually due to starvation. I heard of patients who defied the doctor's orders, found a way to the pantry, ate savagely—and quickly recovered.

Within my own knowledge came another striking illustration of how many diseases science has conquered or almost conquered since my boyhood. A cousin of mine, Dr. J. P. Fearrington had located in Winston-Salem. Once I saw his son (who had been a superb physical specimen and played football in college) in what appeared to be the last hopeless stages of diabetes. He weighed only about eighty-four pounds, and his diet had been reduced to almost nothing—I think it was a cracker and a lettuce leaf. But my doctor-cousin had kept in touch with all the new medical discoveries and was excited by reports of a strange new product called insulin. With his son's life at stake he spared neither time nor money in an effort to get some of the new product—and succeeded. The boy recovered with amazing speed, completed his course at Chapel Hill, and became a successful pediatrician in his home town.

Even for white people the supply of doctors in the 1880's was completely inadequate. As for the colored people, a great proportion of them put their dependence in "conjure" doctors. A typical case was reported by Black Bob when he worked on my father's place. This is what the "conjure" doctor told him: "Put two or three pots of water on the fire. Then put some silver money in the water. Then pour the water into a barrel and bathe in it. At night make a foot-poultice made as I will tell you—and then be sure never, never let your naked feet touch the floor until the 'spell' is over." As a result of this treatment, he was told the witch would leave Bob and settle in a brushpile near his house. Then the next night, Bob, walking backward as directed, went out, torch in hand, to burn the brushheap and thus destroy the witch. This was a delicate operation, but Bob finally completed it exactly according to the magic rules—and was rewarded by a complete recovery from his affliction!

Country preachers were especially important and well-loved citizens in my home community. They were, however, handicapped by poor transportation and poorer pay. A cousin of mine for years served four churches in Granville County. In my father's Bethany Church, I think the preacher received around $200 a year, with many members contributing not more than $1.00 a year. He preached in our church only once a month and had little time for pastoral visiting.

Most of the people in my community were Baptists, Methodists, or Presbyterians, but (as elsewhere) numbers of people did not attend any church. Realizing this and also realizing that it would be hard to get together enough people of any one denomination to operate a strong Sunday school, my Methodist mother and a Baptist uncle organized and directed a union or nondenominational Sunday school. This brought members of all sects happily together and did much good.

Of all the Bible lessons I learned in that Sunday school and elsewhere, the one that made the deepest and most lasting impression on me was the Parable of the Last Judgment. Its supreme lesson has ever since seemed plain to me, namely, that the final test of every soul will be not his adherence to any particular denomination or theological doctrine. Rather, is it not clear that the final testing question will be, not even about faith, but about *love*—love for God as expressed in service to our fellows: "What have you done to help the poor, the hungry, the naked, the prisoner, and [what is most often forgotten] the stranger?"

The highlight of every year was the revival, or "protracted meeting" as it was called. For a whole week there were services morning and afternoon with a dinner served between times. For this each woman vied with all others in making marvelous cakes and pies. During preaching at these revivals one of the sisters would almost invariably become so happy she could no longer restrain herself and would give forth shouts of joy and praise, sometimes delaying the service.

Some preachers emphasized it more and some less, but "hellfire" figured largely in nearly every sermon. Some preachers thought they had gone the limit when they said that hellfire was seven times hotter than ordinary fire— whereas modern scientists talk soberly of fires more than 7,000 times hotter. And some preachers made children of eight to twelve believe that they were in danger of hell if they did not formally repent of their "sins" and assume church membership. As a boy I definitely remember becoming terribly penitent and praying to become a Christian— but then was half scared to death lest that would mean I must be too long-faced and solemn!

While hell was always mentioned as a place of terror, for some reason or other the devil was mentioned rather familiarly as The Old Boy, Old Scratch, or the Bad Man. One small boy, rebuked for saying "devil" too frequently, turned to the phrase, "the gentleman who keeps hell."

I still remember church customs very different from those prevailing today. The women sat on one side of the room and men on the other, the girls and smaller children sitting with their mothers. Crying babies often interrupted the preaching, and frequently the mothers stepped outside to quiet the infant and provide for its refreshment by nature's own method.

In most of these churches there were deacons who were frequently called on to "lead in prayer," the minister calling only on those who could respond with both alacrity and sound doctrine. Calling on a man unexpectedly often led to considerable embarrassment for him and his hearers. I remember one Sunday I was visiting Robert W. Scott, father of Kerr Scott, later governor. Mr. Scott was superintendent of a large Presbyterian Sunday school that almost filled the church and asked me to go along with him. You may imagine my surprise when without warning I suddenly heard the announcement, "Brother Clarence Poe will lead us in divine worship—*now*." Well, "Brother Clarence Poe" was perfectly used to having a brief two- or three-minute private conversation with the Lord each night, including the Lord's Prayer and a few special blessings for himself, *The Progressive Farmer*, and Miss Alice Aycock (or whoever was his best girl at the time). However, in those days for a stranger to be suddenly called on to "lead us in divine worship—*now*," on a Sunday morning, well, that was definitely a horse of another color. It usually meant that the stranger was proficient in delivering a five- or ten-minute oration to the Almighty, based primarily on the assumption that if the Lord were not definitely advised about the desirability of every blessing the congregation might want, He would forget all about it. The test of a prayer was once illustrated by a Negro deacon who was asked how he liked his new preacher and replied, "Fine, fine—why, he axes the Lord for more things than our other preacher knowed He had!" So I gritted my teeth and waded in. But after praying for Hawfields Church, Alamance County, the State of North Carolina, the United States, and maybe the Democratic party (it was "standing in need of prayer" even more then than now), and for the President, the Governor, the coroner, and the county commissioners, and maybe some Indian tribes and faraway cannibals thrown in for good measure, it was certainly a great relief to "Brother Clarence Poe" when he could finally say "Amen" and sit down—and I fancy the Lord Himself was glad it was over if He was listening in, which I devoutly hope He wasn't.

Every church then was also regarded as a sort of religious policeman to look after the manners and morals of its members. To be "turned out of the church" meant a social stigma from which the delinquent never recovered unless he later asked forgiveness and "brought forth fruits meet for repentance."

Unfortunately the churches at that time looked upon dancing, card-playing, and theater-going as grievous sins. I recall that my Grandfather Dismukes would yield a little; he said everybody ought to go to the theater *once!* In other words, no one should make a habit of going but nobody should be cheated out of the pleasure of going once.

It may surprise many readers to know that Negroes and whites who were professing Christians were enrolled together in the membership of a great proportion of the ante-bellum churches. In my own church, the First Baptist Church of Raleigh, there were more Negroes than whites in the membership when it was organized in 1812, and Negroes still predominated in numbers when, sometime after the Civil War, the Negroes asked to be dismissed to establish their own church two blocks away. But it was around 1925 that I no longer saw one old Negro who had elected to stay with his white friends and had regularly sat in a front seat of our church gallery.

The ultimate in religious emphasis in my boyhood came when two women preachers set up a tent and preached "sanctification" or utter sinlessness. They proclaimed that it was not enough to be an ordinary Christian with occasional lapses such as St. Peter himself was guilty of but that to be a real Christian one must be guilty of absolutely no sin whatever—in act or thought. This test must have proved too much for even the best of Chatham Christians, for my recollection is that the "sanctification crusade" lasted only for two or three years.

Many people seemed to feel that a man had fulfilled all the major requirements of Christianity if he never danced, never played cards, never took a dram, never said "damn," and went to church once a month. In some churches card-playing was almost a cardinal sin, and I still remember some flinching of my own conscience when I had to sell a pack of cards in my uncle's store where I was substituting for him one Saturday. Dancing ("hugging set to music" as some called it) was thought even more sinful. Nobody seemed to think that there must have been music and dancing at the wedding feast in Cana and certainly when the Prodigal Son returned to his father. But when it was announced that a piano would be used at a Baptist association meeting in my father's home church, one dear old lady refused to attend the meeting for that reason. "Fiddling" was even more strongly proscribed and hence seldom heard. In speaking of this matter, however, I should mention the different attitude of the Episcopal church. Its greater tolerance sometimes attracted people to it but more often excited the condemnation of other denominations.

Although I left rural Chatham too early to have had many man-to-man friendships with its rural preachers, I know that the minor faults I have mentioned are not worthy to be compared with the immense good done by most of these devout and always poorly-paid ministers of this era. They helped transform and dignify the lives of many men and women. Everywhere they exerted great influence. Not only were outstanding preachers like Patrick Dowd long remembered but people went long distances to hear men like Sam Jones. Eagerly read, too, were the sermons of the Reverend T. DeWitt Talmadge, syndicated in many of the weekly papers, while Baptists read volumes of sermons by one of their great English leaders, Charles H. Spurgeon. Walter Hines Page, as I knew him, could hardly be called a religious man, but in his "Forgotten Man" speech he paid this remarkable tribute to some of these pioneer ministers:

"Not only was the preacher a mighty man in our life, but there was in the old days a type of preacher who was an heroic man, a man who had all the qualities of the pioneer. He was ready any day to face the hardships of the wilderness or to stand in the presence of the Almighty. I doubt if we have ever produced other men as great as our pioneer preachers. They were cast in so large a mold, they dealt so directly with the fundamental emotions of men and with some of the great facts of the spiritual life, that they almost ranged themselves with the giants."

As for myself many people feel that I have rendered few greater services to Southern rural people than by helping them escape from a conception of God as a God of vengeance who punishes with limitless cruelty and for limitless time and giving them the concept of God as love. In a 1962 Christmas message to my friends I expressed the views I had repeatedly expressed in *The Progressive Farmer* as follows:

Never until Christianity is healed of this fatal schizophrenia or "split personality" can Christ be so lifted up as to draw all men to Him and "the beauty of the Lord our God indeed be upon us." How can we effectively so "lift up Christ" with His doctrine of love for all men, if at the same time we lift up the picture of a supposed "God who is Love" but who at the same time permits the endless tormenting of weak creatures of His own making—tormenting them even through long centuries when it could serve no conceivable purpose of reform, restraint, or warning, but mean only the gratification of a merciless vengeance?

Must it not be that the "fires" in which the guilty burn are spiritual fires in a spiritual world—fires of remorse and regret—but only for whatever reasonable length of time such a just but loving Father might require?

Why should we ignore Christ's seemingly emphatic declaration three times repeated. For example, in John 3:15, 16, 36 and in his famous reply to the inquiry "Good Master, what must I do to inherit eternal life?" Do not all these four seem to make him consider eternal life as a reward for the righteous alone—that "the wages of sin is *death* but the gift of God is *eternal life*" (Romans 6:23)?

How can we ever expect either men or nations to cease hating and torturing their enemies when God Himself is represented as doing so and doing so endlessly?

Our whole universe will be forever fairer and all human life forever sweeter when all our churches help teach all men two things: that the Power which rules the universe is love, and that the one supreme duty of every man is love for God plus loving service to man. When these two supreme Christ-doctrines are taught by all Christians then, indeed, will "the beauty of the Lord our God," shining through us as His humble followers, make a New Eden of our now troubled and imperiled world.

CHAPTER FOUR

"Here Once the Embattled Farmers Stood"

WAS IT MERE CHANCE OR WAS IT THE PLAN OF SOME FATE OR destiny or Divine Providence that I should share nearly all the hardships and struggles of our Southern farm people in order that I might be inspired to fight long years for their betterment and at age eighty find as my reward the tribute of a half-illiterate country neighbor, "You have put more bread and meat in folks's mouths than anybody else in the South." I do not know and cannot say.

I do know that somewhat as Moses was helped by sharing the experiences of his people when they were forced to make bricks without straw, I have been helped by having shared the hardships of Southern people in their darkest hours and have sometimes felt some inspiration when I read in the ancient eloquence of Isaiah, "And they that be of thee shall build the old waste places and thou shalt be called the restorer of paths to dwell in." From that hour at nine days of age when I had to fight against the inadequate health facilities of the time and came out conqueror, I have found one challenging struggle after another on which to try my mettle.

Probably earliest of all was the problem of saving the land itself. One of the earliest boyhood hardships I had to share with my family was that too much of the land my father had inherited had been so long cultivated (and with so little knowledge at that time about how to save soil fertility or prevent erosion) that the fields were almost worn out. The land of most other farmers, except river bottoms, suffered from the same cause in greater or less degree.

When my grandfather's estate was divided up, most of my father's brothers and sisters took fairly large allotments of acreage with very little investment in buildings. My father chose to keep the more costly old home, barns, and smaller buildings of his parents and grandparents though this necessitated a somewhat smaller land allotment. Furthermore his land, having been cultivated for two generations, had (as just indicated) become badly eroded and correspondingly infertile as compared with the creek bottoms some of my uncles cultivated.

On sloping land rain was largely uncontrolled. No one then had ever heard of "contour plowing" or the Mangum terrace. Hillside ditches, the only attempt at water control, simply accumulated water on the upper areas of each field to dump it at the end of rows into the next lowest levels, finally reaching gullying proportions at the bottom of the field.

This steady loss of fertility by soil erosion also had vast parallel consequences in human erosion itself of which few then took thought. From one nearby farm three of my cousins left for another state because crop returns had become inadequate. A larger community area once thickly populated with Poes has not a Poe left to bear the name. From a farm adjoining my father's three of my Poe cousins left its impoverished acres in the 1880's, going to Georgia to clear its vast areas of dense virgin pine forest for naval stores—the "tar, pitch and turpentine" which had once been North Carolina's chief exports. ("I almost feel it was a sin," one of them later said to me, "that we laid waste thousands of acres of what would now be invaluable lumber—all in order to get the meager returns of pine sap or rosin.")

Of all the toil and sweat of our farm people when I was a boy it is saddening to think how much was not only useless but definitely harmful. Take corn, for example. After planting it too thick in order to make sure of having plants enough, then thinning it "to a stand" with hoes, then hoeing out the grass by hand, the rows were barred off by a plow that cut many life-giving roots. Next, when the corn was "laid by" with its final cultivation, a plow was used to throw up the soil in high ridges. This ridging not only cut so many roots as to drastically reduce yields but caused the rows to dry out seriously in the event of drouth. Finally, in order to secure feed for horses and mules, the green corn stalks were cut just above the ears and bundled. Later the remaining lower leaves were stripped from the stalk before the grain in the ears had fully matured. One of our earliest campaigns when I later joined *The Progressive Farmer* was against this useless practice of "cutting tops" and "pulling fodder." As we said to our readers, "The next time you are tempted to spend a day cutting tops or pulling fodder, just dig up some big juicy worms, get out your hook and line, and go fishing. You will have more fun—and your corn yield will be better."

Cotton seed was planted in continuous long rows; then more than half the emerging plants were thinned out with hand hoes to prevent overcrowding, and an almost continuous battle with crabgrass followed. In the language of John Charles McNeill—

> But whe'r it freshet or whe'r it dust
> De crabgrass gwine a grow!

Bermuda grass, usually called wiregrass, was an even more persistent enemy. Wherever a sprig fell it was likely to flourish. Some farmers, including Bill Arp, reported, "Even when you try to burn it, wherever the smoke hits the ground, another crop of wiregrass is started!"

In spite of these hardships, however, in ordinary times our friends and neighbors could "make their own bread and meat," but in a year when drouth struck—as it did in 1888— everybody suffered. There was then little need for inviting neighbors to a corn shucking because the yield was so small that each farmer could shuck his crop without help and still need more for feed and food. Many farmers were enabled to survive financially only by cutting all available pine timber for sawmills and by cutting large oak trees as crossties for sale to the railroads.

I still remember a group of my kinsfolk gathered about the fireside in my old home uneasily discussing the situation in 1888. Cheer was found only when one of the younger members, hardly out of her teens, brightened their whole outlook by quoting, "I have been young, and now am old; yet have I not seen the righteous forsaken, nor his seed begging bread."

Not only were my farmer kin and others sustained by the faith expressed in this ancient Scripture, they also began to talk of a new bright hope. Over nearly all the South farmers were beginning to look to a new organization that was spearheading what proved to be an historic crusade for farmers' rights.

Texas farmers were in the fighting forefront in promoting the agricultural rebellion that later took shape as the National Farmers' Alliance. But the movement soon spilled over from Texas and overspread the Southern and Midwestern farming states. Farmers' Alliance orators included Tom Watson of Georgia and "Pitchfork" Ben Tillman of South Carolina, both of whom later became United States senators, and "Sockless" Jerry Simpson of Kansas, a congressman.

Colonel L. L. Polk almost blanketed Kansas in a campaign that surprised the nation by retiring from the United States Senate the famous orator and poet, John James Ingalls. Virtually all rural America was aflame before the crusade ended.

Chatham County farmers had suffered a double blow—a serious crop failure, which was local, and low prices for farm products, which were general. To combat this more widespread second trouble farmers all over the South were looking to the Alliance. It seemed to offer the surest way for farmers to help themselves at a time when the national government did nothing to help.

For at that time there were no Production Credit Associations through which farmers might escape paying usurious prices for credit needed to make their crops. There were no Federal Land Banks to prevent creditors from making usurious charges for land credit or from foreclosing at the end of any ninety-day period that the creditor might think most propitious for his purposes. There were no guaranteed crop "support prices" to soften the blow of violent market changes.

So it was that while our Chatham farmers took comfort in the promises of the ancient Psalmist, they also turned with unusual faith to the Farmers' Alliance movement as a means of helping themselves.

One reason for their doing so was that for them the Farmers' Alliance had become personified in a singularly eloquent and attractive spokesman of their state, Colonel Leonidas Lafayette Polk. Not only had the leading farmers in Chatham been thrilled by Polk's eloquence but he was reaching many homes every week through the medium of the Alliance organ, *The Progressive Farmer*, which he had founded at Winston-Salem in 1886 and moved to Raleigh in 1888. Here was a man who had become acquainted with many farmers as the state's first Commissioner of Agriculture. Some measure of their enthusiasm for him may be glimpsed from a one-sentence remark one North Carolina paper, *The Kinston Free Press*, made about him at the height of this crusade: "Some Alliancemen seem to have more confidence in Colonel Polk than in God Almighty!"

I was too young to join the Alliance but felt a hearty boyish enthusiasm for it. I even wrote some verses published in the county Alliance paper and remember shouting, "Hurrah for Weaver!" as men passed me on their way to the polls in 1892.

With all the fervor of a religious crusade the Alliance organization moved on. "The female of the species is deadlier than the male," Kipling long ago reported, and certainly the Alliance cause in the 1890's recruited a bevy of women orators who out-thundered not only the milder personalities of such men as Colonel Polk but the fiery oratory of Tom Watson and Ben Tillman.

Most picturesque and sensational of all the Alliance orators who came from outside North Carolina to help the Alliance cause here was "tall and stately" Mary Ellen Lease, an Irish-born woman lawyer of Kansas. Her slogan, "Farmers must raise less corn and more hell," caught on and spread like a forest fire. With "a powerful voice, deep and resonant, its effect startling and compelling," as was said at that time, "she hurls sentences as Jove hurls thunderbolts." She was so vehement that she was rotten-egged during a speech in Greensboro, North Carolina, but continued her crusading with undiminished fervor.

No matter how busy they might be, my father and my Uncle Stephen would take time on Saturday afternoons to attend Alliance meetings. In addition to the National Alliance there was the State Alliance, the County Alliance, and, buttressing and invigorating all these, the Subordinate Alliance in each community. Each Subordinate Alliance had to elect a lecturer in addition to other officials. Many an everyday farmer who had thought he would be scared to death if he opened his mouth in public suddenly astonished himself (and others) by finding that after two or three improving efforts, he could speak out his inmost thoughts to his fellow farmers and really "make a sure-enough speech." Other members participating in discussions had similar experiences. From my own county two Alliance farmer-leaders—men of previously unrecognized ability—were sent to Congress and won recognition as worthy representatives there. No merchant, banker, or speculator was eligible for membership in the Alliance but teachers, doctors, and ministers were welcomed. Of a score or more of the ministers serving churches in our Baptist Association all but one were reported to be Alliancemen.

The Alliance also served in gratifying degree as a social organization. Apparently copying much from the Masonic order, it had its own signs, passwords, and even funeral ceremony. Not to belong to the Alliance was in many communities as serious as would now be the case of a steel worker who refused to join his union. The Alliance was also a democratizing agency. Tenancy had increased as landowners lost their land to supply merchants and to other lenders of credit, and tenant farmers were welcomed freely along with large plantation owners. Agriculture was in serious straits and everybody was encouraged to contribute his own thinking as to what should be done. I recollect that my Uncle Stephen Moore even read an out-and-out Socialist paper, *The Appeal to Reason*. Finally, in order to bring about needed reforms, thousands of Southern farmers found themselves willing to break their traditional allegiance to the Democratic party while a host of Northern farmers proved equally willing to break their allegiance to the Republican party. Farmers in all sections began to re-examine old ideas, sectional, political, and economic. I well remember hearing someone read aloud from *The Progressive Farmer* some verses with the refrain—

> But thinking now what I thunk
> I think I thunk a lie.

At the height of its power the National Farmers' Alliance at its 1890 meeting in Ocala, Florida, adopted that "much cussed and discussed" document later famous as the "Ocala Platform." This became the virtual creed of the national agrarian revolt of the late 1880's and early 1890's. Although denounced then as a "wildly radical" program for the nation, most of it has since been adopted in principle if not in form. Here were the chief "demands" in this Magna Carta of Farmers' Alliance: government loans to farmers at 2% on nonperishable farm products and real estate; a volume of money in circulation to equal $50 per capita; the prohibition of gambling in cotton and produce exchanges; free and unlimited coinage of silver; tariff reduction on the necessities of life; graduated income taxes; reduction of government expenditures; public control of railroad freight and passenger rates, and—if control should fail—then government ownership; the election of United States senators by direct vote of the people.

The America of today has grown used to "support prices" for farm products as advocated in the "Ocala Platform"; the Federal Reserve Bank controls the volume of money in much the way favored in Planks 2 and 4 of these "demands." We have long become accustomed to income taxes and to the election of United States Senators by direct vote of the people.

What was especially important at that time was public control of railroad freight and passenger rates. In our now almost "horseless America," which has grown used to automobiles, trucks, and airplanes, who can even visualize the horse-dominated transportation of the 1880's and 1890's? At that time horse-drawn buggies, carriages, wagons, and carts offered the only means for persons to go from place to place or for products to be shipped from farm to market—except where railway lines, often very far apart, provided depots for transporting persons or farm products. And in all too many places railroad-owners, having virtually monopolistic power, fixed passenger rates and freight rates on the basis of "all the traffic will bear"—even though few would have publicly approved the reported Vanderbilt declaration, "The public be damned."

Few people now alive remember how heated were the arguments between opponents and proponents of free silver— "the free and unlimited coinage of silver at the ratio of 16 to 1." One of the then famous but now forgotten political pamphlets I remember reading was *Coin's Financial School,* a brilliantly written yellow paperback defense of free silver as advocated by the Farmers' Alliance and most conspicuously by William J. Bryan in 1896. To illustrate how strong was the feeling on this subject, Fab Busbee, an attorney for the Southern Railroad wished to go to Chicago as a delegate to the National Democratic Convention and asked an Alliance advocate (I shall call him Mr. Benford) for his support. "Well, how do you stand on silver?" Mr. Benford almost thundered. "Well, I'm for it—but I'm not a damned fool about it," answered Busbee, to which Mr. Benford sharply brought down his fist, saying emphatically, "Then you shan't go—you shan't go!" And he didn't.

A most serious complaint of the farmer, moreover, had to do with the ruinous credit system for agriculture at that time. Commercial banks required satisfactory renewals every ninety days. Still more serious was the situation with regard

to production credit—meaning credit to help produce crops
or livestock. The typical Southern farmer grew cotton as
his chief source of money, and since cotton prices did not
meet the cost of production judged by any reasonable living standards, a farmer usually had to have credit to finance
his operations at least from March until November. To meet
this situation an almost universal practice was for the tenant
farmer and many landowners to give, say in March, a "crop
lien" or crop mortgage on a crop newly planted or frequently
not yet planted, the mortgage to mature when the crop was
sold. Meanwhile the borrower bought whatever supplies he
and his family needed on a "time-prices" basis. Careful in-
vestigations I later made through *The Progressive Farmer*
showed that as a general South-wide rule the time-prices
charge for the ordinary "necessities of life" was 20 per cent
higher than the prices at which these necessities were sold
for cash. Thus if time-prices were utilized for only a four-
month period, the extra 20 per cent time-prices charge was
equivalent to paying interest at the rate of 60 per cent a
year! And the tenant farmer could not seek another source
of credit because the time-merchant had a lien or mortgage
on his only collateral. In many cases additional interest was
reportedly added at the rate of 1 per cent after November 1.
Truly, under this system "the borrower was servant of the
lender," as Solomon had said long ago.

It was to help remedy this disastrous time-prices system
that the Farmers' Alliance offered its famous "sub-treasury
plan." Under it the government would lend farmers money
at 2 per cent per annum on properly warehoused products
such as cotton and wheat. These warehouses would therefore
be regarded as dependencies of the United States Treasury,
hence the name "sub-treasury." Of course it has been said,
"All power corrupts and absolute power corrupts absolutely."
The fact that the laws of the state provided absolutely no

limit to the amount a merchant might charge for time-prices
tempted not a few of them to abuse this power outrageously.
I think of one about whom it was told me, "He sent a man
to a widow's house who took the last bushel of her corn
while she stood crying in the doorway." But on the other
hand there were others whose fairness won them the approval and the respect of their fellows. One I knew very
well went into bankruptcy during the depression although
he might have escaped that calamity if he had been hard-
hearted in dealing with his debtors.

Certainly the farmers in the 1880's and 1890's had many
just grievances. William J. Bryan once told me that he regarded the Farmers' Alliance as the forerunner of the Progressive movement in politics, later represented by himself
in the Democratic party and by Theodore Roosevelt in the
Republican party. For a long time it was customary to deride
the remedies the Alliance proposed. But so understanding
a man as Governor O. Max Gardner gave a more truly
correct appraisal when he said at the celebration of the semi-
centennial of North Carolina State College:

"The master mind of this era was Colonel Leonidas L.
Polk, first Commissioner of Agriculture and founder and first
editor of *The Progressive Farmer*. Colonel Polk raised the
issue in North Carolina that the state had gone for more than
100 years without making any provision for higher education for the sons and daughters of our predominant farm
population, that higher education was for the few and not
for the many. This movement culminated in the organization of the Farmers' Alliance and ultimately of the Populist
party. The old-line politicians and the big landowning aristo-
crats of the South were shocked beyond measure by the
revolutionary program of this militant and progressive epidemic of agrarian reforms. They not only jarred the classical
concepts of higher education—they attacked the citadels of

political control. They contended with truth that political power was concentrated in the towns and cities and that the farmer, his family, and especially his children, were neglected and consigned by our government to no opportunity except the dreary task of hewing wood and drawing water."

Early in 1892 the new "People's party" (later called Populist) seemed sure to nominate Colonel Polk for president. After Polk's sudden death in June, the presidential nomination went to James B. Weaver of Iowa, a famous Union general. He had nothing of Polk's eloquence or personal attractiveness but nevertheless carried four states and received more than a million votes at a time when we had much fewer men voters—and no women voters at all. A Confederate general had been named for vice president on the ticket with him. They carried my county, and my father and most of my kin voted for them.

Allan Nevins, noted historian and biographer of Grover Cleveland, has made this sound judgment of the Farmers' Alliance movement:

"Few social movements in American history have possessed as much justice as the Agrarian Revolt of the Nineties. It is the special glory of this revolt that it carried into American politics a broad program of progressive ideas that almost without exception have since been written into law."

CHAPTER FIVE

A Country Boy Makes City Friends

As CLEARLY AS IF IT HAD HAPPENED YESTERDAY I REMEMBER A
day when I was fourteen and declared aloud to myself what
had then been a gradually developing resolution about my
life work. Taking a pen in hand I vowed:

*"No matter how great the seeming obstacles now, I shall
become a writer and shall make this my life's work."*

In the next two years I wrote articles for our county paper
and some stories and verse for *The Progressive Farmer*. Then
two years later in May, 1897, something happened that
proved to be one of the turning points of my life.

The North Carolina legislature had proposed that each
school district or township vote on the question of levying
an additional tax for public schools. In this I saw a great
challenge to improve educational opportunity for every other
country boy like myself—and incidentally to help every country teacher such as my mother had been. I therefore wrote
as moving and heartfelt a plea as I knew how to make and
sent it to *The Progressive Farmer* for publication. Along
with it I sent a personal letter saying I hoped some time to
be an editor myself. The result was a prompt request that
I come to Raleigh for an interview. It was not the definite

offer of a position, but the business manager and editor at least wanted to talk with me. Eagerly I arranged to see them.

The article that brought me to the attention of *The Progressive Farmer,* perhaps because it was written by a sixteen-year-old farm boy who desperately wanted more education, reads as follows:

THE PUBLIC SCHOOL QUESTION

A question more important than the chief ones discussed during the last campaign now presents itself for the decision of the people of North Carolina. I do not think the above statement is unwarranted. The questions discussed during the last campaign were chiefly of a monetary nature. A decision of those questions affects us financially, but a decision of the public school question will affect us financially, mentally, and morally. It affects us individually and collectively. It affects our welfare, our children's welfare, and our state's welfare.

Why? It affects us financially because the ignorant are at the mercy of the learned, and morally because ignorance is the mother of superstition and credulity. It affects us individually, because it affects the welfare of our children and our neighbor's children, and it affects us as people because on the welfare of the children hangs the destiny of the country.

In education, North Carolina is far behind her sister states, and the state that is behind in education is behind in progress and in power.

In the battle of life our school children—the future citizens of North Carolina—will have to compete with the children of the Middle Atlantic and New England states. Let us consider for a moment the great disparity between the educational advantages of North Carolina, and those of the sections mentioned above, and the inevitable result will be only too terribly apparent.

But we need not go to the Northern states alone to find states ahead of ours in education. Let us take our own Southern states. Reliable statistics show that 28 per cent of the white persons over ten years of age in North Carolina can neither read nor write. No other Southern state makes such a discreditable showing.

North Carolina lowest in the scale of knowledge! Think of it! "The Old North State," which has so often led in the cause of right and liberty—so often led other states in battle—now in the cause of education takes the rear!

"Knowledge is power" and North Carolina is behind in power. And if her people fail to avail themselves of the opportunities given them by the last legislature, they are depriving their children and their state of power and of influence!

If they allow these opportunities to pass unimproved they are saying: "We will not give our children the advantages which their future rivals in life enjoy. We care neither for their destiny nor for the future of the state."

Shall they say it? Some may think that they are utterly careless and indifferent, but we do not believe it. North Carolina is slow but she is sure. With apparently stoical indifference she hears, but she ponders well. She has taken a Rip Van Winkle sleep on the school question but the time for the awakening has come. Let us take her from the rear and place her in the van.

This is a matter which demands immediate attention. It admits of no postponement. Old North Carolina must "awake, arise or be forever fallen."

Is there a man in North Carolina so selfish, so groveling that he will vote against the measure because he has no children to send, or is going to send them to higher schools?

If such a man there be, may God pity him! Has he no interest in the welfare of his country and his neighbors? Is his heart too small, his soul too shrunken, to admit a love for the advancement of civilization and Christianity? Does he care not if the "Old Ship of State" sinks in the waves of oblivion and his country becomes the land of the tyrant and the slave? If his heart has never stirred with patriotic emotions; if he considers barbarism better than civilization, and Paganism better than Christianity; if he cares more for a few paltry cents than for the benefits of knowledge, let him vote against it. But, as Scott exclaims:

> If such there breathe, go, mark him well;
> For him no minstrel raptures swell;
> High though his titles, proud his name,
> Boundless his wealth as wish can claim,—
> Despite those titles, power, and pelf,
> The wretch, concentred all in self,
> Living, shall forfeit fair renown,
> And, doubly dying, shall go down
> To the vile dust, from whence he sprung,
> Unwept, unhonor'd, and unsung.

The question is one which affects the welfare of us all, and it follows as a natural consequence that it is one in which we are all interested and for the proper solution of which we should all labor.

It lies before the people and awaits their decision. May they not prove recreant, but may they, actuated by the same broadminded patriotism which has made their past record so fair seize the opportunity and give the children of North Carolina the same advantages which the children of other states enjoy—place our beloved "Old North State" in a position creditable to herself and to her people.

Then, and not till then, should we be willing to quit the fray, on the result of which depends so much of the future glory and prosperity of North Carolina and North Carolina's sons and daughters.

Clarence H. Poe
Gulf, N.C.
April 10, 1897

So much for my appeal as published in *The Progressive Farmer* on April 27, 1897. When the people went to the polls a little later only eleven townships out of the many hundreds in the state's nearly one hundred counties voted for the tax —an absurdly low number! Perhaps the disastrous result can be attributed in part to the fact that the proposal had been submitted by a legislature dominated by Republicans and Populists. But an appalling indifference to the value of education must have been the major factor—heavily underlining the magnitude of the task Charles B. Aycock was to assume three years later.

On May 25, 1897, I packed my bags, thanked my neighbors and kin for their good wishes and congratulations, and embarked by slow train for Raleigh and the much-anticipated interview.

About the first thing Editor J. L. Ramsey did was to ask me to write an editorial on "Be Systematic." I evidently passed this test for it appeared in the next issue. Then after meeting other tests I was employed as assistant editor. I was launched on a career that has lasted over sixty-five years and has never ceased to be absorbing and satisfying.

As evidence of my greenness I might mention that when someone on the staff gave me a letter to mail and pointed toward a spot where there was a mailbox and a fire alarm box, I was about to make my entrance to Raleigh historic by turning in a fire alarm when I was only supposed to mail a letter!

The Progressive Farmer had been founded in 1886 by Colonel L. L. Polk. When I came to work on it, it was owned by his widow and edited by J. L. Ramsey, with Polk's son-in-law, J. W. Denmark, as business manager. Mr. and Mrs. Denmark kindly invited me to board in their home which I did for several years.

Mr. Denmark was a Confederate veteran. Not old enough for regular combat service, he had enlisted as a drummer boy and suffered all the hardships of war and near-starvation. "Once," he told me, "I fell in a hole in the rear of our retreating forces. I was so weak, helpless, and hopeless I positively resolved just to stay there and die. Fortunately some passerby pulled me out, set me on my feet, and I worked on until the Surrender." He later managed to graduate from Wake Forest College and then married Colonel Polk's daughter. Their three school-age children added interest to the home life. I enjoyed sharing their games and studies. But reading was my main joy and occupation. All my leisure time, the time a boy would now spend on radio, television, and sports, I gave to books—mainly the English and American classics.

Both Mr. and Mrs. Denmark were active in church and Sunday school work. This was natural in view of the fact that Colonel Polk had himself been president of the Baptist State Convention and one of the foremost promoters of a Baptist college for women, first called by the grandiloquent title "Baptist Female University" and now Meredith College. Mrs. Denmark was also an artist of not inconsiderable ability, winning top honors for her exhibits at the state fair, which was then the main showplace for achievement by North Carolina artists.

When I came to Raleigh it had 13,000 people and 23 saloons. If it had as many saloons now in proportion to population, there would be about 150. However I had definitely become a teetotaler by reason of precept, example, and I think especially because of having studied the injurious effects of alcohol in a school textbook, Steele's *Physiology and Hygiene*. Hence I have always recalled with some amusement the only time I remember entering a Raleigh saloon. A business visitor from another town, having finished his interview with me late in the afternoon, asked if I would go with him while he got a drink. He asked for apple brandy and the bartender replied he had none; he asked for some Scotch whisky and the reply was the same. My friend then called for Old Crow or some similar brand, only to hear there was none of it. Definitely exasperated, my friend exclaimed, "Well, give me what you drink yourself!" Without speaking a word the bartender turned on a spigot and handed my friend a glass of water!

Although Raleigh was dominated socially by old families of more or less renown, I soon found them ready to give a cordial welcome to anyone with a definite and even eager interest in history, literature, and North Carolina progress. Since I had such interests it was not long before I was invited to join local groups dealing with them. I did not, however, give much time to clubs that offered merely social contacts but no useful activity. Having joined the Capital Club, which was of the social type, I remember finding at the end of the year that my membership had cost me a dollar for each minute I had spent in it!

Having mentioned families of old-time wealth and distinction, I am reminded of how many of them never recovered from the reverses brought about by the Civil War. For example, one popular lady whose father had been a Congressman and a Confederate general, was reduced to the necessity of taking in boarders but always insisted on keeping up the appearance of merely having "guests." I spent several years in her home but never once handed her a check or a piece of money. Rather, at the end of each month I slipped a check or cash for the month's board and room under my plate when she was not looking.

In those days Southern men set great store by military titles, earned, honorary, or imaginary. Even the somewhat insignificant title of captain was prized and nurtured by Confederate veterans. For example, as long as he lived my old kinsman Samuel A. Ashe was invariably referred to as "Captain Ashe." I also recall with some amusement that when I once made a commencement address at Mississippi A. & M. College and had then not even received an honorary doctorate the college president could utilize, he introduced me everywhere we went as "Colonel Poe"! In Raleigh I once boarded with a man quite generally referred to as "Colonel," when the nearest military justification was found in his statement, "If the war had lasted two weeks longer I would have been of the right age to enter!"

Long after Raleigh's social leaders had ceased to make little if any distinction between descendants of those who had been slaveholders and those who had not, they still maintained an emphatic prejudice against families who had made money by traffic in slaves. This fact is illustrated by a remark made by Mrs. Robert H. Jones, daughter of Confederate General L. O'B. Branch, which I jotted down on April 2, 1909. When the name of a particular lady was brought up in conversation Mrs. Jones said: "Do you know who she was? Her father made his fortune selling Negroes on the block, and of course the family were not recognized in good society at all—no 'nigger-traders' ever were." I do not recall seeing anybody in Raleigh whose father had seriously challenged anyone to fight a duel. But Mrs. Jones did tell me that her father, when in the United States Congress in the 1850's, challenged a fiery abolitionist Congressman, Galusha A. Grow from Pennsylvania, to a duel. Grow rejected the challenge. I think Mrs. Jones used the phrase, "refused to fight," probably not having outlived the antebellum Southern idea that failure to accept a challenge indicated a lack of bravery. Anyhow Mr. Grow took the attitude of an Irishman my mother used to laugh about who said under similar circumstances, "Sure and begorra, and I'd rather be a coward five minutes than be dead all my lifetime!" In Mr. Grow's case he not only "lived on" but became a Republican Congressman-at-large from Pennsylvania as late as 1894-1903, dying in 1907 at age eighty-five.

In some respects more people then were willing to be unconventional than now. Their profiles, it seems to me, were drawn in bolder lines with rougher edges than those of conforming modern man. Notable for example was the craggy figure and thunderous voice of old man Swift Galloway in our state legislature. When prohibition was discussed he said if it was adopted he would like to take frequent brief vacations in hell. He once indicated his zest for living by saying, "I want to live to be four hundred years old—and be hung for rape!" Nearly every county seat had some man whose individuality sometimes took such a turn as William Polk reports about old Judge Alfred Crabtree who "hated so many people that he couldn't keep them straight and so used to sit on his porch and ask his wife as some foe passed by, 'What am I mad at that damned scoundrel for, Marina?' "

I am also reminded of an ancient kinsman who had a weakness both for rhyming and joking. Once when some visitors showed up at a well-laden country supper he amazed his guests by "asking grace" as follows:

We thank thee, Lord, for Thy kind relief
Thou hast set before us both pork and beef—
But, oh, it fills our heart with sorrow
We'll eat today and have none tomorrow!

Of course the visitors knew what a prankster he was and were unrestrained in their appetites!

Names in those days were certainly unconventional! A cousin of mine named his twins Joe Tom and Tom Joe. The first Raleigh doctor I knew had the unusual name of Wisconsin Iowa Royster and a brother, Vermont Connecticut Royster. Another brother was named Arkansas Delaware, and two sisters were Indiana Georgia and Virginia Carolina. (Incidentally, the grandson of this Vermont Connecticut and his namesake is now the Pulitzer prizewinning editor of the *Wall Street Journal*.) Another later example of unconventionality occurred when a "first family" Raleigh lady became head of an organization of "Women Opposed to Woman Suffrage"!

At that time Raleigh was generally known as "The City of Oaks," but many trees had been lost in leveling streets and from other causes. At one time Raleigh's main street, Fayetteville Street, had been lined with beautiful elms but these had been cut down when some misguided advocate of "progress" insisted that Raleigh "ought to look more like a city" and its main street more like Broadway!

The vicissitudes of transportation in this period are illustrated by one or two experiences I had when I went back to Chatham County to visit my family. There was a little six-mile railroad track in Chatham from Cumnock to Colon which gave the people of our rural community access to the Seaboard Railroad. It carried one passenger car along with several box cars and operated on an amazingly casual schedule. Once when I was returning to Raleigh this little train was late, and the conductor-fireman, seeing that I was plainly anxious, asked if I *needed* to make the Colon connection. I told him I did.

"Well, we'll just drop off all the heavy boxcars that slow us down and you get up in the locomotive with me."

Then with raucous complaint, the rusty couplings between cars and engine were disconnected and we sped on our way. Another time some of the train cars overturned and the same accommodating engineer, who knew by then that I was always in a hurry, carried me to the station in an open handcar! These handcars were operated by two men pumping handles up and down like a seesaw.

At that time when no such facilities as radio and television were available, many distinguished statesmen, scholars, and orators traveled from city to city delivering the same speech at various places. The Chautauqua was the most famous agency bringing selected groups of speakers to cities in this way. The subjects of Chautauqua addresses were usually important subjects relating to individual and national welfare. These were, however, occasionally broken into by touches of humor.

"Cuba or the Battle Cry of Freedom" was the dramatic title of a fiery oration in the Chautauqua series I heard Thomas Dixon deliver early in 1897. Sentiment against Spain's domination of Cuba built up until one morning a few months later I was awakened by the news, "The Spaniards have sunk the *Maine!*" Of course the Spanish-American war was soon the dominant interest of all America. Great sentimental value was given it as evidencing the reunion of North and South, with Southern boys now wearing the blue whose fathers had once worn the gray. Vividly I recall attending the funeral of Worth Bagley (a brother of Mrs. Josephus Daniels) whose death excited nation-wide sympathy and comment. He was the first naval officer from the South to die in battle as a representative of the now re-united nation.

For four years after I came to *The Progressive Farmer* all the typesetting was done by hand. This meant that for each letter of the alphabet there was a tiny piece of lead about half the size of an old-fashioned match with a letter—*a, b, c,* etc.—embossed at the top. These leaden pieces were kept in twenty-six separate compartments on the printer's elevated desk, all these letters being in lower case Roman type. A similar desk just above contained twenty-six letters all in capitals. There were two other "fonts," as they were called, which carried italic caps and lower case. The printer's duty was to pick up one of these tiny pieces of lead for each letter in the word the copy called for. Next he would separate the words with tiny pieces of lead without heads in order to produce the necessary blank spaces. Picking up any paper or magazine now we are amazed to consider how many thousands of separate motions every old-fashioned printer had to make in setting type for a single issue of even a small publication—and how easy it was for errors to occur. Perhaps it was because of this fact that so much profanity spontaneously developed. Always the printer's helper was called "the printer's devil" and all broken type was thrown into a box called "the hell box."

Naturally it was with real regret that *The Progressive Farmer* gave up old friends who had so long labored with handset type when we installed instead a new Mergenthaler machine to do the typesetting. Fortunately, I think it was not hard at that time for these men to get other employment. But the event brings sharply to mind the situation today when automation so seriously threatens to throw many men and women out of work faster than new jobs can be found for them.

Since few typewriters were in use at that time manuscripts were sent to us by practitioners of every known style of chirography and this increased the possibilities of error. Fictional, of course, was a commonly reported story of a distinguished but sometimes bibulous North Carolinian. A writer intended to describe him as "battle-scarred" only to have the word appear "bottle-scarred"—and when an attempted correction was made, "battle-scared"! But the most emphatic opposition to the change from handwriting to typewriting was expressed by the unconventional Judge Risden Tyler Bennett. Getting a typewritten letter from a friend who had always before written him in longhand, Judge Bennett sent the letter back to the writer with the one-sentence criticism, "Damn this metallic age!"

I am also reminded that while today nearly every business and bank on Raleigh's main business street belongs to some chain or group, such a thing was then wholly unknown. Nearly every important grocery or drygoods store was operated under the name of one or two individuals. Each Raleigh bank was known generally by the name of its largest owner or officer. There was Colonel Johnson's bank, Joe Brown's bank, Ben Lacy's bank, and John Pullen's bank.

Another important business difference was this: it was then very common for a merchant first to ask a certain price for an article, for the customer then to offer a somewhat lower price, and for this bargaining to go on for quite some time until the sale was made—frequently at much less than the price originally asked. I remember when one leading clothier finally advertised his as "The One-Price Clothing Store" and he probably received more business and respect for doing so.

As a young editor I made mistakes, of course—as I have done in later years. But one mistake brought me a friendship I long treasured. The venerable ex-senator, General M. W.

Ransom, had been listed on the program of a state meeting of importance. In reporting it I criticized the committee for his appearance, saying that he was clearly in his dotage and should not have been asked to preside. I have always been glad that next week I frankly and fully apologized for what I had said, adding that the venerable Senator's long service to the state, whatever his condition at the meeting, should have prevented me from making so ungenerous and even unjustifiably harsh remark. "Your frank acknowledgment of an error was the beginning of my warm friendship for you," Dr. E. C. Brooks later told me. At that time I think I may have been too anxious to be known as an "outspoken editor." In later years I came to value more fully a quality illustrated by my friend Dr. W. W. Long of South Carolina—"the ability to disagree without being disagreeable."

Before I came to Raleigh employment opportunities for women outside the home were tragically limited. Teaching was almost the only important avenue open to educated women, and teachers were poorly paid. The present Woman's College at Greensboro was first called "The State Normal and Industrial College" to indicate some broadening of opportunities. But these came slowly. I had been on *The Progressive Farmer* several years before we had a woman employee. We first had a woman bookkeeper. Properly trained stenographers were rare. Incidentally, one of my first was a granddaughter of one of the famous Siamese twins who had become North Carolina citizens quite some time before.

About the same time "business colleges" became popular for young men seeking business employment. Their standards were not very high but at any rate a "degree" from one of them gave a young man some specific label to suggest business instead of merely social qualifications. A common story told at the time was that of a Charleston youth who sought employment with a North Carolina banker who promptly asked for a recommendation from his former Charleston employer. The reply dealt effusively with the young man's social standing, the fact that his father had been a colonel, his mother a leader in the D.A.R. and Colonial Dames, etc. Thereupon the following reply was transmitted to Charleston: "We appreciate your letter of the 27th instant. Unfortunately, however, we do not want a young man for breeding purposes. We want him to keep books."

One of the greatest friends I was to make in Raleigh was not a man or a woman. It was the State Library. As I remember it now, it was shabby in appearance and the librarian, a one-legged Confederate soldier, was in no sense a scholar. Yet to me it had all the glory of a prince's palace because there I could find such welcome friends as Homer, Plutarch, Dante, Epictetus, Milton, Adam Smith, Carlyle, Emerson, Thoreau, Tennyson, and Browning. Before I was nineteen I had read with real joy nearly all the foremost books of literature and history that were required reading for college students. Biography, history, and poetry especially interested me. I still recall the new world that was opened up to me by Darwin's *Origin of Species* and *Descent of Man,* and the thrill I received from my first reading of Tennyson's *Ulysses:*

> Yet all experience is an arch wherethro'
> Gleams that untravell'd world, whose margin fades
> For ever and for ever when I move . . . .
> To strive, to seek, to find, and not to yield.

Reading all of Adam Smith's *Wealth of Nations* was amply repaid if I had found in it just the one sentence that I later used in all my fighting for "equality for agriculture." That sentence runs like this: "The policy of all great nations since the downfall of the Roman Empire has been more favorable to commerce, the industry of the city, than to agriculture, the industry of the country." And I insisted that our own nation had too often practiced the same discrimination.

Of light literature the library contained little though I think it included the popular book-length poem, *Lucille*, from which I have always remembered (and always with approval) only two lines:

If a woman is pretty to me doesn't matter
Be she blonde or brunette so she lets me look at her!

I became one of the library's most constant visitors and one of Librarian Sherrill's special friends.

If by this time somebody asks if my friends were confined to persons of the masculine persuasion—or to the neuter Library—some proofs to the contrary might be mentioned. About the same day I reached Raleigh, three young ladies from another town, one of whom I found especially charming, arrived for the commencement festivities at A. & M. College, now State College. At that time one of the year's most important social events for most young people was the annual Sunday school picnic of the church they attended. This often meant a railroad trip for which several coaches were added to the regular train. The following week I accompanied the young lady (and dozens of other young people, though I gave them little notice) to Chapel Hill for the annual Sunday school outing. It was only thirty miles to Chapel Hill, but to get there we had to go from Raleigh on the main line of the Southern Railway to University Station and transfer on a short line to Chapel Hill, four or five miles away. Then followed a delightful day in which I saw among other things the Old East Building which was there when my grandmother's brother enrolled in 1817 and was still a major feature when my two cousins had studied there in the 1880's. But the major interest was the young lady herself, and before she left Raleigh I composed a poem in her honor, half humorous and half adoring, which won excited praise from her and her friends but which neither of us took too seriously later on. At least *she* did not, for not long afterward she went over the nearby South Carolina line and married a more ready or aggressive suitor. Of course young love at sixteen is never regarded seriously in later years and I may have soon consoled myself by a cynical remark which was almost a proverb among young men at that time, "Never run after a street car or a woman. There will be another one along in fifteen minutes." At that time I was in easy walking distance of Meredith, Peace, and St. Mary's Colleges and soon met many attractive young ladies at their social affairs and public lectures.

When summer came it meant that a great many of my friends would be "going to the Springs." Nearly all these springs were supposed to have medicinal value though most doctors later insisted that the physical benefits resulted mainly from drinking more water than usual plus the rest and recreation these annual trips to the Springs involved. Governor Aycock, his relatives, and kin mainly went to Seven Springs near Goldsboro whose multiplicity of numbers might suggest some kind of magic. In western North Carolina, Cleveland Springs was a favorite summer resort. But when I was in my early twenties most of my Raleigh friends, including J. W. Bailey and his sister's family, went to Buffalo Lithia Springs in Mecklenburg County, Virginia. Many Virginians from Richmond and elsewhere were sure to be found there and other visitors from as far away as Texas. Since there were then no automobiles and since travel preparations and railway schedules were a constant nuisance, the families who came to "enjoy the water" usually stayed from two weeks to two months and therefore formed many friendships often renewed year after year. As

I remember it, the four main forms of amusement were bowling, drinking water, dancing the Virginia Reel, and courting pretty Virginia girls. I made respectable scores at bowling and enjoyed all four forms of delight in some degree (especially the fourth) but the nearest praise I ever received for my dancing was the remark, "It is fortunate for Poe that his salvation doesn't depend on how he dances the Virginia Reel!"

By that time I had also learned that my boyhood hobby astronomy might be used not only to enrich knowledge but romance. For what young man of my time on summer evenings failed to find the other sex interested in seeing and naming some particularly beautiful star, then saying in happy unison, "That is now our star—and as long as we live we will think of each other whenever or wherever we see it." And now what aging man fails to find the star (or several stars, I might confess) still there—glittering on in an eternal youth which, alas, neither he nor any fellow spirit of his earlier days has been able to retain.

All in all the cordiality with which Raleigh received a young man who had only recently been doing all kinds of farm work is highly indicative of the democratic transition that was occurring all over the South in the 1880-1920 period. Gradually new businesses were springing up at a time when small businesses had an opportunity to grow and flourish, in a manner such as the domination of big units does not now permit. The domination of society and commerce by the former wealthy slaveholding group had been relaxed. A new recognition of merit in the non-slaveowning group had, indeed, been imperative ever since the South realized that this once-contemned group had not only made up the overwhelming bulk of the men in the Confederate army but had fought with a courage and daring certainly in no degree surpassed by their wealthier comrades. Furthermore, as I frequently pointed out, the victorious North had won this victory largely because it had chosen as leader a man from the South's slaveless, landless, and almost school-less class and that his successor had also come from the same class. Their potentialities the New South must recognize and utilize as the Old South had unfortunately failed to do.

CHAPTER SIX

Building The Progressive Farmer

LAUGHINGLY, I USED TO TELL MY SMALL CHILDREN, "I BECAME editor of *The Progressive Farmer* on July 4, 1899, and ever since then every time you go into any town on any July 4, you'll find all the main streets gay with flags!" While my becoming editor was in no whit responsible for any flag ever seen on that day, it was a truly memorable date in my life.

For several years before this date, I had toyed with the idea of going to college. Under present conditions, of course, North Carolina State College would be a natural choice for anyone in agricultural work. Then, however, A. & M. College, as it was called, did not have in any impressive degree the faculty, curriculum, or prestige that it has since so brilliantly achieved. Most of its courses, I should say, were little more advanced than those of many a good high school today. Hence in order to get a better rounded or classical education I was urged by some friends to go to Wake Forest. Other friends, notably J. W. Bailey, himself a Wake Forest graduate, strongly urged me to stick to editorial work as a greater opportunity and greater intellectual challenge. But Dr. J. B. Carlyle of Wake Forest was persistent in his appeals and helped me prepare to meet entrance requirements. Hence early in 1899 we carried an advertisement to pay for my first year's tuition at Wake Forest. I suppose I should still be entitled to take advantage of it—if I should present my claims—but I have never done so.

When this advertisement appeared I was only an associate editor of *The Progressive Farmer.* J. L. Ramsey, listed as editor, was still holding a government position. Within the next few weeks his government service expired, and Mr. Denmark and the Polk family decided I had fully demonstrated my ability to succeed him as editor-in-chief. They offered me the position and I accepted—instead of going to college. In announcing my promotion I simply stated in one paragraph in *The Progressive Farmer* that I had already been doing most of the editorial work for some months and would continue the same policies I had been following.

Many have since asked me if I have regretted my decision to become editor rather than go to college. I often think of Thomas Carlyle's famous saying at that time, "The true university of these days is a collection of books," and while I didn't go to college, in some degree at least two colleges did come to me. What I mean is this: two of my more fortunate older first cousins went to the University of North Carolina at Chapel Hill and two others to Trinity College (now Duke), and from them I had passed on to me college textbooks on literature, history, science, mathematics, and language. These I did not have to *make myself* study for I always *enjoyed* tackling hard studies. After coming to Raleigh I rejoiced in having all the added treasures of the North Carolina State Library at my disposal. All my life I have been an avid, rapid, and persistent reader.

Furthermore as editor I did continue to "study agriculture" with greater depth and expansiveness than I could have ever done as a college student of that period. I also resolved to keep a continuing and up-to-date study of agricultural research by applying its principles in the operation of a cotton-tobacco-dairy farm (which started with 89 acres and eventually included 700), supplemented by frequent visits to agricultural colleges and experiment stations both in the United States and the countries I visited.

When I became editor, *The Progressive Farmer* was a small weekly paper of about 5,000 circulation, with a subscription price of $1.00 a year. It had the same size page as that of most daily papers today. After 1901 it became sixteen pages of its present-day page size and eventually became not a "paper" but the magazine it is today.

In the years just after 1899 *The Progressive Farmer* absorbed several state farm papers of small circulation and also conducted vigorous subscription efforts by mail. At one time when the paper was still a weekly we made a special introductory offer of "Ten Weeks for Ten Cents" and asked every subscriber to get ten friends to give ten cents for a ten weeks "get-acquainted" subscription. Of course *The Progressive Farmer* was sent to these persons only for the ten-weeks period unless they renewed for a longer period.

At that time, however, it was standard practice for publishers to continue sending their publications (when the reader subscribed for a year or more) beyond the time paid for. In such cases it was thought the subscriber's duty to notify the publisher when he wished his subscription stopped, and a subscriber's failure to make payment for the extra period was treated as a failure to pay an honest debt. One editor even attained some fame by his formula for collecting such a debt as expressed in the following verse:

> The man who cheats his paper
> Out of a single cent
> Will never reach that heavenly land
> Where old Elijah went.

> But when at last his race is run—
> This life of toil and woe—
> He'll straightway go to that fiery land
> Where they never shovel snow.

In my earliest years with *The Progressive Farmer* I was as frugal as possible and saved nearly every cent I earned. Part of the time the paper was not able to pay my salary and a relatively large sum accumulated that was due me. At any rate, in 1903 by using all my savings and borrowing $1300, I was able to buy *The Progressive Farmer,* taking 46⅔ per cent of the stock myself while four friends bought the remaining 53⅓ per cent.

On December 23, 1903, the four men I had chosen to join me in this enterprise met with me to complete plans for organization and operation. These were Dr. B. W. Kilgore, director of the State Experiment Station; Dr. Charles W. Burkett, head of agriculture at A. & M. College; T. B. Parker, long a leader in the State Farmers' Alliance and active in Farmers' Institute work. All these were chosen because they were not only my good friends but were active leaders in the state's agricultural progress. J. W. Bailey was added because of his keen personal interest in me and because of his experience as editor and chief owner of *The Biblical Recorder* and because of our joint interest in the Mutual Publishing Company which did printing for both his paper and mine.

It is interesting now to recall that just six days before our meeting, December 17, 1903, an event occurred that was to change the history of the world and the fate of millions of people. Yet I do not remember hearing anybody ask, "Have you heard anything about what those two Wright fellows did down at Kill Devil Hill last Thursday?" What they had done we thought little more important than the development of a somewhat improved balloon. So we went ahead and transacted our business, undisturbed by any thought of what future airplanes might do, or speculating on the changes that might be brought about in Southern farming which Dr. Seaman A. Knapp characterized as being "mainly a series of motions inherited from Adam." The total capital stock of our new company was $7,500 of which $6,200 was paid J. W. Denmark for *The Progressive Farmer* and $1,300 put into the treasury for promotion purposes. A charter I had written was accepted and I was unanimously elected president and editor at a salary of $1,000 a year. Two voices were heard in tones of enthusiasm about the outlook. Bailey said, "We are getting a $10,000-a-year man for $1,000!" But what started incredulous laughter was Dr. Burkett's comment referring to our $7,500 total capital stock, "I tell you, gentlemen," he said, "I tell you the time will come when this company will make $7,500 in a single year!" If some angel with divine authority had remarked to some of us, "The time will indeed come when it will make $75,000 a year," the angel himself might not have been believed. And if the angel had added, "There will come a period of depression when you will lose $75,000 in one year," we might also have been saved from believing that!

After organizing our company and becoming president, I also took over the functions of circulation manager and advertising manager until the time we could grow enough to justify employing an individual for each position.

As circulation manager I still remember some of the unorthodox methods I used. For example, one circular letter to prospective subscribers began with a verse I had heard somewhere, possibly in some non-commercial connection:

> There was a young lady in Siam
> Who said to her lover named Priam,

"To kiss me of course
You'll have to use force—
But the Lord knows you're stronger than I am!"

Then followed a report that *The Progressive Farmer* was making amazing growth by voluntary methods and we hoped the recipient would join without our having to use force.

To subscribers who had let their subscriptions expire we had envelopes printed with a large line in heavy script reading, "A Letter to the Prodigal Son," the subscriber's name and address appearing written below. In this we explained that just as the Prodigal's old father had yearned and looked for his boy's return so we had yearned for this particular reader to come back into our fold. A few reports did reach us of farmers who disliked having themselves publicly mentioned as "prodigal sons," but on the whole the letter brought such a good response that for several years we used it to win back subscribers temporarily lost from our list.

After we had *The Progressive Farmer* well under way we discovered that another publication with precisely the same name had been started and was being promoted in the Southwest. Fortunately we had had our title copyrighted and were eventually able to scare our threatened competition into not using it. He then resorted to the name *The Aggressive Farmer*, which would have meant endless confusion in the case of fast-talking subscription agents. But this "double-talk" difficulty did not last long.

The Progressive Farmer has always been a crusading publication. The very first issue in 1886 had announced a crusade for a land-grant agricultural college (now State College) in North Carolina. Only two or three years later, through Colonel Polk as its editor, it was leading in the campaign to organize farmers in the National Farmers' Alliance movement. Almost immediately after becoming editor in 1899 I found one opportunity after another for promoting causes in which I was deeply interested. The first crusade I joined was for better public education such as I had yearned for when at age sixteen I wrote my first article for the paper.

We supported the Suffrage Amendment to the state constitution adopted by popular vote in 1900 providing an educational test for voters and the later Aycock program of universal education. Until that time many good citizens such as my Uncle Dan Riddle had said flatly, "It is not fair to make me pay to educate another man's children." One very large group said, "It is not right to make white people educate Negro children." Both these philosophies were deep-rooted and hard to eradicate. For months their advocates seriously threatened to repudiate and politically destroy Aycock who had faced both issues with headlong opposition and refused to budge. In the matter of Negro education all over the South another blockbuster charge had been made, principally by United States Senator Vardaman of Mississippi: "Educated Negroes show a higher percentage of crime than uneducated Negroes." This declaration I not only believed false but proved false by the facts and figures I gathered from state prisons all over the South. The results of this research were published in Northern and Southern publications, and from that time on little was ever heard of this once widely accepted error.

The Progressive Farmer also battled along with our educational leaders not only for increased local taxation but for state appropriations and to increase the required minimum constitutional school term from four months to six months. We joined in an even more bitter fight about compulsory school attendance. The right of parents to govern all the activities of their children was generally regarded as something divine and inalienable, subject to no outside authority.

For years "compulsory" was a dirty word to most politicians. They stood aghast at the mere mention of it. Especially was it argued, "Farmers will never approve compulsory education because of the spring and fall need to use children for cotton chopping and cotton picking." But the educational forces had not been idle nor had those of us on *The Progressive Farmer*. Not long after the Farmers' Educational and Cooperative Union reached a membership of 40,000 in North Carolina and held its state meeting in Raleigh, to the amazement of all weak-kneed politicians the news went out, "The Farmers' Union has emphatically declared for compulsory education!"

We fought for libraries for small public schools and they at last became a reality. To my great gratification the legislature provided funds on a state-county matching basis. Furthermore we induced the State Department of Agriculture to provide matching funds for reproducing famous masterpieces of rural art to hang in rural schools.

When I bought *The Progressive Farmer* and organized our company I wrote this significant paragraph into our bylaws:

"The paper will be kept absolutely free from all partisan politics and political scheming. Its chief and highest aim will be to inform and help our Southern farmers with every vital problem affecting their interests—at the right time, in the right way, by the right men. In addition to this, however, I shall expect perfect freedom to discuss current events and current problems in a clear and fearless manner, but without bitterness or partisanship. The paper should be not only a farm journal, but a farmer's journal—interested in rural mail delivery as well as in cotton growing, in good rural schools and good country roads as well as in fertilizers and soils. In short, it will be devoted to everything that makes for the uplift or betterment of farm life."

J. W. Bailey once wrote, "*The Progressive Farmer* is a good paper not only for farmers but for progressive people generally." In the early years of our publication this was especially true. In thousands of homes ours was the only publication the family received—with the possible exception of the denominational organ and the county weekly. There were few national magazines of quality and these few were beyond the price-range of the average farmer's budget. "Hence," we declared, "it must be a major purpose of *The Progressive Farmer* not only to enrich the farmer's pocketbook but enrich country life." No other farm publication gave so much attention to problems of farm organizations, health conditions, the rural church, and cultural influences and agencies.

Being an avid poetry lover I inserted one or more poems of excellence in every issue of *The Progressive Farmer*. Most notable of all was one that appeared in 1899, the year I became editor, and that I instantly recognized and editorially acclaimed as sure to make history—Edwin Markham's "The Man with the Hoe." The intervening years have proved it the most potent and prophetic single poem of the last hundred years. Taking as his text the toil-burdened figure in Millet's painting, Edwin Markham saw in the downtrodden peasant masses of the world the force that would ultimately destroy tyrants, emperors, and kings.

> O masters, lords and rulers in all lands,
> How will the Future reckon with this man?
> How answer his brute question in that hour
> When whirlwinds of rebellion shake all shores?
> How will it be with kingdoms and with kings—
> With those who shaped him to the thing he is—
> When this dumb terror shall rise to judge the world,
> After the silence of the centuries?

The downfall of Czarist rule in Russia, the end of English domination of India's millions, and the exploitation of the poor wherever found in the Old World or the New—these were all foreshadowed in Markham's poem. It made him famous overnight. Later I was especially glad to become his personal friend and to receive from him autographed copies of "The Man with the Hoe" and of one of the most famous quatrains in American literature—

CIRCLES

> He drew a circle to shut me out;
> Heretic, rebel, a thing to flout;
> But Love and I had the wit to win—
> We drew a circle that took him in.

Even more impressive was the phrase I once heard Markham use in a conversation I had with him in Raleigh. "Man's supreme needs," he said, "are represented by three B's—Bread, Beauty, and Brotherhood." By bread he meant the material things we need; by beauty he would include all that is beautiful in art, music, nature, poetry, and human conduct; and brotherhood, of course, involved a cordial and vital principle, "Thou shalt love thy neighbor as thyself." In speeches for years afterward I frequently acclaimed this doctrine of "The Three B's" as did my younger son after me.

The first editor of a rather adequately supported "Home Department" of *The Progressive Farmer* was Mrs. Juanita Polk Denmark. A daughter of Colonel L. L. Polk, she wrote under the nom de plume "Aunt Jennie." Naturally this first Home Department differed radically from what it has become in later years. Very largely it emphasized the family life, rural community life, and social relations, especially the problems of parents and of young people of both sexes.

Mainly the articles printed were letters from farmers' wives and from young people accompanied by "Aunt Jennie's" comments—comments that combined kindliness and common sense in much the same way that Dorothy Dix later practiced.

Interest in home economics grew constantly. Sometime after Colonel Polk's daughter gave up writing for *The Progressive Farmer* in 1906, the Home Department took another forward step. A highly trained home economics specialist—Mrs. F. L. Stevens—became our home editor, giving about half her time to the work and inaugurating scientific "Home Reading Courses" in home economics. This was a valuable contribution to Southern homemaking, for at that time few schools offered home economics courses, and home demonstration work for women and girls had not then been inaugurated. In a few years, however, Dr. and Mrs. Stevens left for positions at Purdue University.

Then it was that *The Progressive Farmer* did something no other Southern farm publication had ever done: we employed a highly trained woman to give her whole time as editor of the Home Department—Mrs. W. N. Hutt. With such a full-time editor the Home Department soon blossomed. Mrs. Hutt not only continued discussions of home economics problems (adopting an easy conversational style of imparting information) but promoted community organizations of farm women all over the South, "The United Farm Women," and provided programs for them. She also recognized the importance of young people's problems in her "Teens and Twenties" department. In a letter offering her the position I had said: "We want the department to be full of instruction, but we want it also to be full of inspiration and human interest and good fellowship. A textbook, as you know, may be full of information, and yet be as dead and uninspiring as an Egyptian mummy. . . . We want the women to feel that they are partners in the department, responsible for its success, helping with the suggestions they give as well as being helped by the suggestions they get, and that the woman who edits it is not way above them but one of them. . . . We should emphasize better homemaking as well as better housekeeping—better training of children . . . more beauty and music and games and reading and comradeship in the family circle . . . the financial and social partnership of husband and wife and children . . . better schools, better churches, better roads, better public health work, more libraries and women's institutes and lyceums and reading clubs and all the agencies of a fuller social and intellectual life."

Not long after county agents were named to help farm men, the farm women demanded that county home agents also be named to help them. These home agents had many rich experiences in various parts of the United States. In Texas my friend Miss Sallie Hill (who later became editor of our Home Department) "rode herd," as she calls it, over a territory that included fifty counties from Waco to El Paso! "My circuit," she used to tell me, "for I was really 'a circuit rider,' involved 1,920 miles! Some of my border trips were vast stretches where I seldom saw a house—only some sheep herder in the distance and an occasional filling station—fifty to sixty miles in some instances. I must confess those trips by myself seemed endless. One day I realized I was being followed by a car. I could even see a gun lying across the driver's wheel! I sped up as fast as I could go and went into a filling station at Langtry. The man who had followed me came up beside me and said, 'Lady, I didn't know any Ford could go that fast! I am a border patrol and was trying to ride alongside you to tell you not to be afraid, but I couldn't catch up with you!' In explanation of my speed I must say that we could see the Rio Grande River, and border depredations from Mexico across the river were reported from time to time. Another time I had to drive across Diablo or Devil's River on stepping stones in about two feet of water. I was advised not to get off the stones; I did not."

Once when Miss Hill and I were reminiscing about changing times she said, "Today we just take for granted so many services. We tend to forget earlier conditions in farm homes. When a homemaker successfully kept peaches or tomatoes forty or fifty years ago she attributed it to luck—so little was known about the importance of complete sterilization and bacteriology. Another conversational item in those early days on farms was: 'I can't get my hens to set.' Then we always felt that the hens rebelled against setting; we now know that the hens were sorely beset with vermin and so we treat the hen first. But then that was a 4-H hazard every member had to take! The goal was forty-five baby chicks from three setting hens. As a home demonstration agent and as a supervisor I would hear the chorus in late spring, 'I have no baby chicks; my hens won't set.' One intrepid farm daughter set out to outwit the hens. She tied two bricks together with a heavy cord and put the cord just over the setting hen. Quite obviously the hen could do nothing but set—and in due time produced a goodly hatch! I mention this not as a recommendation but as evidence of the determination of some of our earlier 4-H members to complete a project! As for our women, they began to get courses and information in everything they desired: art appreciation, home building, furnishing, and even hanging the pictures!"

For some years, I suppose, after organizing our company I made the mistake of thinking of *The Progressive Farmer* too largely as my own property. True I had carried it through a considerable period when only my failure to collect my small salary had enabled it to survive and for some time some people called it "The Poe-gressive Farmer." But it was only by getting strong men associated with me that the company attained the distinction and success it later achieved.

Powerful editorial and managerial help came in 1908 when, at my urging, my friend Dr. Tait Butler became vice president of our magazine and editor of the *Southern Farm Gazette* of Starkville, Mississippi, which we had acquired. This paper, which Dr. Butler had founded in 1895 and operated for several years before leaving it for official agricultural work, was soon named the Mid-South Edition of *The Progressive Farmer*. Dr. Butler was an outstanding leader in the livestock field and won international prominence for his leadership in eradicating the cattle tick scourge that had so long prevented Southern farmers from selling their cattle in Northern markets. So at an agricultural meeting in Washington when some "expert" claimed that cattle ticks could not be eradicated in the South, Dr. Butler rose up and exclaimed, "But I have done it!" and explained how.

He was a deep thinker, a forceful speaker, outspoken but scrupulously fair in his views. As a director of *The Progressive Farmer* he was equally clear in expressing his own views and in accepting the rule of the majority whenever his own viewpoint was not sustained. In addition to helping get rid of the cattle tick, he did an almost monumental work in ridding Southern farmers of ridiculous superstitions about livestock diseases. For generations many weak, emaciated cattle had been generally diagnosed by farmers as having either "hollow horn" or "hollow tail." For hollow horn the owners bored into the horns of the cattle and applied some supposedly helpful mixture. For hollow tail the owner split the cow's tail and inserted salt in abundance. For all such superstitions about both diseases and remedies Dr. Butler had only the bluntest ridicule. "Your cattle," he said, "are not suffering from hollow tail. *What they are suffering from is hollow bellies!*" And this was gradually accepted as a fact.

The meagerness of Southern pastures and the failure to give pastures either good land or good fertilizer likewise exasperated him. The average Southern pasture he satirized as being "a piece of land surrounded by a wire where no grass grows."

In all my own activities as president of the *The Progressive Farmer* company I have constantly aimed to be not a boss but a leader. I have also urged all our editors and department heads to keep this distinction in mind, illustrating it by a paragraph I read long ago in a Clemson College bulletin:

The boss drives his men; the leader coaches them.
The boss depends upon authority; the leader on good will.
The boss inspires fear; the leader inspires enthusiasm.
The boss says "I"; the leader says "we."
The boss assigns the tasks; the leader sets the pace.
The boss says "Be on time"; the leader is there ahead of time.
The boss knows how it is done; the leader shows how.
The boss says, "Go"; the leader says, "Let's go."
The boss makes work a drudgery; the leader makes it a game.

Nobody in our organization more strikingly illustrated the best qualities of leadership than Dr. B. W. Kilgore. It was sometimes said he could walk over a basket of eggs without breaking a shell! For years as director of agricultural extension work conducted by a joint committee of conflicting personalities in the state agricultural college and state department of agriculture, he carried forward the state's agriculture at a rate of speed few other states could equal. Later he—and still later his son Ben, Jr.—became editors of our Kentucky-Tennessee Edition, young Ben dying of a sudden heart attack after a promising but too strenuous campaign to become governor of Kentucky.

Since conditions did not justify Messrs. Bailey, Burkett,

and Parker in becoming full-time associates with me in our company, I am indebted to them for having sold their stock (at prices wholly satisfactory to them) to Dr. Butler as my editorial associate and to my long-time personal friend, John S. Pearson, as our general business manager, each of these men thereby acquiring 20 per cent of the company's stock. Pearson combined executive ability, rare modesty, and a seemingly effortless capacity for making a trusting friend of every person he met. This capacity for appraising clearly and fairly all angles of any personality conflict and then making each man see the other man's position helped our organization in many a situation that might otherwise have caused serious loss. Nearly every upset employee was willing to accept John Pearson's final judgment and go back to his work contented. The late Senator J. W. Bailey wrote of him in 1946: "When I consider all I have known, he holds his place second to none, a gentleman beyond compare."

Nor should I fail to mention here my long-time associate editor, Professor W. F. Massey. Many others had preached the economic value of soil conservation but no one had ever so strongly preached soil-saving as *a moral duty*. "The earth is the Lord's and the fullness thereof," he would quote, and add, "We are tenants of the Almighty and responsible to Him for the use we make of His soil which must feed and sustain all the long generations of men." When well past eighty he wrote, "For forty years my morning prayer to God has been that I might that day help someone to a better care of His soil."

In later years Eugene Butler, Dr. Butler's son, became editor of our Texas Edition and succeeded Dr. Butler as vice president. To this service (and to his later larger service when he succeeded me as president and editor-in-chief) he brought not only marked ability inherited from his father but the wit, humor, and ability that characterized his mother even when she was past ninety.

Meanwhile a large staff of editors, experts in various phases of agriculture, had been employed and stationed at our four editorial and business offices: Raleigh, Birmingham, Memphis, Dallas. At our Birmingham office where copies of all our editions have been printed since 1911, no other editor surpassed or equaled Alexander Nunn, who still renders distinguished service as vice president and executive editor in cooperation with President Eugene Butler and General Manager Fowler Dugger. Both Mr. Butler and Dr. Nunn have won national recognition for agricultural statesmanship and have been especially effective in helping shape the research and extension policies of our Southern agricultural colleges and the United States Department of Agriculture. Mr. Butler one year received the coveted Hoblitzelle Award for agricultural leadership which carried a cash award of $5,000. Several of our other editors eagerly offered to swap their non-cash honorary doctorates for his big Texas-size hunk of cold cash—especially since the Hoblitzelle Award implied achievement equal to or surpassing an ordinary doctorate! Dr. Nunn has also been especially active in church activities, having been sent to one or more international conferences of Methodist leaders in London. Mr. Butler and Dr. Nunn made important contributions to a fairly recent book, *This Is the South,* which is perhaps the most effective review of all the most important aspects of its present-day life and culture.

For a long time all important policies of our company were decided by the Poe-Butler-Pearson-Kilgore quartet. Later some shares of stock were sold to other key men in our organization. But I now realize that for some time we did not make as full use of their talents as we should have made. Then we learned the importance of having committees to deal with special phases of our activities, bringing in on these committees W. C. Lassetter and younger men such as Eugene Butler, William Poe, Alexander Nunn, Paul Huey, the two remarkable Dugger brothers, and J. L. Rogers, to mention only a few. All these men were encouraged to express their views regardless of whether or not these views coincided with those of the Poe-Butler-Pearson-Kilgore quartet. We also gave a number of our ablest men a greater sense of identification with our company by naming them as directors or vice presidents, and they in turn got the best opinions of men working under them.

Meanwhile all of us redoubled our efforts to increase circulation. Five years after we bought the company we rejoiced in a subscription gain from 5,000 in 1903 to 38,259—adding "And We Have Just Begun to Grow!" By 1911 we had passed the 100,000 mark. A merger with the *Southern Ruralist* of Atlanta in 1931 enabled us to pass the 1,000,000 mark. And in a relatively short number of years after we bought *The Progressive Farmer* it chalked up the following pioneering accomplishments.

Ours was a leader in publishing separate editions. This meant that a *Progressive Farmer* reader in any one of our five edition-areas, Texas, Carolinas-Virginia, Georgia-Alabama-Florida, Kentucky-Tennessee, Mississippi-Arkansas-Louisiana, would read an edition reporting the latest and most vital agricultural news and counsel based on the best research and soundest farming experiences in his own particular part of the South—with some major features, of course, appearing in all five editions.

By guaranteeing the reliability of all advertisements we carried we took an even more remarkable step. Then many publishers—as all too many now—sold their advertising space just as they might sell space on a billboard, allowing the buyer to put on it any kind of claim or message, no matter how utterly false or misleading. At that time, too, a far larger and lower variety of crooks, frauds, and quacks sought victims through advertising. Even prominent church papers carried much such advertising. Especially serious were the misleading patent medicine cure-all advertisements that *The Progressive Farmer, Collier's Weekly,* and *Ladies' Home Journal* took the lead in exposing and denouncing. Many adolescents and others were half-scared to death by quacks who treated really insignificant symptoms as serious and then lured their victims on to greater and greater expenditures for some worthless, so-called remedy.

"The country's best diversified farm journal" was another claim made for *The Progressive Farmer.* It carried poems and stories by distinguished new writers like Jesse Stuart, encouraged the reading of the best ancient and modern books, fostered an appreciation of beauty in homes, schools, churches, and highways—and with it all included a saving dash of humor. As Edward K. Graham said, "It combines culture and agriculture."

John Pearson made little or no effort to influence editorial policies but he did more than once say, "We ought to condense any article as much as we can and then ask 'Is it worth $64 an inch?' " Sixty-four dollars an inch was the price we required advertisers to pay for space. For my part, I supported Dr. Butler's "passion for accuracy" by saying, "If we make one mistake in an article and that mistake is printed in one million copies of our magazine, have we not really made one million mistakes instead of just one?"

In this chapter without using too many statistics I have sought to summarize the major activities by which we built *The Progressive Farmer* from a small paper to a distinguished magazine. Like many other business men at that time I usually worked six days a week, stopping early enough

for a horseback ride with Bailey or Pearson and other friends
of both sexes.

Pearson frequently said, "Poe has proved that hard work
can be good fun!" And why shouldn't this have been true?
I had youth, energy, constant new goals to aim toward,
steady progress in reaching those goals, the daily comradeship of dedicated fellow workers, and the unusual satisfaction of knowing that we were helping people who not only
needed help but appreciated it. For over and over we heard
the report about *The Progressive Farmer,* "You can tell by
a man's farm whether he reads it or not." Under such circumstances one's daily work could indeed become what
Sidney Lanier said one's work should be, "a singing with
the hand."

In concluding this chapter I think I should say one word
for the encouragement of boys and girls who cannot go away
to college. Although I entered journalism instead of going to
college, through books, constant study at home, and travel
on three continents, I so applied myself that in 1914 Wake
Forest awarded me its Litt.D. degree, later the University of
North Carolina and Washington College conferred their
LL.D. degrees, Clemson its Doctor of Science, and North
Carolina State College its Doctor of Agricultural Education.

CHAPTER SEVEN

"To Be Young Was Very Heaven"

"WHAT WERE THE TEN BEST YEARS IN AMERICA AND THE WORLD since 1900?" This was the question a student of history recently put to himself. And he came up with this answer, "The years from 1900 to 1910."

With this opinion I believe most thoughtful persons—at least those of my generation—would agree. These were years in which man learned to fly but did not even dream of using flying as a means of murdering millions of his fellow creatures. Rather it was a time when the distinguished Dr. David Starr Jordan, lecturing in Raleigh in July, 1912, declared, "Peace will continue, for war is now impossible. It is a luxury no nation could afford since it would mean national bankruptcy." Even persons who did not share this view nevertheless thought mankind was moving toward the fulfillment of Tennyson's dream—

Till the war drum throbbed no longer and the battle flags
    were furled
In the Parliament of Man, the Federation of the world.

Such enthusiasm, too, was buttressed by a dynamic religious faith that caused a famous bishop to say, "The best things are ahead of us, not behind us. Only an atheist can be a pessimist. The movement of humanity under the rule of an all mighty, all gracious, and all loving God must be forward, not backward."

Few people thought the peace would be broken anywhere in Europe or Asia. If a break should occur anywhere, the might of the English navy applied at the right points could be expected to put it down. And for us here in America, how well I remember hearing John Temple Graves, noted Birmingham lecturer and columnist, exclaim, "Let us thank Almighty God for the two great oceans, one on the east and one on the west, which will forever protect us from attack by any other power." Such was the mood of America as a new century was hailed the certain forerunner of a far more brilliant record of human achievement.

Nationally the United States was still exulting over our amazingly easy victory over the forces of Spain, long a dominant figure in world affairs. We had freed Cuba—and thought it a much more glorious achievement than some of us might think it at the present date! We had taken over the Philippines and Puerto Rico, thus becoming a colonial power. In the 1900 presidential campaign dashing young Theodore Roosevelt, the "Rough Rider" hero of San Juan Hill, was the most colorful figure. In both state and nation the reins of power had passed forever from the hands of men who had fought in the Civil War.

In North Carolina it was, indeed, a new era and nearly all its leaders were personal friends of mine. The challenge of an up-and-coming new century seemed to turn all eyes forward. "Bliss was it in that dawn to be alive, but to be young was very heaven!" the poet Wordsworth had written about another era in another land, and I feel somewhat the same way about this period in North Carolina. It was a young man's world and I was among the youngest of the active workers. One of the state's most dynamic young men,

Charles Brantley Aycock, was elected governor in 1900 when he was just out of his thirties. Another young man in his thirties, Dr. Charles W. Burkett, became the first head of agriculture at State College. Charles D. McIver, still in his thirties, had but recently earned his title "A Steam Engine in Breeches," and Walter H. Page, who had placarded our reactionary leaders as "mummies" and said one of the state's major needs was "a few first class funerals," was only forty-one when he aroused all North Carolina by his appeal for "The Forgotten Man." Young Josephus Daniels, in his thirties, was making the state's biggest daily a champion of progress, and J. W. Bailey, still in his twenties and a real progressive, was putting excitement into the state's largest religious paper. Meanwhile down in Scotland County a young poet in his twenties, John Charles McNeill, was writing the songs of a new state and at Chapel Hill, two young Grahams, Edward Kidder and Frank Porter, were giving out the first flashes of their later brilliant educational leadership.

It is quite significant, I think, that of all these friends with whom I was most closely associated, not one had chosen a commercial career or planned to set up money-making as a major purpose of life. In America today when the lust for money is making its baleful influence felt in all areas of life—in business, politics, and even in sports—one element of my early training comes significantly to mind. My parents, teachers, and friends incited me to the highest endeavors but I never heard one suggest that I should try to be *a rich man*. A good man, yes, a useful man, and with an earned degree of prominence—but never did anyone suggest that money-making be my chief aim. "To live a rich life rather than die a rich man" was then a major purpose.

It was just sheer coincidence of course. Still to me it is quite significant that within a fortnight after I came to Raleigh, Walter H. Page made his still unforgotten address on "The Forgotten Man." He made this address at what was then called the "State Normal and Industrial School" at Greensboro (now Woman's College of the University of North Carolina).

My friendship with Page began about midnight in a Southern Railway passenger depot when we talked unceasingly while we waited two hours for a delayed connection and found ourselves in hearty agreement about the needs of North Carolina and the South. After that time he practically made me a member of the staff of his new magazine, *The World's Work*, repeatedly calling on me for articles relating to Southern and agricultural progress and problems.

In his speech on "The Forgotten Man," Page powerfully rebuked the South's neglect of the man at the bottom and our failure to provide the schools and training needed for his progress and development. Page pointed out that North Carolina was spending per pupil in the public schools less than any state except South Carolina, forecasting Aycock's later famous phrase—"Thank God for South Carolina which keeps us from the bottom of the educational ladder!" As compared with North Carolina's $3.40, Page said poor North Dakota spent almost exactly ten times as much—$33.50; Minnesota, $30; Wisconsin, $21; Michigan, $20; Indiana, $20; Virginia, $9; Georgia, $6.50.

It might be said that Page made half of North Carolina mad and stirred the other half to new effort and determination. Much talked about for a long time afterward, his speech helped lay the groundwork for Aycock's educational campaign a few years later. About that time some wit said, "North Carolina is so slow that if the angel Gabriel sounded his trumpet and proclaimed, 'Come forth!' North Carolina would come fifth!" To me it seems that the state has never been long asleep since Walter Page so eloquently pleaded the cause of our "Forgotten Man."

Even more like a bugle call was a speech I heard him make at the Conference for Education in the South in Birmingham on April 27, 1904. I can truthfully say that of all the speeches I have heard no other so greatly influenced and inspired me. I paid it an unprecedented compliment of reproducing it in full in *The Progressive Farmer* under the following head and subhead:

HOW THE SOUTH MAY REGAIN LEADERSHIP
IN INDUSTRY AND STATESMANSHIP

The Training Not of Leaders Only, but of the Mass of Men, is All-Important—Cheap, Unskilled Labor is a Curse to any Community—Free Training and Free Opinion Will Give the South a Commanding Position in the Affairs of the Nation and the World.

Page began by saying: "There is a class of men in the Southern states who have a stronger love of their country than any other men anywhere feel. . . .

"It is to the Southern men of this mettle that I wish to speak, directly to them and to them only. I address those then who answer to this description of a Southern gentleman—a man who is frank and fearless and generous to his fellows. The weaker the man is with whom he has to do, the more scrupulous is his justice; the weaker the woman is with whom he has to do, the more scrupulous his honor."

Page then went on to make a powerful appeal not only for education but for the kind of education that would train men and women for what they were to do in their life work, saying: "The secret of the unrivaled progress of the United States is the training of the mass of the people. So commonplace is this fact that many a man misses its meaning because they use words that confuse them. 'Education' is one such confusing word. To 'educate' the people means one thing to one man and another to another. Let us call it plain 'training'; for training is the thing that has made the world a new world, that has vindicated Democracy, that has opened the door for opportunities as fast as we can seize them— opportunities not only industrial and diplomatic but intellectual and moral also.

"A satisfactory society in our modern democracy cannot be made up of 'educated' men and 'uneducated' men. So long as education is regarded as a privilege and not as a right and a universal necessity, the community will stand still in activity, in thought, in character. And it is this non-privileged structure of society that has given the Northern and Western states the lead of the Southern states. We run now squarely into the doctrine of universal training at the community's expense (compulsory if need be), which is necessary in a democracy. We must train the child of every hillbilly, of every politician, of every Negro."

What Walter Page was saying in this address was not directed to farmers alone but he was summoning all classes of people to a crusade for the only means of doubling Southern farm income and similarly increasing the income of other classes.

To encourage young advocates of progress in the South and to show what could be achieved by the cooperation and organization of such young men, Page and other like-minded men had started an organization they called the Watauga Club. I joined it in 1902 and served as president from about 1926 to 1950.

Page was still in his twenties when he helped organize the club in 1884 and Josephus Daniels only twenty-four when he became a member in 1886. Charles D. McIver, who seems to have joined the same year (he was then teaching Greek, Latin, English literature, and bookkeeping at

Peace Institute) was only twenty-four. Apparently the chief founder of the club was another young man in his twenties —William J. Peele. Dr. Charles W. Dabney, then director of the State Experiment Station and later president of the University of Cincinnati, was only twenty-nine. All these men later became my friends.

The major aims and purposes of the club were set forth in this creed written by Page:

"I believe in this land—our land—whose infinite variety of beauty and riches we do not yet know. *Wake up, old Land!*

"I believe in these people—our people—whose development may be illimitable. *Wake up, my People!*

"I believe in the continuous improvement of human society, in the immortality of our democracy, in the rightmindedness of the masses. *Wake up, old Commonwealth!*"

Nobody old enough to have been in the Civil War was admitted to Watauga membership. There was a reverence for those men, but the first aim of the club was to look forward. And unfortunately all too many of the old soldiers, and especially the generals who had been elected to public office years before and stayed on, looked backward; at their age it was perhaps psychologically impossible for them to do otherwise.

For several years after I began work on *The Progressive Farmer,* the young man who most largely shared my interest in literature, poetry, history, current events, and Southern progress (although seven years my senior) was J. W. Bailey, brilliant young editor of the *Biblical Recorder.* Even before I came to Raleigh he had impressed me by his constant and zealous advocacy of better public schools, and he deserves much more credit than he has received for preparing the way for the educational advance of the 1900's. As our offices were in the same building and there were no automobiles to divert us, we took long walks about Raleigh and into the surrounding rural country, and later still we took longer horseback rides all through the Wake County countryside and fished together at Penny's Pond. He was progressive in spirit, as I was, and tremendously anxious to arouse North Carolinians to their great unrealized possibilities.

As editor of the *Biblical Recorder,* Bailey received a salary of $1500 and once told me, "I tell you, Poe, if you get married and have a home on fashionable Blount Street, you can't get along on less than $1500." (The governor's salary at that time was $3,000 a year.)

At that time young men in my group were not accustomed to addressing one another by their given names but by their surnames. J. W. Bailey addressed me as Poe, and I addressed him as Bailey. Hence I often speak of him as "Bailey."

It was in the Bailey tradition to be unconventional. His father, when editor of the *Biblical Recorder,* encountered an old uncle of mine he had previously met, who said, "Dr. Bailey, you don't remember me?" "Remember you—why, I would know your hide if I saw it in a tanyard!" When Miss Susie Heck was about to marry Dr. Alphonso Smith it was hardly surprising to find Will Bailey asking her, "Do you really love him—love him enough to cut his toenails when he is sick?"

Bailey always declared that the greatest appeal of the Baptist church to him was the complete freedom it gave each individual to make his own decision about theological matters, it being almost the only great denomination imposing no written creed to restrict freedom of this kind. Having been taught biology by Dr. W. L. Poteat, Bailey had accepted the doctrine of evolution that was later to cause such a stir in Baptist circles and even nationally in the Scopes trial. For my own part, in addition to having read Darwin, I had also read Dr. Lyman Abbott's *Theology of an*

Evolutionist and Sir Henry Drummond's *Ascent of Man* and wholly accepted Dr. Poteat's viewpoint.

Josephus Daniels and I, I think, always had a great understanding and interest in each other because we both became editors at the same age—eighteen. His paper was the *Wilson Mirror*. An old story has it that a stranger called and found Daniels, broom in hand, sweeping out his office. "I want to see the editor," said the stranger—and threatened to throw young Daniels out of his way as an impostor before becoming convinced that the eighteen-year-old *was* indeed the editor!

If I were asked to select one story to illustrate Mr. Daniels's abiding motive it would be that of the young preacher who wished to run out the bootleggers in the community only to have a deacon advise, "I'd say let 'em alone; doesn't the Bible tell us, 'The wicked flee when no man pursueth?'" "So it does," replied the preacher, "but they certainly make better time when somebody is after them!" All his life Mr. Daniels was "after" somebody he thought deserved that kind of treatment. He liked the phrase "Nuisance Disturber" as a synonym for *News and Observer*. In one famous case he "went after" Federal Judge Thomas R. Purnell with such vigor that Purnell sentenced him to a brief imprisonment for contempt of court—but later allowed Daniels to serve the time in the Yarborough House, Raleigh's leading hotel. And in prestige the sentence hurt Purnell and helped Daniels.

Thousands of people who have since been bedeviled by expenses for automobile purchases or for monthly payments for gasoline, oil, repairs, license tags, and the stupidity of *other* drivers must also have agreed in their hearts with what Mr. Daniels said early in the automobile era: "There are only two classes of people who ought to have automobiles—millionaires and fools."

Even in his later years I do not think Mr. Daniels would

have claimed that he had always been quite fair to one
underprivileged class—our Negroes. But in this matter he had
been simply a product of the policies and passions of that
time. He later fully supported Governor Aycock's universal
education campaign and defended the Negroes against ex-
tremists who wished to limit Negro school support to taxes
paid by Negroes themselves.

In spite of the fierceness with which he could attack an
enemy in print, Daniels seemed unvaryingly pleasant in his
social contacts. I found great pleasure in working with him
in Governor Aycock's educational campaign, in the 1912
efforts to get the presidential nomination for Woodrow Wilson, as a fellow member of the consolidation committee and
executive committee of the Consolidated University, and on
the State Hospital and Medical Care Commission of which
I was chairman.

Mr. Daniels lived to be eighty-five and fortunately was
active in editorial work to the last. But he never liked to
have anyone call him old. About that he said, "I am like
Admiral Ramsey of the British Navy. Once he issued some
order which angered all the sailors and midshipmen—so
much so that when the Admiral was walking the deck a day
or so later he heard a sailor at some distance say, 'There goes
the damned old bastard!' Thereupon the keen-of-hearing
Admiral called the sailor to him and said, 'Young man, I
heard what you said—*I heard what you said*. And if ever
again you call me *old* you'll be shot at sunrise!'"

A picturesque old-timer was Josiah Turner who came in
to see me more than once when a new generation had forgotten the magnitude of his editorial services in the Reconstruction period. Day after day in that period as editor of
the *Raleigh Sentinel* he had thundered against one iniquity
after another, and when his list of major iniquities ran out
added them all up together under the heading, "The Same

Old Editorial." Harry Truman's "give 'em hell!" was mild tea compared with what Josiah Turner dished out by spoken and written word as long as any carpetbagger remained in office. He was not only editorially but physically combative and provocative, inviting to physical combat any and every man he criticized. My cousin, Ed Fearrington, once told me of hearing Turner curse reconstruction Judge Albion Tourgée almost to his face as Tourgée was proceeding to enter the courthouse in Pittsboro—speaking in a voice so loud Tourgée could not have failed to hear him.

When I came on the journalistic scene a distinguished kinsman (the kinship was distant but as in the case of many old-time Southerners he frequently reminded me of it) was Captain Samuel A. Ashe. A memorial marker and bust in our Capitol Square recite his services to the state. After reaching the age of eighty he completed a two-volume *History of North Carolina* and was a frequent contributor to "Letters to the Editor" in the *News and Observer* that he had so long edited. He once wrote for me a nostalgic article about rice growing in the Wilmington, North Carolina, area as he knew it when a boy.

Another picturesque editor was the Reverend John H. Mills, known as "Jack" Mills, editor of *Charity and Children,* who once made an observation that I have always remembered—"It is astonishing how much ignorance some people can accumulate in one short lifetime!" His successor, Archibald Johnson, also made his paper lively by blurting out his independent and uncensored convictions pertinent or impertinent about any subject. His more famous son, Dr. Gerald W. Johnson, tells a characteristic story: "My father had taken a forthright position on some subject only to receive a communication showing that the facts called for a radically different position. My father printed the letter only adding the comment, 'Well, I had rather be wrong than nothing!'"

Another fellow editor who entered the profession while still in his teens was Clyde R. Hoey, editor of the *Shelby Star* and later governor and United States senator. Writing, however, was not so pleasant an occupation for Hoey as public speaking. For that he had an uninhibited flow of thoughts, words, and adjectives that poured forth with the certainty and continuity of the geyser "Old Faithful." I believe it was some Southern senator who, when asked how long he could speak, answered, "If it is a subject I know nothing about, one hour; if other subjects, unlimited." Anyhow it was claimed you could wake up Governor Hoey from a sound sleep at 2:30 A.M., ask him to speak ten minutes on any subject whatever, and he would meet the test adequately. Long after they became unfashionable, Governor Hoey wore a long-tail coat, high collar, and a carnation in his lapel.

Among the friends with whom I spent numerous happy evenings in my home discussing the problems of the South and the books and poets we both loved, I have an especially vivid memory of Dr. Edwin Mims who was professor of English at Trinity College (now Duke) and the University of North Carolina, served as chairman of the English Department at Vanderbilt University, and after his retirement wrote a history of Vanderbilt. His first book, *The Life of Sidney Lanier*, added greatly to the prestige of both the author and the subject. One of the most impressive Southern books of his time was *The Advancing South* in which he made such an extensive review of my life and work up to 1927 that anyone interested in my career would do well to look it up.

Another man who profoundly influenced the progress of the South, and especially its educational progress, was one whose friendship I long enjoyed—Dr. Edwin A. Alderman. In the late 1880's he and Charles D. McIver went all over North Carolina campaigning in behalf of better schools for all the people. He later maintained this interest through his succeeding years as president of the University of North Carolina, Tulane University, and the University of Virginia. I attended his inauguration as president of the University of Virginia—and still remember the remarkable color and pageantry of the occasion, much like a coronation in the Middle Ages, made still more remarkable by the fact that the institution was the creation of a great American whose faith in democracy and the common people Alderman shared. For a combination of depth of thought and eloquence of expression Alderman has seldom been equaled in the South. He loved life, and when I was in my thirties and he in his fifties I remember his poignant remark, "What would I not give for your youth!"

About Alderman a mutual friend told me this significant incident: "By his rare elegance of manner and eloquence of expression Alderman had drawn to him a host of admiring friends including myself. But I sometimes wondered, 'Is there steel in the man? How would he stand up under a great disaster?' Well, it was my privilege to find out. His physician found that he had contracted tuberculosis, then one of the most dreaded and fatal of diseases, and ordered him to go to Lake Saranac for a long and lonely combat with what might prove his mortal enemy. Yet the night before Alderman left, a group of us had dinner with him and seldom had he seemed in higher spirits or more ready to meet with dignity and cheer whatever the morrow might bring."

Of all the friends I had in the early 1900's the one who most nearly deserved to be called a saint was John T. Pullen. As a vocation he was president of a small savings bank, but the avocation to which he gave his heart was the welfare of distressed people who were down and out—or nearly so. This was no doubt true because he himself had seemed at one time to be a hopeless alcoholic. As a young man he had joined the First Baptist Church, but soon fell victim to repeated lapses of drunkenness. Finally he had been turned out of the church so often, and so often taken back on repeated promises of better behavior, that the entire church seemed ready to disown him once and for all. But Colonel L. L. Polk, himself always a fighter for the underdog, eloquently pleaded that young Pullen be given one more chance—and Pullen then made good by many years of consecrated service to the poor and unfortunate. He was virtually a one-man Salvation Army. A frequent custom of his when he found some family unable to buy needed food was to send word, "I am going to have supper with you tomorrow night and bring the steaks." It would be impossible to say how many seemingly useless down-and-outers were saved by John Pullen—and indirectly by Polk's eloquence which gave seemingly hopeless young Pullen one more chance.

Next I might refer to some friends among our lawyers and judges. I first think of Judge Henry G. Connor who successively graced our Superior Court, Supreme Court, and Federal Court. Judge Connor was thin as a rail and liked to tell this story on himself. "One of my first courts was in a mountain county. About the third day I was walking away from the courthouse when I overheard one mountaineer walking behind me ask another, 'How do you like this here new judge?' 'Well, I think he's a right smart judge—but don't he look like Before Taking?'"

Senator F. M. Simmons dominated North Carolina politics for a quarter of a century. Many people disagreed with him, his views and policies, but no one ever doubted his integrity.

Bailey once told me of hearing Simmons say, "I have never in all my life been able to understand how any man of sense could be willing to have no higher purpose in life than just piling up dollars." Simmons also told Bailey how he got a start as a lawyer: "I knew of course I would have mighty few clients for a long time. So I bought the entire collection of *North Carolina Reports*—the opinions handed down by the Supreme Court of the state up to that date—and resolved to read every one of them. It took about a year but it brought its reward. Thereafter whenever any prospective client came in with any kind of problem, I could almost invariably turn pretty quickly to some decision which helped my client—and me!"

One of my most highly esteemed lawyer friends was Judge John J. Parker who lacked only one vote of being confirmed as a member of the United States Supreme Court. Several times thereafter it was suggested that a president should rectify the injustice Parker had suffered. This was never done but the situation probably served to bind his friends even closer to him. Although a Republican, he was held in equal esteem by the foremost men in both political parties and was among the older men for whose friendship I was always especially grateful.

Probably because families were larger a generation or so ago I then knew several trios of distinguished brothers. First were the Page brothers—Walter Hines, editor, publisher, and ambassador; Robert N., congressman; and Frank, banker and outstanding road builder. Frank Page created a colossal state highway system with great efficiency but always resented it whenever anyone added, "and with nobody anywhere at any time ever believing there was a single cent of graft." As he was wont to say, "I do not think a public official should ever think it a compliment to be called honest or for a lady to be called virtuous; all that should be taken for granted." The true story behind Frank Page's highway achievement was revealed by a close friend, Ben McNeill, after Page's death. Page had lost a brilliant young son in World War I, and in one of his rare moments of self-revelation said, "I know my son would have done some great work for North Carolina if he had lived. I am trying to do for him what he would have done."

The Kitchin trio included William Walton, congressman and governor; Claude, a long-time congressman and minority House leader; and Thurman D., first a distinguished physician and later president of Wake Forest College.

Of the Winston trio I saw most of Judge Robert W. Winston, for several years a law partner of Charles B. Aycock. At the age of sixty Judge Winston, still at the height of his powers, retired from the law and became a student (in selective subjects) at the University at Chapel Hill. The other students enjoyed his fellowship and he soon produced a work of high importance in American historical literature. When I consulted the *World Almanac* recently and glanced through its biographies of presidents, I found it listed Judge Winston's *Andrew Johnson: Plebeian and Patriot* as the chief source book about this famous son of North Carolina. Winston's brilliant brothers included Francis D., lawyer and lieutenant governor; and Patrick Henry, a lawyer who emigrated to the state of Washington while it was still wild and woolly. Patrick Henry Winston is probably best remembered for his reply to the question, "What are the main industries where you live?" "There are two," he answered, "grand larceny and petty larceny." His head was as bald as a peeled onion and once while making a speech he was interrupted by a man who had kept all of his head of hair and had added a two-foot-long beard swaying over his breast. "I demand, Mr. Winston," said this hirsute citizen, "that you tell us what you would do about the unequal distribution of wealth in this country." "I will," answered Winston, "if you'll just tell me what you would do about the unequal distribution of hair in this country!" As a book reviewer Winston might also have won distinction if he had kept the pace he set when describing Jefferson Davis' *Rise and Fall of the Southern Confederacy:* "It's the damndest book I have ever seen; I read 1999 pages and on every page the Yankees were running like turkeys. Then I turned to page 2,000—only to find Lee had surrendered!"

The three Dixons included Frank, a noted lecturer, and two famous preachers, Thomas and A. C. Dixon. A. C. was called from an American pastorate to the famous London church at which Charles H. Spurgeon had won international renown. Thomas, a prominent preacher and author of several novels, most notably *The Leopard's Spots,* won national fame by his pioneer movie "The Birth of a Nation." His early brilliance is attested by the fact that he was elected to the state legislature before he was twenty-one years old and, I think, while he was a ministerial student at Wake Forest College. In his last years he lost practically all the rather large fortune he had accumulated from novels, movies, and plays by a too-daring venture in real estate. He bought up and partially developed an enormous acreage in the mountains of western North Carolina on the assumption that he could almost single-handedly create a beautiful mountain resort for authors, artists, and musicians. He once gave our Watauga Club members an exciting review of his widely varied life interests. No less gifted than the three Dixon brothers was their sister, Dr. Delia Dixon Carroll, one of the earliest and eventually best-known women physicians of our region.

Three eminent Poteats included two brothers and a sister. Dr. William Louis first won distinction as a biology teacher in Wake Forest College and later was its president. About this time the extreme fundamentalist campaign against teaching evolution reached its furious peak. For a time it threatened to dislodge him as Wake Forest's president but he stood his ground with patience, wisdom, and especially with serenity. He was a guest in my home once just before he was leaving to face a fiercely hostile group in the Southern Baptist Convention, but I have never seen a man less concerned about what might happen on the next day. I was glad to stand with him and have been given much credit—perhaps too much credit—for influencing the farmer-Baptists to do so. One other thing comes to mind about Dr. Poteat. I was in Memphis early in 1912 when a telegram from the *New York World* asked him (among other college and university presidents), "Whom do you think the Democrats should now nominate for president and why?" (Bryan, of course, had been named three times—unsuccessfully.) Poteat's laconic reply was, "Woodrow Wilson—he has not acquired the habit of failure." Dr. Edwin McNeill Poteat was president of Furman University, and his sister Ida attained distinction as head of the Art Department at Meredith College.

It was one of the ironies of fate that in 1900 when North Carolina elected as governor a young man barely forty, sworn to promote a new program of universal education, it elected as the state's chief educational official—called "Superintendent of Public Instruction"—a very estimable but feeble former Confederate general nearly twice Aycock's age. General Toon was not one of the "mummies" unconcerned about educational progress, but he was obviously too old for the work awaiting him and died only a few months after taking office.

It was this unexpected fatality that gave the new governor one of the most important opportunities of his life. To succeed General Toon, he named a lifelong friend and university classmate, Dr. J. Y. Joyner, who was then a distinguished member of the faculty of the State Normal and Industrial School at Greensboro and was about Aycock's own age. No better choice could have been made. All through Aycock's administration and for nearly ten years afterward, I worked with Joyner as he proved himself a wise and far-seeing captain of North Carolina's educational forward march. In less than three years he was able to report these marks of progress: number of local tax districts—increased from 30 to 229; public school funds—increased from $700,000 to $1,700,000; 840 new school libraries—where none had existed in 1901; number of log schoolhouses—decreased from 1,132 to 508.

A product of farm parentage and rearing, Dr. Joyner throughout his administration sought to tie the public schools to agricultural progress and to double farm income. For years before vocational agriculture became a national policy, Dr. Joyner helped establish in North Carolina a group of "Farm Life Schools"—high schools mainly directed to training boys to be better farmers. More agricultural subjects were introduced into the state curriculum. Saying that most examples used in common school arithmetics were related to town and city subjects, Dr. Tait Butler and Dr. F. L. Stevens prepared an arithmetic dealing especially with the farmer's daily work. Walter Hines Page welcomed an article of mine he published in *The World's Work* entitled, "Farmer Children Need Farmer Studies."

About this time another heartening development occurred illustrating the truth of what a Southern mountaineer once said when some friendly Northerners visited his county studying conditions and asking questions—"Mixin' larns both." To Robert C. Ogden, one of New York's merchant princes, a brilliant idea had occurred. Having progressive friends in both sections of the country he decided

to organize "The Conference for Education in the South."
For this purpose he chartered a train of Pullman cars each
spring and brought south with him some of the North's foremost editors, educators, and thinkers to meet a similar group
of Southern editors, educators, and public men. I attended
meetings at Richmond, Birmingham, and Winston-Salem,
became an officer of the Conference, and was delighted to
hear and talk with such leading Northern editors as Dr.
Lyman Abbott of the *New York Outlook,* St. Clair McKel-
way of the *Brooklyn Eagle,* Page, and Dr. Albert Shaw of
the *Review of Reviews.* I met also from the South such
leaders as the distinguished Dr. J. L. M. Curry of Alabama
(incidentally the only Mexican War soldier I ever remember
meeting), Dr. S. C. Mitchell of the University of South
Carolina, Governor Montague of Virginia, and O. B. Martin,
later a leader in Texas. These are merely a few of the scores
who came from both North and South to exchange ideas for
advancing education in the South and to discover, indeed,
that "mixin' larns both."

Another man whose friendship I was glad to make at these
meetings was Dr. H. B. Frissell of Hampton Institute for
Negroes. In the field of Negro education he rendered a
service hardly less important than that of Booker T. Washington who was then building Tuskegee Institute and promoting racial peace by saying, "Our people of the two races
may be as separate socially as the fingers but as united as
the hand in doing all the jobs needed for promoting the
welfare of both races."

These were the people and this was the setting that made
North Carolina and the South in the decade 1900-10 a
Golden Age for me. This explains the answer I gave Page
of *The World's Work* and Albert Shaw of the *Review of
Reviews* when, within a few months of each other, each man

called me to New York to consider taking a position with his company. Each wished to promote an illustrated national magazine devoted to country life, work, and recreations. The salary offered, $3,000 a year, does not now seem large, but in 1900 this was the salary of the governor of North Carolina and added to this I was offered a share in magazine profits.

In an interview after returning to Raleigh I said of the South, "I believe that there are now opportunities here such as there have never been before, and that it is not going to be such a strange thing hereafter to see young men turning down offers in New York in order to share the labors and the rewards of the industrial and literary awakening among our own people."

CHAPTER EIGHT

We Fought the Man in the Moon

I GREW UP IN THE YEARS OF THE SOUTH'S DEEPEST POSTWAR poverty and trials and so shared the struggles and sorrows of humble men and women who knew hardship but also had pride, faith, heroism, and honor—unsung heroes who were not great men but who lived great lives. To help such people has ever since been my greatest joy.

Very soon after I became president of our company I called for a South-wide campaign to increase average Southern farm income $500 a year (which of course would be equivalent to several times that amount now). And to further this campaign the needed weapons would almost seem to have been providentially put into my hands.

In studying agricultural data from the preceding 1900 census I found exactly the authentic official justification I needed. This data showed that we needed to increase average farm income in both our South Atlantic and South Central states at least $500 a year in order to equal corresponding incomes that farmers in the states immediately to the north were already enjoying. Highly visible and spectacular were the two bags of money of relative sizes I repeatedly pictured in cartoons in *The Progressive Farmer* reporting 1900 Northern and Southern farm income averages as follows:

North Atlantic States	$984
South Atlantic States only	484
SOUTH BEHIND	$500
North Central States	$1,074
South Central States only	536
SOUTH BEHIND	$538

Along with these telltale money bags, one labeled $484 and one $984, and the other $536 alongside $1,074, I laid down three propositions that I repeated over and over again, not only in *The Progressive Farmer*, but in speeches I made to state farmers' meetings, educational meetings, press associations, and even to state legislative bodies. I covered the whole South from Maryland to Texas. At one time I wore myself down by a continuous series of speaking engagements until my doctor thought he detected an "extremely incipient tuberculosis." But after slowing down a few weeks I was ready to go again and have never been troubled since.

The three major propositions that I proclaimed with what Shakespeare would call "damnable reiteration" were as follows:

"1. To bring up its earning power $500 more a year for each Southern farm is the supreme task and opportunity of our generation.

"2. It is not only our supreme task and ambition, but it is a realizable ideal, a workable, practicable program of progress.

"3. It is not only our supreme task, and a realizable one, but it is one upon whose success depends the prosperity not only of the South as a section and Southerners as a whole but also (and more important) the prosperity of you yourself as an individual and of every individual Southerner— the farmer no more than the banker, the merchant, the railroad man, the lawyer, the preacher, the teacher, the statesman."

To emphasize the fact that in the South there were then more people engaged in agriculture than in all other occupations combined, I added a humorous note quoting a schoolboy who was asked, "What part of speech is woman?" and answered, "She ain't no part of speech—she's the whole thing!"

"I do not know whether or not it has ever been worked out as a principle of political economy, but anyhow it is unquestionably true that wealth is by nature not aristocratic but democratic," I declared. "The poorer every other man is, the poorer you are. The richer every other man is, the richer you are."

Never in all our crusading for doubling farm income did we forget the fact that the permanent foundation of the structure depended on having a higher degree of general education for all our people. And this led me to close and constant association with educational workers all the way from country teachers and teachers of special "moonlight schools" for illiterates to university presidents, not only in North Carolina but in the entire South. All of us had to face and combat an aristocratic concept of education—an attitude that had found expression when an ante-bellum governor of South Carolina urged education for the relatively few gifted persons in the university rather than education for the masses in the common schools by saying, "One sun is better than a million stars."

Because this aristocratic concept had been so long dominant and farmers had been too poorly educated, in our crusade to double farm income we had to fight not only earthly obstacles but the Man in the Moon himself. For at that time a majority of farmers put more faith in the signs of the moon than in any reports from agricultural experiment stations. They would not plant corn or other crops, kill a hog, or castrate a pig or calf, unless someone checked the almanac and reported, "The sign is right." When I inquired the reasons for their faith, they squelched me with the answer, "Everybody knows the moon is one of the most powerful forces in the universe. It controls the tides of all the seas. And if it has power to control the mighty oceans, why doubt that it can control life in the plants and animals around us? Furthermore our daddies and granddaddies believed this and we are no smarter than they were."

Faith in the Man in the Moon was no doubt further increased by the fact that he seemingly had the power to smile on us whenever he wished with the cheerful round face of the full moon, withdraw his pleasure and turn his back on us, and then gradually come back in full good humor.

The seriousness of this superstition is illustrated by the following letter I once had from an inquiring farmer: "I pity the poor farmer with 250 acres of beans, or corn, or potatoes to plant. It is getting late in the spring, and finally his land is ready to plow. He gets it in perfect shape, but lo-and-behold! he finds it is 'the wrong time of the moon,' or the 'sign is not right.' He will wait until 'the sign is right,' and by then his seedbed is muddy again. A man could miss out on a full year's crop in this way."

I remember seeing fields of corn where the stalks were excessively high but ears small and hearing the explanation, "Jim didn't plant when the moon was right." And corn is only one example. I remember very well that our farmers might delay hog-killing because the sign in the zodiac was not right. Women had to make soap and plant their flower seed in accordance with lunar conditions. One old lady who was given some zinnia plants to set out said, "I'll wait till the sign is right," by which time the plants were dead.

This belief in the wisdom of farming by the moon and zodiac was so deep-rooted that even as late as September, 1962, I had a neatly typewritten and well expressed letter from an intelligent farmer who strongly questioned the belief but wanted to be reassured by me and *The Progressive Farmer!* Not only did the moon theory have no scientific support in America but the world-famous French astronomer, Camille Flammarion, conducted extensive tests and found that the moon had absolutely no effect on either plants or animals.

Even after experiment station results became widely used, I have heard their recommendations questioned by farmers who would say, "My experience has been different and I would rather depend on my own experience." I remember that Dr. Butler once wrote a devastating reply in *The Progressive Farmer*, "One Experience or One Million?" pointing out that an experiment station recommendation was never based on one man's experience or tests made in a single year but represented conclusions growing out of perhaps 1,000 carefully checked test-plot experiences under varying conditions and seasons. I illustrated the folly of depending on one experience by telling of a woman nurse who said, "In treating a carpenter who was sick, I gave him cowpeas and he got well. But I gave cowpeas to a sick blacksmith and he died. This proves that cowpeas are good for carpenters but will kill blacksmiths!"

Tradition, even when it came from high authority, might not be adapted to all situations. For example, I remember farmers used to quote Benjamin Franklin's *Poor Richard* couplet:

Plough deep while sluggards sleep
And you shall have corn to sell and to keep.

Actually deep plowing was fine advice for breaking land for planting crops but bad advice for cultivation where it might cut or damage the whole root system.

We should realize that even after making allowance for the greater purchasing power of the dollar around 1900, the average one-horse or tenant farmer in the South received so few dollars that at that time he was virtually a peasant. In setting out to remedy this situation we had not just one, two, or three enemies to conquer (in addition to the Man in the Moon) but a dozen enemies. If I had then been asked to make a catalogue of the other difficulties and evils we must battle, I think I should have listed them somewhat as follows:

Most serious of all was what I called our "one-armed" system of farming. There are still many farmers living who tell of hearing me speak at farmers' meetings and illustrating by gestures my concern about this No. 1 weakness of our farming system. "There are two great arms for producing agricultural wealth," I would say, *"plant production* and *animal production."* Raising one arm I would say, "This represents plant production or crops." Then raising my other arm, "This represents animal production—livestock, dairying, and poultry.

"Now in the richest farming states farmers get almost equal income from both arms—$100 from animal production for every $100 they get from plant production. But here in the South we average only about $20 from the animal production arm for each $100 we get from crop production. Our plant production arm is well muscled and constantly used. Our animal production arm is little used, flabby and feeble. Practically speaking, we have a one-armed system of farming. Our supreme need is a system of two-armed farming by which we will get as much from animal production as we now get from plant production, and so more than double cash income." All over the South from Virginia to Texas I preached this gospel of "Two-Armed Farming" and of course I preached it as constantly in *The Progressive Farmer* as in my public appearances.

Not only was the South practicing a one-armed or "crops only" system of farming but the trouble went much deeper. Except for limited areas in the Carolinas, Virginia, Georgia, Kentucky, and Tennessee where tobacco was depended on, the South was virtually a *one-crop country*. Cotton was indeed king and the South was constantly referred to as "The Land of Cotton." And cotton required planting, cultivation, and picking only from April till November. Hence it did not give the owner enough income or profit-making days. Rather, as I often said, it was as if a man tried to make profits from a factory that was shut down five months of the year. I once debated with a man who said, "God Almighty has made the South to grow cotton and other states to produce 'supplies' for those who grow it—and we should follow His plan." Shipment of Southern cattle to Northern markets was prohibited by quarantine until Dr. Tait Butler found a way to exterminate the vampire cattle ticks that had been frequently so thick as to almost cover the hide of an otherwise marketable steer. There had also been little research to show the South's grass possibilities. Hence farmers spent much time killing grass by spring and summer cultivation and bought enormous quantities of high-priced Western grass (in the form of hay) to feed their livestock in winter. On many a carload of hay brought in from the West (so merchants told me) the freight charges were more than the Western farmer had received for producing it.

Soil-saving was a major need. This meant saving the thin crust of fertile topsoil that nature had laid down through untold centuries of leaf-cropping and decay. When this thin layer of topsoil was lost by gullying or sheet-erosion, the farmer who wished to prosper had to clear "new ground" from woodland at home or leave for new land in the West. And the lack of proper water control made soil-saving virtually impossible for the average farmer on sloping land.

First *The Progressive Farmer* popularized and advocated the Mangum terrace, invented by a farmer, P. H. Mangum, of Wake County. He designed the row system by which water was made to "walk off" the land instead of "run off." Later the U.S.D.A. and other agencies adopted the "strip crop" system, whereby wide strips in row crops alternated with strips in permanent pasture.

Cotton farmers suffered from other special disadvantages. As I found from my own experience the "hog round" system of buying cotton (paying the same middling price for all cotton of "middling" quality or better) offered growers little incentive to produce cotton of superior length and staple. When I grew a crop of such superior qualities, the cotton buyers would pay me nothing extra for it, saying, "We can get increased prices from cotton mills or exporters only when we assemble large quantities of the same grade and staple." Of course they did the "assembling" and the individual farmer took the losses. In far too many cases, too, when the farmer offered his cotton for sale, there was no competitive bidding. As I was told of one cotton market, "Buyers congregate at a corner where cotton is bought. Then the buyer who first sees an oncoming farm wagon with cotton, will call out 'Ducksoup!' or any other word agreed on. This would let other buyers know that he would get that farmer's cotton at whatever price he could, and other buyers should let him alone and wait their turn to pluck another grower." In producing cotton the poorer tenant farmers also had to pay frightful usury in the form of "time-prices" credit for all the supplies they bought while

...ng the crop—a form of usury that often amounted to as much as 60 per cent a year.

In 1920 and immediately thereafter, Dr. Kilgore, Dr. Butler, and I almost blanketed the cotton South in speaking campaigns and other publicity, first in helping organize and later in supporting the newly organized cotton growers' cooperative associations. Before that time if a cotton farmer presented a bale of cotton for sale, he might be asked, "What is the staple [length of lint]? What is the grade [condition]? What is the weight? What price is being paid for cotton of this grade and staple?" To all these questions most farmers could only answer, "I don't know." Now, as a result of campaigns in which I was glad to help, the government quickly reports to the farmer the grade, staple, and current market price of that quality in addition to checking at reasonably brief intervals on the accuracy of the cotton buyers' scales.

The Southern farmer also suffered from several unfair governmental policies. The protective tariff made him pay higher prices for nearly everything he bought whereas his cotton was sold at world prices. For a full generation freight rates were grossly unfair to the South, giving Northern manufacturers cheap access to Southern markets while freight rates on his shipment of products to Northern markets were considerably higher. For example, Southern buyers of iron and steel had to pay freight rates based on the cost of shipment from Pittsburgh, although Birmingham steel and iron were right at hand.

From all I have now said it should be plain that the fight for "An Extra $500 a Year Per Farm" offered such difficulties as should have made the Man in the Moon relent even before progressive farmers grew wise enough to laugh at him. Certainly all of us in this crusade had our work cut out for us. But every month and every year we made some advances that meant better farming and better living, and every worker to this end could say, paraphrasing Browning, "What I am not but aspire to be, comforts me." Nor were the farm people backward in showing their appreciation. It is still true as Emerson said, "He who gives us better homes, better books, better tools, a fairer outlook, and a wider hope, him will we crown with laurel."

At this point I should be both unfair and ungrateful if I did not single out a few of the men who did most as friends and co-workers in our efforts to bring about the revolution in Southern farming conditions. Unquestionably the chief of these was Dr. Seaman A. Knapp, 1833-1911. He was indeed a unique figure and I was closely associated with him in promoting throughout the South his policy of "farm demonstration work," of which all official agricultural "extension work" is the outgrowth. Everyone should know his life story as an example of an historic triumph over personal handicaps, a lifetime dedication to unselfish service, and a rarely matched degree of nationally recognized achievement after he reached the Biblical three score years and ten.

Just to see Dr. Knapp was to be impressed by him. Large of mold, with a distinguished head and a forceful but kindly expression, he "looked like one of Plutarch's men." His greatness lay not in any new scientific discovery. Rather his greatness derived from the fact that he discovered a new way of disseminating all the vast treasures of scientific truth others had developed. We may grant that in learning from him farmers in some degree heard what numerous other men had been *saying* for forty years; the point is that all too many of these others had been "crying in the wilderness of ineffectuality" while Dr. Knapp actually reached the ear and the heart of the man behind the plow. By a program of *seeing*, not *saying*, he actually carried the message to Garcia.

In 1902 Secretary of Agriculture Wilson appointed Knapp as "Special Agent for the Promotion of Agriculture in the South." It was as such he began the historic work of revolutionizing Southern agriculture by his "Cooperative Demonstration Work." "I will not," he said, "undertake experiments. My task is solely to get people to practice what has already been well tested."

The way he tackled the problem had the genius of simplicity. He found farmers in each county who were outstandingly successful because they were using good farming methods. He got them to agree to use even better methods and to make their farms serve as "demonstrations" for themselves and their neighbors. Eventually he saw the necessity for giving one man the responsibility of supervising each county's agricultural program and so employed a "county farm agent" to help with farm problems. Even the most backward farmer was curious to see what was going on at each "demonstration" farm—and what he saw was worth a thousand lectures or textbooks. "Seeing is believing" is a phrase Knapp constantly repeated.

But the basic idea of demonstration work as a way to convert farmers to better farming methods would not have won success half so quickly or completely if it had not been for one tiny insect. This was the boll weevil, usually called the Mexican boll weevil. Puncturing and half destroying the growing cotton bolls the insect cut cotton yields so disastrously that many growers were reduced to bankruptcy. It was this situation that caused a mass movement of farmers to Dr. Knapp. As one Negro farmer put it, "We wuz driv by compelment!" Dr. Knapp at least offered an alternative to the system (or lack of system) the farmers had been following. And farmers felt that they at least would not be worse off by adopting it. As one farmer said, "I would swap a rotten egg for anything!"

So the boll weevil, only partially controlled by poisoning, spread from state to state year after year until it had infested the entire cotton belt from Texas to Virginia. But the Knapp idea of better farming spread equally fast. Eventually one Alabama town erected a monument to the boll weevil because farm demonstration methods—originally made to check or destroy the weevil—had made all farming more profitable than it had been before boll weevils came.

Dr. Knapp's supreme gift was probably the gift of sympathy. This quality he had in that unusual degree possessed only by men and women who have themselves suffered and therefore understand what suffering means to others. So powerful of physique was he in his later years, so untiring of strength in his seventies, I was amazed after his death to learn that in early manhood two accidents had so crippled him that for seven years he had been dependent first on a wheel chair and then on crutches!

The next great quality in Dr. Knapp was the ability to inspire men and states and regions with new faith in themselves. He did not waste time rebuking the mistakes of the past; rather he pointed to all the rich possibilities of the future. As I heard him declare at the Southern Educational Conference in Pinehurst in 1907:

"Some years since, a traveler said that Southern farms looked like a bankrupt stock ready for the auctioneer; the soils impoverished . . . and even the graveyards seemed not to believe in a resurrection! This viewpoint is not mine. To me the Southern states surpass all of the countries of the earth of equal area in material resources, mainly undeveloped."

Furthermore, Dr. Knapp went on to declare our farm people not only capable but teachable. "Some declare farmers a hard class to reach and impress. But I find they are the most tractable of people if you have anything substantial to offer—but they are from Missouri, all want *proof*."

Nor did Dr. Knapp's demonstration work stop with adults. Even the boys and girls on the farm—first in boys' corn clubs and girls' tomato clubs—became partners in a campaign of progress. These clubs later evolved into the widely renowned 4-H clubs of today. Many a corn-club boy made bigger yields on his allotted acre than his daddy had ever made on any acre. Dr. Knapp liked to laugh about one such farmer who had reluctantly let his son Bill have an acre to cultivate by 4-H methods and, as the boy's acre far outstripped his own, would say to all his neighbors, "Jest look what me an' Bill done!" One such South Carolina boy, Jerry Moore, made an astonishing yield of over 100 bushels of corn per acre and thereby won South-wide applause. President S. C. Mitchell of the University of South Carolina told of a rural Sunday school teacher who asked his class, "Please tell me what you know about Jeremiah," only to have a bright-eyed youngster reply, "I don't know nothing about Jeremiah—but just let me tell you what Jerry Moore done!"

Dr. Knapp and I were close friends until his death in 1911 and I have seldom appreciated any tribute more than his: "*The Progressive Farmer* suits me. It is a fast team with a good driver. I do not have time to watch all the race, but maybe they will let me tie on the ribbons!"

Most county farm agents whom Dr. Knapp selected were not agricultural college graduates, but they were men who had been constantly studying the best agricultural literature they could get from the farm press and bulletins from experiment stations all over the South. They had demonstrated that they both knew and had practiced better methods than most other farmers, and their successful practical farm experience gave them ready acceptance in many places where a man of greater scientific knowledge would have been rejected for too much "book farming." Governor Aycock once said, "A man who wishes to be a leader of his people must be ahead of them—yes, but not out of sight." The successful extension workers never forgot this principle.

Along with Dr. Knapp one of my closest friends and allies in the revolutionary change in Southern farming was America's pioneer apostle of soil conservation, Dr. Hugh Hammond Bennett. In the late '80's when young Bennett was chopping cotton in his native county of Anson, North Carolina, and when I myself was chopping cotton a few hundred miles away, the gospel of soil-saving had hardly even begun to be preached. That the land a farmer was cultivating would "wear out" like his coat or his plow—or like the farmer himself—was commonly accepted as if it were manifest destiny or providential decree. The work Hugh Bennett did in changing this attitude towards the soil was monumental. His agricultural statesmanship benefited not only his native South and his native America but almost the whole world. In Alaska, Mexico, Brazil, Cuba, Venezuela, and Africa he investigated soil situations and needs. It has been well said, "He stopped gullies in four continents." And the moral duty of saving soil for future generations was constantly impressed on all *Progressive Farmer* readers by our repeated inquiry, "Can you hear it rain with a clear conscience?"

Santford Martin has given us a picture of Hugh Bennett coming into a Congressional committee hearing dragging a Mack Gowder plow without a mould-board—the kind that doesn't turn under crop residues but leaves them on the surface as mulch. "He usually came lugging some such device into the committee room himself, with his hair ruffled, tie twisted, vest half buttoned, and trouser cuffs dragging. But Congress liked it. And so did the people."

Of one specific appearance before a committee, Martin quotes Bennett as saying: "I spread out a thick bath towel on a table, tipped the table back just a bit, and poured a half pitcher of water on that towel. The towel absorbed most of the water, preventing its flow from the table to the rug. I then lifted the towel and poured the rest of the pitcher on the smooth table top, watching all of it rush over the edge onto the rug. I didn't say anything right away—just stood there looking at the mess on the floor. Then I looked up at the committee and explained that the towel represented well-covered, well-managed land that could absorb heavy, washing rains. And that the smooth table top represented bare, eroded land with poor cover and management on it. They seemed to understand, because we got our appropriation."

To one more remarkable friend and co-worker I feel I must pay a brief tribute—Dr. Liberty Hyde Bailey, long dean of agriculture at Cornell University. Many of my friends and co-workers, graduates of Southern agricultural colleges, gained both information and inspiration by taking postgraduate courses under Dr. Bailey. His books, including *The Holy Earth*, exerted immeasurable influence over them and me. The first agricultural book I ever studied was his *Principles of Agriculture*. A few years later I was looking at an exhibit of apples at our state fair when I suddenly recognized him from pictures I had seen. "Aren't you Dr. Liberty Bailey?" I asked, and his reply was seasoned with characteristic humor. "Well, I am," he replied, "and your recognizing me just proves it'll never be safe for me to go on a spree—no matter how far I get from home!" The brief story of Dr. Bailey's pioneer farm boyhood as he told it is so typical of the rural pioneer days recalled by many of the South's older farmers when I was growing up that it is incorporated here in his own words:

"My father moved from Vermont to the wilderness frontier of northern Michigan in 1842, carrying everything he owned in a pack on his back. The Bailey clearing in Michigan was 52 miles from the nearest post office. When mail began to reach us twice a week my father said that once a week was enough for mail. . . . I grew up with Indians, woodsmen, and pioneers. We herded cattle on horseback and carried our guns when we went to the fields. . . . There is no memory of my youth that is more precious to me to this day than the splitting of fence rails. . . . Passenger pigeons flew in such enormous numbers in the spring that the sky was darkened. I was with the Indians on many mornings trapping passenger pigeons in great nets."

My last letter from Dr. Bailey, written when he was past ninety, ended with these two significant sentences: "The years with me indeed are many but they are still good ones. It has been a wonderful journey."

Dr. Bailey's comment that his ninety years had been "good years" naturally leads me to this final question: Of all the men I have known in my own four score years, who would seem to have been happiest? I think it may have been my long-time friend T. J. W. Broom. In early life he had a chance to become a partner with a friend who went on to win great wealth as one of the South's merchant princes. But after weighing the tempting offer carefully, Broom turned it down and later wrote me one of the most remarkable letters I have ever received. Discussing his work as county farm agent in Union County, North Carolina, he wrote this unforgettable paragraph:

"When I travel up and down my county and see the progress our people have made and which I have had the privilege of helping them make, a feeling of gladness comes over me and there is a song in my heart all the day long."

Few of the men who worked to bring about the revolution in Southern agricultural practices and outlook would have expressed themselves as eloquently as Broom. But to many of us who worked on *The Progressive Farmer* or did field work in Knapp's amazing crusade, has come at times such a feeling of gladness as indeed put "a song in our hearts all the day long."

CHAPTER NINE

The Ananias Club—and Other Causes

"WELL, MR. POE, I WANT YOU TO JOIN THE ANANIAS CLUB."

This was the most startling proposal any promoter of a new organization ever made me. And the man making it— it was around 1900, I believe—was the beloved dean of Raleigh newspapermen, Colonel Fred A. Olds.

"Say that again," I said, and he repeated.

"Yes, our Raleigh newspapermen are getting up a club and we are calling it the Ananias Club." Then he amazed me still further by saying the distinguished and dignified Reverend Dr. T. N. Ivey, editor of the *Raleigh Christian Advocate,* had agreed to join!

After waiting a minute for this to sink in, Colonel Olds continued, "Of course most folks don't know that there is more than one Ananias in the Bible. The one most people know about we have no use for. But there's another Ananias who was one of the best men in the Bible—the Ananias who opened the eyes of Paul. Acts 9 and 22. And since it is the first duty of all newspapermen *to open the eyes of the people,* what better patron saint could we have for our club?"

The argument was convincing, and Colonel Olds might have added that the father of Virginia Dare, the first English child born in America, was Ananias Dare, no doubt

145

named for our Ananias. I joined the Ananias Club and all the members not only had good fellowship in meetings but great sport in startling our friends by the unusual name of our organization. Most of us stuck by it, but Dr. Ivey, who had accepted the membership in innocent merriment, found too much pressure from his chief priests and elders and finally withdrew. Anyhow, the Ananias Club was purely social, and I must turn to more serious organizations.

I cannot claim to have had such a congenital virtue as one historian attributed to John Quincy Adams by saying, "The impulse to do his duty was always strong in Mr. Adams, and when that duty was unpleasant the impulse became absolutely irresistible." But I think my early hardships gave me an almost irresistible eagerness to help every underdog anywhere such an underdog might be located. The result has been that I have been placed in positions of leadership in a number of important movements not restricted to farm people.

The first I remember was the North Carolina Reformatory Association, organized about 1898, in which A. L. Chamberlain and John Nichols were prominent. At that time all young criminals were herded into the state penitentiary or put in stripes on chain gangs or in convict camps. Young boys in their teens were placed in association with the most depraved and vicious of hardened criminals. A teenager's first mistake might lead not only to severe physical punishment but also to a mark of degradation that would leave a scar on his whole life. The purpose of our group was to arouse public opinion so that provision would aim first at reformation rather than punishment of such young offenders. It would now be hard to think of a civilized state lacking some such reformatory for salvaging human worth and potentiality. No longer, anywhere I know, are convicts degraded by having to wear stripes—a condition that caused Governor Bickett to quote a verse showing the tendency to self-righteousness of which most of us are guilty:

> When the donkey saw the zebra
> He began to switch his tail.
> "Well, I never!" was his comment,
> "There's a mule that's been in jail!"

The old barbaric system of leasing convicts to work in chain gangs for businesses or individuals was also later discontinued over nearly all of the South.

Another hideous blot on Southern life at that time was the fact that little children were not only worked at a tender age in cotton factories, which should have been prevented, but they were worked for unconscionably long hours and little pay. As there was no compulsory school attendance law, there was nothing to prevent either indifferent parents or desperately poor parents from working their children in the mills under such conditions. As a result of this situation the North Carolina Child Labor Committee was organized, and I gave it my eager support. Eventually I was made chairman and had to work in opposition to some of the wealthiest and most powerful industrial leaders in the state—not only against them but against their highly paid lobbyists and attorneys. Some of these manufacturers I know favored improved legislation in this field but went along with their organizations in the opposition. Because of this experience I have long remembered the sage observation of a famous Englishman—"Individuals often rise above selfishness, but organizations never." The North Carolina Child Labor Committee did succeed in getting the minimum age for child workers raised to thirteen years and the hours per week lowered to sixty before the National Child Labor Act wiped out child labor as a national evil.

The next organization for improving social conditions which attracted my interest was the state Anti-Saloon League. As the name indicates, its original purpose was to abolish the saloons—the unregulated public drinking places operated for private profit. In these saloons thousands of men, victims of the liquor habit, spent the hard-earned wages desperately needed by their wives and children. Certainly the victim of the drink habit was an underdog—and his whole family with him. There being no statute to regulate the activities of saloon keepers, many a man upon entering a saloon was urged to drink more and more as long as his money lasted. Quite often, too, the saloon became an active ally of vice and prostitution, seriously undermining the morals of the community.

To remedy this situation was, as I have said, the original first line of attack of the Anti-Saloon League, and even eliminating these grosser evils of the saloon system would have been a marvelous advance in public welfare. Very soon, however, the decision was made that saloons—scattered but not as widely as filling stations are now—could not be "controlled" and that prohibition was the only effective remedy. One of the first important gains in anti-liquor legislation was the adoption of an act outlawing saloons in rural districts. The theory here was that saloons could not be tolerated in places where the people had no police protection. Then followed local option elections by which one city after another, and later whole counties, voted prohibition on themselves. Eventually, in 1908, prohibition for the entire state was emphatically approved by a state-wide referendum of voters.

About this time I was called on to act as chairman of the

executive committee of the state Anti-Saloon League whose leaders almost immediately began pressing for nation-wide prohibition. With this I disagreed. I predicted that in states like New York where opposition to prohibition was so powerful not even the national government would be able to enforce prohibition. One argument I gave was this: "Just after the Civil War the extremist element in the North sought to give voting privileges to masses of ignorant Negroes just out of slavery. The result is that fewer Negroes are now voting than would have been allowed to vote if a policy of gradualism had been adopted permitting Negroes to vote as rapidly as public sentiment would tolerate." Of course national prohibition did bring about in some states just such lawlessness as I had foreseen, but not so much in the South as many critics of prohibition predicted.

I also questioned the policy of treating the sale of beer and light wines as austerely as hard liquors. Today there are very few so blind that they cannot see that ever-increasing alcoholism, especially among the young and among women, is one of the most serious perils to health, morals, and human safety in our automobile age. For many years I have realized that true friends of temperance lost their supreme opportunity when the question of repealing the Prohibition Amendment was proposed in Congress. At that time I am confident opponents of prohibition would have accepted an amendment prohibiting all forms of liquor advertising. The ABC stores are a vast improvement over the old-time saloon. But should not private profit be eliminated from the manufacture of alcohol as well as from its sale?

In 1912 another forward step was taken. Along with a few other kindred spirits I helped organize the North Carolina Conference for Social Service (sometimes called "the Conscience of North Carolina") and served as president for its first, second, and third years. When the Conference was organized, I wrote for it the following Declaration of Purposes:

"To have the population of the state the best equipped of any in the Union, and to insure here and now an environment of physical, mental, and moral healthfulness that will prevent human waste and make for the full development of every individual within our borders—this is its aim. And in working toward this result, it will seek to unite all the now scattered forces of social service upon this threefold program: investigating conditions, awakening the people, and securing remedies."

To implement this ideal, active committees were set up on church and social service, illiteracy, reformatories, criminal procedure, orphanages, feeble-mindedness, improvement of country life, child labor, prisons, liquor problem, race questions, public health, taxation, women and social service, and associated charities.

The golden anniversary session of the Conference in 1962 was cheered by a message from the President of the United States saying: "I am certain the long vision and pioneering energy of Clarence Poe and the other founders will continue to sustain you." The Governor of North Carolina made a more specific tribute as follows:

"North Carolina has traveled a long way in many areas of human need since this organization was founded under the leadership of people like Clarence Poe and J. Y. Joyner. Then chain gaings were considered an essential part of our penal system. Child labor was defended as necessary in industry. Mental patients were locked away in filth and misery. Compulsory vaccination for smallpox and other communicable diseases was unknown. There was no program to care for the dependent child, the lame, and the aged. Workers hurt on the job received sympathy and very little else for there was no workmen's compensation law in those days."

From 1916 to 1931 I was chairman of the board of trustees of North Carolina State College. When the consolidated university program was proposed by Governor Gardner, Josephus Daniels was made chairman and I vice chairman of the committee to work out consolidation policies. Frank Graham was tremendously helpful in this. The great respect with which he was regarded by trustees of both institutions helped mightily to solve our most vexing issues. Later I served on the executive committee and special sub-committee on agriculture of the consolidated board until my retirement in 1955. In both of these positions I found opportunities to help what I regarded as underprivileged groups. I think I may justly claim that mine was the first voice to urge support of junior colleges as supplements to the state university. I know that as a State College activity I especially urged the establishment of two-year courses in agriculture. For this I made the following argument: "All too many bright young men on the farms cannot afford to pay the costs of a four-year course. Furthermore, they might find little opportunity to utilize such an extensive treatment of farm subjects. But they would be greatly helped by two-year courses, and these would be economically justified." I also realized the great value of short courses on special subjects, such as dairying, beef cattle, and poultry raising, and reported that farmers of other states who took such courses became warm supporters of the college in its contests for appropriations.

Another group for whom David Clark and I (while differing on many other matters) made earnest appeals were those boys who flunked out in their first or second year of college work. We stressed the fact that dropping them as college students had a serious psychological effect, creating a spirit of defeatism and humiliating them when they returned to their homes and home communities. Furthermore, the state had already made a considerable investment in their tuition costs. For these reasons we urged that special tutors be employed to try to reclaim such young men and enable them to complete their college courses.

Perhaps I should not call them underdogs, but certainly no group anywhere has suffered more than those who have given life and limb in wars not of their choosing. Of all the causes I have fought for in my lifetime there is no one to which I have brought greater zeal and intensity of purpose than the long, long effort to help preserve world peace.

This yearning for peace seemed nearest fulfillment when Woodrow Wilson called on America and other nations to join in fighting "a war to end all war." In the ensuing months, when some outstanding farm leaders were calling it "a war to enrich the munitions makers and international bankers," I worked without ceasing to sustain the war effort and later to establish and maintain the League of Nations as the fulfillment of Wilson's hopes. In addition to this editorial activity I served as a member of the executive committee of the State Food Administration and as a speaker in support of bond campaigns and other war defense efforts. After awhile, however, I wondered if I should not volunteer for active combat service and finally wrote my friend Secretary of the Navy Daniels as follows:

"For several months I have had a feeling that I ought to get out and take some real post of danger in connection with the great war. It kind of stuck in my craw last year when Dr. H. Q. Alexander, who was trying to arouse opposition to the war among North Carolina farmers, wrote me that it was all right for *me* to talk war because *I* would not go.

"Of course, I know that a year ago I could serve America infinitely better by my editorial work—counteracting German propaganda, putting all the facts about the war before our subscribers, and stimulating food production. Right now, however, I am wondering if I could not do more good by setting up an example as a volunteer. In this situation, it has occurred to me that you, as Secretary of the Navy, or Secretary Baker, or President Wilson may now and then have need of a man of my type for some mission not without peril—for I am not seeking a bomb-proof position somewhere here in the United States. If it is to go to the uttermost parts of the earth, I am willing."

Mr. Daniels, however, knowing how important it was to maintain the loyalty and activity of our farm population thought I should stay on my editorial job. This I did and I have now before me a card from the "War Department Provost Marshal General, Local Board for Division No. 2" addressed to me and carrying the following notice, with the first two words in large caps—

BE ALERT   *Keep in touch with your Local Board*
              Notify Local Board immediately of change
                          of address
CALL AT THIS OFFICE ON NOV. 14, 1918

Since I then lacked only a few weeks of reaching the age of thirty-eight and was head of a family of five, I have no idea that the draft board would have let me leave my editorial work. Nevertheless I used to laugh when I showed this card to my children and said, "Now you see just what happened! This card was mailed on November 11, 1918. So on that day Kaiser Wilhelm heard I was coming three days later—and up and surrendered!"

I shared Wilson's heartbreak when he fell a martyr to the cause of peace in Colorado, but I still hoped that the United States Senate would accept certain reasonable limitations and have the United States become a member of the League of Nations. Perhaps his stubborn Scotch-Presbyterian blood might not have admitted it but I still think that if Wilson had not been incapacitated by disease some such result might have been attained.

Disappointed as I was at the Allies' failure to make World War I "a war to end all war" I nevertheless saw in the subsequent brutal rise of Hitlerism a challenge not only to world peace and democracy but to the dignity of humanity. Even before Pearl Harbor I had served on the National Committee to Defend America by Aiding Our Allies headed by William Allen White, and after our entry into war I was a member of the Council of National Defense and chairman of the North Carolina Farm Manpower Commission. When World War II began my older son, Charles Aycock Poe, had already been an active F.B.I. agent and was kept in this position. My younger son, William D. Poe, volunteered and served until the war's end. While the war was in progress my daughter, Jean Shepperd Poe, married Colonel Gordon Smith, Jr., who was then serving in the Pentagon but was later transferred to Puerto Rico.

I still remember vividly how, as World War II was nearing what proved to be its end, the Allied Forces were preparing for a massive attack on Japan that was estimated to lead to half a million casualties, and William was among these prospective invaders. While bombs dropped on Hiroshima are generally given credit for ending the war, I have often wondered if the same effect might not have been attained if we had dropped bombs on some almost uninhabited island and then after demonstrating their effectiveness demanded Japan's surrender.

With the ending of hostilities my hope for world peace was again revived by the formation of the United Nations. The precariousness of its position in view of Russian intransigence is often disheartening. But almost every day when I look through the glass on my desk at the following eloquent paragraph from Winston Churchill, I dare to hope with him that our generation may yet see the day envisioned in his words:

"It may be that we shall move into a happier sunlit age, when all the little children growing up in this tormented world may find themselves not the victor nor the vanquished in the fleeting triumphs of one country over another, in the bloody turmoil of destructive war, but the heirs of all the treasures of the past and the masters of all the science, the abundance, and the glories of the future."

My own efforts to bring about the fulfillment of the vision so eloquently proclaimed by Winston Churchill (whom I once heard speak in the British House of Commons) found their culmination in my service on the International Development Advisory Board and the Point Four Program of President Truman. The story of this program and my part in its inauguration seems worth summarizing here.

On January 20, 1949, my son William and I left our offices early and went to my home in Longview Gardens. Our object was to hear President Truman make his inaugural address after his generally unexpected election in November. His inaugural began in rather traditional lines with nothing to excite us. But suddenly a single sentence startled us into eager attention and interest. That sentence began—

"*Fourth,* we must embark on a bold new program for making the benefits of our scientific advances and industrial progress available for the improvement and growth of underdeveloped areas." William and I were delighted as Mr. Truman went on to say—

"Our aim should be to help the free peoples of the world, through their own efforts, to produce more food, more clothing, more materials for housing, and more mechanical power to lighten their burdens. . . . Greater production is the key to prosperity and peace. And the key to greater production is a wider and more vigorous application of modern scientific and technical knowledge."

At that time I had no thought that I could do more to help such a truly "bold new program" than to urge its acceptance and development by Congress. Later, however, I was named as a member of the International Development Advisory Board (or IDA-B as we called it) and the commission won increased prestige because of the distinguished men named as my fellow members. One of these was Nelson A. Rockefeller, who served as chairman; another was an equally unpretentious inheritor of great wealth, Harvey S. Firestone. Representing labor were two men for whom I formed great respect, Walter Reuther and Jacob S. Potofsky. As an agricultural member my ally was Dr. John A. Hannah of Michigan State University.

Mr. Rockefeller, dynamic, handsome, and engaging, was then at the height of his powers—young enough to be untiring but mature enough to have developed a rarely equaled understanding of what was needed to help America go forward for its own welfare and in cooperation with other nations. The phrase most often on his lips was "an expanding economy." "Partners in Progress" was a phrase he liked. We should not try to hand down something to other nations as charity. Rather we should promote such progress through educational, health, agricultural, and industrial development to enable other peoples to stand on their own feet. All of us especially approved the declaration in the Jewish *Talmud*, "The truest charity is that which helps a man help himself so he will no longer need charity."

Leading American experts in many fields helped our board members realize the desperateness of the conditions under which more than half the members of our human race lived. My own rather extended first-hand study of conditions in the Orient in 1910-11 had given me a somewhat better understanding of these conditions than most other members possessed—conditions it would be impossible to set forth more concisely than in the statement I prepared in summarizing the studies made by our board as follows: In the so-called "underdeveloped areas" of the world, including Africa, Central America, South America, and all of Asia except Russia and China, there live more than one billion people; most of these people are tenant farmers and farm workers; their conditions of income, health, education, and life-expectancy, compared with conditions of people in the developed areas (U.S.A. and Europe), are substantially as follows:

	Developed Areas	Underdeveloped Areas
Illiteracy, per cent	5	78
Per capita income per year	$461	$41
Doctors, per 100,000	106	17
Persons in each 100 living till 15	92	54
Persons in each 100 living till 60	70	15
Life expectancy, years	63	30

Just how important was it then—and how important is it even now—to educate the American people to the appalling situation statistically summarized in the table just given? I doubt if one American in ten has even a half-way adequate understanding of how "the other half" of the human race has to live. A truly remarkable revelation of the misunderstanding that exists among people even in places of high authority occurred at one meeting of our board I well remember. In discussing the needs of poverty stricken, underprivileged groups in India so distinguished a member as the Honorable James W. Gerard, who had been ambassador to Germany, exclaimed, "Why, India is a rich country—there is no need to put it in the class with the poverty-cursed nations!" Actually, of course, "the wealth of the Indies," as I had learned first hand, is a phrase that had long misled millions of people. They had not realized that its "wealth" is concentrated in an area no thicker than an orange peel as compared with the vast area of dire poverty beneath the thin peel of the orange. It is this vast disparity between the few who are inordinately rich and the millions who are desperately poor—it is this disparity which constitutes the greatest asset of Russian communism and the greatest peril to the Free World.

In this connection I remember with especial satisfaction my part in urging the board to give especial attention to Africa "as the next area of world-shaking explosions." To this end I proposed a special committee on the conditions and possibilities in Africa to be headed by the only Negro on our board, able Dr. Robert P. Daniel, then head of A. & M. College in Virginia and previously president of Shaw University.

In reporting to President Truman on March 7, 1951, our board made the following significant review of conditions and needs:

"The free people of the world over are awakening to the fact that defense, in and of itself, is not enough—that there must be a *positive* force as well. . . . It might even be that winning world peace is even more difficult than winning a world war. . . . The Free World community must have the strength to preserve law and order—without which it cannot live in peace. However, law and order alone are not enough. Their needs can only be met by expanding production, new businesses, more jobs, new schools and hospitals, and opportunity for all. . . . Basic to defense and to human well-being and the promotion of free institutions is increased production—not in one part or country alone, but in all parts and in all countries . . . an expanding economy which creates opportunity and increased earnings, better living conditions, hope and faith in the future."

Mr. Rockefeller handled all business in a most expert, courteous, and friendly manner. He impressed me as a man highly informed, forward-looking, unselfish, and with an overriding desire to help the underprivileged peoples of the world. Especially outstanding was his interest in South America. In my contacts with Rockefeller I frequently recalled to myself that I had once seen his celebrated grandfather, John D., Sr., founder of the Rockefeller fortune and dynasty, at a church service we both attended in Ormond Beach, Florida, and the amusement I could not refrain from feeling at hearing the richest man in the world join in the prayer—

"Lord, give us this day, our daily bread!"

CHAPTER TEN

Governor Aycock As I Knew Him

THAT GOVERNOR CHARLES BRANTLEY AYCOCK WAS THE BEST loved man of his generation in North Carolina is a fact that seems to have universal acceptance. And the reason I think so is found in the simple statement of his long-time friend Archibald Johnson, "Governor Aycock was the most beloved man because he was a great lover."

Certainly Governor Aycock loved all classes of North Carolina people. Many at this point might ask, "Did he really love colored people—the Negroes he so largely helped disfranchise in 1900?" My answer is, "I am sure he did." He felt that the Negroes at that time—so recently out of slavery and whose schools had been so inadequate—were not prepared to exercise wisely the privilege of suffrage, for their own sake or anybody else's. But even in his campaign for governor he declared:

"May the era of good feeling among us be the outcome of this contest. Then we shall learn, if we do not already know, that while universal suffrage is a failure, universal justice is the perpetual decree of Almighty God, and that we are entrusted with power not for our good alone, but for the Negro as well. We hold our title to power by the tenure of service to God, and if we fail to administer equal and exact justice to the Negro whom we deprive of suffrage we shall in the fulness of time lose power ourselves, for we must know that the God who is Love trusts no people with authority for the purpose of enabling them to do injustice to the weak."

Immediately after becoming governor, Aycock threw into the balance all the popularity he had won by long years as a Democratic leader so that Negroes might be given a chance to educate themselves and thus prepare to meet the literacy test the new Constitutional Amendment required. So intense was the opposition to "educating niggers" even in his old home county that I heard it said, "Charlie Aycock couldn't now be elected constable in Wayne County!"

But about this matter he was entirely adamant. Once when the opposition seemed to be so sure of victory, I, as one of his most constant admirers, went to see him in the Governor's Mansion to suggest that he consider a compromise. "Why not require the equal division of school funds between the races up to the constitutional requirement of a four months school term—but then give either race a chance to vote a special tax on itself to extend the term beyond this constitutional requirement?" I asked. This, however, he courteously, but firmly and irretrievably, put aside. He wanted the white people to show their concern for our colored people by sharing equally with them whatever funds the wealthier race, along with their own, might be willing to provide for schools.

And so the battle went on. It reached its climax in the Democratic State Convention in Greensboro in 1904. There the question of approving or repudiating Aycock was the supreme, if not publicly stated, main issue. So bitter was the feeling that some of Aycock's closest friends urged him not to risk a public appearance or speech in defense of his policy, saying he would be howled down—as some other

leaders had been. To Aycock, however, this was not a
situation to run from; it was a challenge to face. His prepared speech as printed gives no idea of the spontaneous
and extemporaneous eloquence with which he swept the
delegates off their feet and thus committed North Carolina
—perhaps forever—to an attitude of racial good will. And
all this occurred at a time when all too many other Southern
governors and senators profited by fomenting fires of racial
bitterness.

Perhaps Aycock's most famous phrase is the one most
often misunderstood—the phrase from his last prepared
address and now carved on his monument, "The equal right
of every child born on earth to have the opportunity to
burgeon out all there is within him." This phrase was not
intended to apply only to school children. What is of great
significance is that Aycock in this connection was speaking
not merely of equality of educational opportunity alone but
particularly of better economic opportunity for the poor of
all races. For the phrase was not used in an educational
address. It was prepared for and used in his address announcing his candidacy for the United States Senate—an
address dealing with the basic economic and social problems
facing America and national policies he thought necessary
for their solution.

Of course Aycock was most immediately touched by the
inadequacy of the state's service to its children in the field of
public education. On the fiftieth anniversary of his inauguration as governor, Cameron Morrison told of a visit to Aycock
while Aycock was United States district attorney for eastern
North Carolina. The case was that of a man accused of some
violation of a federal statute and Aycock inquired about his
educational opportunities. Finding that the state had given
the man almost no schooling to fit him for any advancement
in life, Aycock exclaimed, "I cannot demand the full penalty

of the law when the state itself has so shamefully neglected its duty toward developing a citizen."

The universality of Aycock's love for people is probably indicated by the fact that even through his fiercest campaigns he maintained an undiminished friendship for such leading Republicans as Judge W. S. O'B. Robinson, Marion Butler, and E. C. Duncan.

Of course, for a fuller understanding of Governor Aycock's life and character one should read the appraisals of him made by many of his contemporaries in *The Life and Speeches of Charles B. Aycock*, edited by Dr. R. D. W. Connor and me, and the recently published *Charles Brantley Aycock* by Dr. Oliver Orr. But I have often thought that the authors of both books wrote when they were too young to realize how deep were two tragedies in Aycock's life that they lightly passed over. The first was the death in 1889 of the gifted and lovable young woman he had taken as a bride in 1881 when he was twenty-two and she nineteen. (Her death at the age of twenty-seven seemingly occurred from a ruptured appendix.) The other tragedy was the death from spinal meningitis of his gifted nineteen-year-old son and namesake while a promising junior at the University of North Carolina. In his address, "How the South May Regain Its Prestige," at Athens, Georgia, in 1903, Aycock expressed his conviction that only by sharing with his fellow men some great loss or tribulation can anyone develop in his heart that depth of sympathy for all others which true greatness requires.

But if his sorrows mellowed Governor Aycock they never soured him. Not inappropriately his beloved mother was named Serena, and serenity was almost a major quality in his makeup. To cherish grudges was impossible for him. In his speech prepared to announce his candidacy for the United States Senate he went out of his way to pay a gracious tribute to each one of his three prospective opponents.

In his home life Governor Aycock was especially happy, perhaps loving his second wife all the more because she was the sister of his first. The easy comradeship of all members with one another was manifested by the nicknames by which each member was called. His wife Cora was Code, Alice was Daught, Mary was Muff, Frank was Ditbo, Louise was Tardy, Brantley was Pot.

In his book *Idle Comments,* Ervin Avery speaks of Governor Aycock as smoking a short-stemmed pipe but "short" was a slip of the pen. At night it was a privilege to see him get out and light up his old-fashioned long-stemmed pipe with a reed as long as his arm. One of my happiest memories is of one such night when he, Alice, and I sat beside an open fire while he read passages from Tennyson's "The Brook" and commented on the characters in it. Another happy memory is of the night when he entertained at dinner the members of the bar participating in a case of outstanding importance. Among those present was Junius Parker who had written a remarkably significant and thoughtful paragraph for which Aycock expressed great admiration (and which because of my own great liking for it as a guide all editors should observe I have kept under the glass on my desk for years):

"Power of any sort, whether of wealth or intellect or education, or social position, or accident, brings duty—the duty of truth, the duty of fairness, the duty of courtesy, the duty of sanity; a duty to the weak not to oppress them; a duty to the credulous, not to mislead them; a duty to one's friends, not to flatter or cajole them; a duty to one's enemies, not to malign them; a duty to the rich, not to be a sycophant; a duty to the poor, not to be a demagogue."

Of course Aycock's fame now rests upon his achievements as governor and political leader, but a generation ago his fame rested in large part upon his achievements as a lawyer. For Aycock the lawyer, one of the most amusing tributes was paid by a man who for some reason, probably political, fell out with Aycock and quit speaking to him. However, when this man got into trouble a little later and needed a lawyer he asked Aycock to represent him. Aycock used to add laughingly, "I did represent him and he paid me my fee— and never spoke to me again!"

Long afterward, when he had received fees ranging in four figures, he remarked: "The first year I practiced law, I made $144, and it was the hardest $144 ever made in my life. I worked night and day and week after week and month after month to make it. I had to pay $12 a month for my board and what little clothes I had I had to borrow the money to pay for. I made $144, and that is what I ought to have made."

One particular early experience he always enjoyed telling. "I had prepared and delivered what I thought was a pretty good speech," he said, "and I had a young fellow's pride in my effort. In fact, I made it convenient to fall in with Judge Dick, before whom I had appeared, to see if he, too, wouldn't say it was good. Sure enough, he began: 'Mr. Aycock, that was a fine speech you made this morning, a very fine speech'; and I swelled with pride. 'There were marks of real eloquence about it,' he continued. 'In fact, the first time I heard it I could hardly refrain from expressing my admiration. The second time I heard it, it still sounded good. But the third time I heard it, it simply made me tired.'

"The judge taught me a lesson," Aycock would say. "I had repeated myself too much. It is a fault I have ever since sought to avoid."

Aycock was gifted to an unusual degree in one particular way—the faculty of making his client's cause his own cause. He not only put himself in his client's place, he probably did better; for it was natural for him to believe in the best in every man, and he probably believed his clients to be a great deal better than even the natural self-deception of some men permits. "Aycock never had a client who wasn't an angel," someone has said. But a better explanation seems to be this: Aycock's first thought in any case was not of what legislative act or Supreme Court decision covered his case, but on what natural principle of right or justice his client might base his claim. Immediately he became the armed champion of that righteous principle—a principle without flaw or blemish or human frailty—and his client, as a symbol of that immaculate right, became himself its flawless incarnation.

As a lifelong friend has observed: "He loved the law practice and contests in a court room better than anything else. It made no difference to him whether the fee was $5.00 from a poor client or $5,000 from a rich client, he put himself into a case with the same forgetfulness of self and devotion to the interest of the man he represented."

Aycock did not come out best in all his encounters and always enjoyed telling stories of cases when he was outwitted. On one occasion Aycock was relying on the testimony of an old Negro whose reputation for veracity was none too good. Aycock had steered him skillfully through the testimony, however, until the opposing counsel got hold of him. "Where were you during the war?" he was asked. "I wuz with Marse Robert." "Which Marse Robert?" "Marse Robert Lee. I wuz his body-sarvent." "Well, tell us about it." "Well, he was the best man I ever seed. Never seed him doin' nothin' wrong but onct." "When was that?" "That was arter the S'render. Gen'l Grant he tuk Gen'l Lee's swored away from him, and Gen'l Lee he got mad and grabbed it back and broke it in two. Then he flung half of it right in Gen'l Grant's face and cussed. Yassuh, dat time he cussed!" The

examination had progressed to this point before the astonished Aycock had thought to object, but he immediately
arose and said: "Your Honor, I move that we extend a vote
of thanks to the old Negro for his contribution to Southern
history!"

One of Aycock's greatest legal triumphs was his appearance before the United States Supreme Court in the railroad
rate case. Governor Glenn, Aycock's successor in office, was
present and later wrote an unusually vivid description of the
scene—the eight Supreme Court justices in their black robes,
with the venerable Chief Justice Fuller with his classic face
and white hair in the center:

"Aycock began to speak in a low voice so inaudible that
men were leaning forward to hear what he said, and the
Chief Justice remarked, 'A little louder, Governor, if you
please.' He raised his voice slowly, and deliberately began
to lay down the contentions of the state, with forceful logic,
apt and numerous court decisions, persuasive voice, and
masterful oratory. As he spoke his form seemed to expand,
his eyes sparkled with fire, his hands moved in commanding
gesture, until he closed in one of the grandest perorations
I have ever heard, while each judge sank back into his chair
seemingly relieved from a great tension. For a few moments
there was a hush in the chamber, and then friend and foe
crowded around the ex-Governor pronouncing it one of the
ablest speeches ever heard in the United States Supreme
Court. Later when I met Justice Fuller in Washington, he said
to me: 'You have a wonderful man in your state.' I replied,
'Who, Chief Justice?' and he said, 'Ex-Governor Aycock,' and
added: 'Tell him I say that while he did not succeed in convincing all of the justices so as to win his cause, he did
convince them, as they admitted in our consulting room, that
he had delivered one of the greatest speeches ever made before the court. And tell him further that my dissenting opin-

ion was almost entirely based upon his argument.' How great praise was this when we remember that Justice Fuller's dissenting opinion is now considered one of the ablest ever handed down!"

A whole book might be given to stories of Aycock's legal career, but space remains only for a word—and in a somewhat different vein—about his work from the standpoint of business. So considered, Aycock was a man to vex the soul of Job. He was never methodical in his business. He would take a case and throw his whole heart and soul into it, but meanwhile everything else might "go hang." He often attended to his correspondence after the fashion of Napoleon who said that if one would let a letter lie two weeks it would answer itself. Even checks sent to him were sometimes uncashed until financial pressure required him to give them attention.

Dr. Luther Gulick has said, "Do the big things first," but not even with this principle to aid him could his warmest friend have accused Governor Aycock of being systematic in his labors. All detail work—answering miscellaneous correspondence, investigating titles, preparing proceedings—was to him a weariness of the flesh. Consequently, his business suffered in many respects—or his correspondents did—whenever his law partner was not watchful; and an efficient secretary was very necessary to his success when he was governor.

Aycock was a true countryman, loving the good earth and all country things. On walking from the Governor's Mansion to his office I found he always took the unpaved sidewalks as far as he could. He loved fox-hunting and used to hunt rabbits on the hill where my home now stands, expressing with almost poetic phraseology his admiration of the beautiful view across nearby Crabtree Creek and the Neuse River. He was one of the first to advocate agricultural teaching in country schools. I know, too, that he fully shared a beautiful sentiment once expressed by his second wife to me. The season for summer vacations was ended and she said, "This year I have not been able to see the scenery of the mountains or the scenery of the ocean. But I have greatly enjoyed the scenery of the sky." I think I have ever since had a heightened appreciation of "the scenery of the sky" as shown in sunrise and sunset, the tints and shades of varicolored clouds, and the glittering stars at night.

Turning to a slightly different subject, I should mention how very fortunate it is that a stenographer was present when Governor Aycock delivered in almost its entirety his famous speech on "Universal Education" just before he fell dead in Birmingham, April 4, 1912. One part of that speech, however, is nowhere available in its perfection. But I think it should be remembered and I think I can give it almost verbatim as follows:

"Yes, I am asking you to pay more taxes for schools— and I know just how much you hate taxes. I can never forget the anguish and distress on the face of an old farmer as he goes into the sheriff's office and asks, 'Sheriff, Sheriff, how much is my taxes?' Then drawing out an old, half worn-out billfold tied all the tighter with four or five strings, he unwraps each string as painfully as if he were having a tooth pulled, then counts over the whole amount of taxes three or four times to make sure he has not inadvertently paid the state one extra penny, parting with each coin or bill as dolefully as if he were bidding the last farewell to a friend ... and finally leaves the sheriff's office looking as if he had been to a funeral. Yes, I know how deep is your aversion to taxes but I know one thing is deeper—and that is your love for your children and their future."

In few reports of Aycock's educational speeches has enough attention been given to his emphasis on the curse of "cheap labor" and the importance of using education to increase wages and income. "When you buy manufactured articles," said he, "you buy them from Massachusetts, and pay for labor worth $4.00 a day; but you pay in the products of your own labor, which is worth 50 cents a day. Now, what does this mean? Why, that you must give eight days of your labor for one day of labor by the man in Massachusetts. And why? Simply because Massachusetts has educated her people to work efficiently and North Carolina has not."

Just how strenuous were the campaigns Aycock conducted in his day is hard for anyone now to conceive. There were, of course, no automobiles, railroads were far apart, and connections were a tribulation to the flesh. I have heard Josephus Daniels tell of Aycock's coming in by train about midnight from some speaking engagement and then having to catch a 3 A.M. train for another long trip by a slow train that stopped to receive and discharge passengers at every little station before reaching the place for his next political engagement.

Aycock enjoyed every contact with his friends. The good fees he received as a lawyer gave him especial pleasure because they enabled him to give money to numerous causes and persons, and his law partner Judge R. W. Winston had to cooperate with his private secretary to keep him from giving too much to persons not wholly worthy. Any old Confederate soldier he found hard to resist—and there were many while he was living. An annual delight was paying his friend Z. L. M. Jeffreys for a full carload of watermelons to be sent to the children at the Baptist Orphanage at Thomasville. But Aycock never resorted to the insincere affectations of friendship so often practiced by back-slapping demagogues. As his brother-in-law Dr. Albert Anderson said, "You can feel and know that he is your friend without his resorting to such tricks of the political trade."

Regarding Governor Aycock's personal life, few people

knew him better or for a longer period than Captain Samuel
A. Ashe, editor of *The Biographical History of North Carolina*. For this, Ashe, able and scrupulously veracious, wrote
the sketch of Aycock concluding, "He is a man of exemplary
habits, being entirely free of those weaknesses and excesses
that sometimes stain the character of public men." This was
in 1905. If, for some relatively brief periods later he slipped
in any degree, should not this additional fact be mentioned
as of equal or greater significance—that when he found
drinking was hurting him, he demonstrated a courageous
self-mastery fully in keeping with his character and reputation, quitting it entirely and forever by his unaided will?

It was at a bridge party in 1910 after Governor Aycock
and his family had returned to Raleigh from Goldsboro that
I first became acquainted with my future wife—and when
she said, "I choose Mr. Poe as my partner," I was not long
in deciding that I wanted to "make the temporary organization permanent." As I walked home that night I said to
myself, "If that girl is what I think she is, I am going to
marry her." A visit to her had top priority when I returned
from my trip around the world in March, 1911, and a delightful summer vacation party at Blowing Rock a little
later enabled us to become more fully acquainted with each
other in very happy surroundings. Returning to Raleigh
after the vacation ended I continued seeing her at her home,
at parties, on horseback rides, buggy rides—and at least once
on a sleigh ride! I later liked to tell her teasingly that her
Salem College course in home economics had been one of
her trump cards and that one of her most effective recommendations had come from a cook in her family. To one of
my friends this cook had remarked casually that she had
never seen anybody with such a uniformly sweet and happy
disposition day after day as "Miss Alice."

I have never forgotten, too, that when I went to ask for

his daughter's hand, Governor Aycock was somewhat pressed for time because he was very shortly due to leave to speak at a banquet. After I somewhat hesitantly talked about the weather, politics, and the general state of the union, the Governor relieved me by taking matters in his own hands. "Well, I know why you have come to see me," he said, "and it is all right." After Governor Aycock's lamented death before the date of our planned marriage, Alice's little brother Brantley, about four years old, asserted his rights in my case. "You shan't marry Daught," he said, "unless you give me a bicycle." So I have often teased my wife by saying that I bought her with a bicycle—the best investment I ever made.

Numerous letters Governor Aycock wrote me have been turned over to the Department of Archives and History. One, however, I kept as a family heirloom. Written in longhand (in reply to a letter of my own sent the day after he had given his consent for Alice's marriage) and addressed to "Clarence H. Poe, Esq.," as was a common salutation among gentlemen at that time, it reads as follows:

"I thank you for your courteous and kind letter of this date. It is a beneficial letter to me in that it makes me earnestly desirous to be fully worthy of the estimate which you make of me. My regard for you has been of long standing and has grown with the years. I make no doubt that the closer relation in which we have now come will more and more endear you to me. I shall hope for a real companionship unmarred by our difference in years. Alice and I understand each other like sister and brother and I shall count myself greatly blessed if you and she and I shall keep step together, even if youth has to slow its steps a little for the sake of age and age shall have to hurry just enough to keep up with the joyousness of unrestrained youth. I am certain that you and she will both do your duty toward each other, bearing burdens together with hope and patience. May God guide and keep you both and make us all the happier and wiser in our new relation. Mrs. Aycock joins in love."

In some reminiscences of her father written by my wife a few years ago, she mentioned some revealing incidents as follows:

"He was a lover of the Latin language and having heard him quote it so often and talk about it so much, I was in my second Heaven when I reached the grade to start Latin. While I liked it, too, I did find it hard, but whenever I couldn't translate a passage of Caesar or Cicero and went to him for help I always found a delighted and helpful teacher. . . . He liked baseball very much and always liked to sit on the top row in the center section. His seat could very easily be seen from the outside and he once said laughingly that he could never enjoy the first part of the game for every few minutes he'd hear a voice say, 'Daddy, throw me down a quarter to get in the game.' It would be one of my numerous brothers! . . . He often rode a bicycle and on the day I got one of my own asked me to go out with him to ride around the track. When we reached the track and rested awhile he said, 'Let's race around!' Imagine what a thrill I got when I beat him! I was so excited about it that I told everybody and it was a long time afterward before I realized that of course he had *let* me win! . . . He was a great lover of nature. Our home in Goldsboro faced the west and he would often go out on the porch even in wintertime to admire a beautiful sunset. . . . There were almost no automobiles when he was governor or before and he enjoyed taking long walks, after office hours, with close friends. . . . When I was about seventeen or eighteen I decided I would like to learn to play bridge. When I told him this he said, 'Fine, but remember this—if you do play I want you to be a *good* player!' . . . He was folksy and friendly and I cannot remember ever feeling that he was stern. We loved him, were proud of him, and all but put him on a pedestal—but we were not afraid to reach up and pat him on the back! He was a very affectionate person but not demonstrative. . . . When he was governor he found it a great burden to have the pardoning power. He would come from the office and tell how an aged mother had been to see him about her son in the penitentiary, or a young mother with a babe in arms would see him about her husband, and he lost many an hour's sleep over cases like these."

A friend recently brought me the original copy of a letter Governor Aycock took time to write a little girl in the month that he had been elected governor, August, 1900. This letter so significantly reveals his character that I think it worthwhile to add it here. Addressed to Miss Ione Fuller, Winston, N.C. (before Winston became Winston-Salem) reads:

Goldsboro, N.C., Aug. 25, 1900

My Dear Little Girl:

I would write to you with my own hand in reply to your beautiful letter of August 4th but you write so much better than I can that I am ashamed for you to see my hand writing. It is very sweet of you to express your pleasure at my election. When you come to Raleigh you must not only come to the Capitol to see me, but you must go to the Mansion to see Mrs. Aycock and my house full of little children. I have seven and among them a little boy who is a fine little fellow and just about the right size for your sweetheart. I remember with much pleasure the flowers which you were kind enough to pin on my coat at Mocksville and, of course, I have not forgotten you. I thank you for remembering me and for writing me the letter.

With best wishes, I am

Very truly your friend,
C. B. Aycock

CHAPTER ELEVEN

The Worlds Across the Seas

GOING ABROAD!

Even today, when travel has become incredibly faster—
and when so many enjoy what once so few enjoyed—the two
words have a touch of magic. For me in 1908 at age twenty-
seven, when I had my first chance to cross the seas, they
had a multi-splendored fascination. By that time my work
on *The Progressive Farmer* had taken me all over the South,
and I had also had a chance to see the great agricultural
areas of the Middle West and the grandeur of our western
mountains and the Pacific coast. But it was my good fortune
to see Europe before World War I when, in Sir Edward
Grey's famous phrase, the lights went out all over it. And I
was also privileged to see much of Asia in that same period,
before the wars and revolutions of the twentieth century
brought it headlong out of its ancient past.

✓ The most compelling motive for my first trip to Europe
was my wish to see how many lessons in farming ideas and
practice I might learn for the benefit of the readers—then
nearing 100,000—of *The Progressive Farmer*. The idea of
such a trip also had many attractions from the viewpoint
of sheer personal pleasure. Few people enjoyed the works of
the great English and European poets, thinkers, and artists

more than I, and the thought of seeing the homes and birth-
places of Shakespeare, Burns, Carlyle, Tennyson, Browning,
and Hugo, and seeing the original works of great artists
such as Michelangelo, Rembrandt, Renoir, and Thorwald-
sen gave me an anticipated pleasure that was more than fulfilled in actual experience. I knew too that the differences
between our New World of 400 years and the Old World
countries of 4,000 years would be little less than startling.

Especially was I pleased to think of Europe as being the
"Old Home" of nearly all white Americans. Hence I looked
forward especially to seeing England as the home of my
Poe, Moore, Hackney, and Shepperd ancestors; Scotland as
the home country of my great grandmother, Charity Patterson; and France as the home of my mother's family,
Dismukes (spelled Des Meaux in France before it was Angli-
cized in this country). With especial interest I studied the
history, customs, and traditions of these ancestral lands and
loaded up a suitcase of books about them to carry along
with me.

Nor was it for these reasons alone that the prospect of the
trip excited me. While I had planned to make a European
trip for "some time," the idea did not take definite form
until a charming young lady who had just graduated from
Trinity College (now Duke) told me, "My cousin Sue Bar-
row and I are getting ready to join a party Mr. Longley is
getting up to leave for Europe in a few weeks." The young
lady was Miss Mary Reamey Thomas of Virginia. My recollection is that she had talked first of a bicycle trip through
England, but the idea soon expanded into a full-length,
traditional "continental tour."

Our party also expanded to include Dr. W. P. Few, then
head of the English Department at Trinity, who had fallen
rather desperately in love with his brilliant former pupil.
The Longley party was large and nation-wide, but the four

of us segregated ourselves into a delightful Southern quartet which all found mutually enjoyable—and the Thomas-Barrow-Poe trio continued as a unit after Dr. Few reluctantly returned home to prepare for his fall session work. He later had the good fortune both to win Miss Thomas (who is as alert now as then) and to become president of the newly christened Duke University. His love of the classics did not prevent his enjoying more down-to-earth stories such as one about a too-industrious farmer in his native South Carolina who used to arouse his boys at daybreak Monday by hollering, "Get up, get up, get up! Here it is Monday, tomorrow Tuesday, next day Wednesday—half the week gone and no work done yit!"

I had no sooner landed than I was charmed by the beauty of the English countryside and particularly by the neatness of the homes, fields, and gardens. I remember having the impression that no one seemed really poor. The tiniest cottages were surrounded by trim hedges and a profusion of flowers.

We enjoyed seeing the Shakespeare country, the Wordsworth country, and Warwick Castle—where I was permitted to put the helmet of Oliver Cromwell on my head! I was especially interested in seeing the rude Scotch cottage in which Robert Burns lived—Robert Burns of whom Jesse Stuart has written: "He was educated with an ax, a hoe, a plow, a wheat cradle, a flail, and a mattock." Standing on the spot in Oxford where Cranmer, Latimer, and Ridley were burned at the stake for conscience' sake gave me a new appreciation of the value of religious liberty that all of us in America now take for granted. Looking on the original copy of the Magna Charta in the British Museum in London led me to reflect upon the long, hard-fought, and yet unretreating struggle through which the idea of "liberty, equality, and fraternity" had been conceived. I also wished to help dispel a still general prejudice, perhaps handed down from the Revolutionary War, that Britain was king-ruled and not a democracy like our own.

"The pleasant land of France" was my next destination. Here as in England I was almost jealous when I saw its meticulously cultivated fields entirely unmarred by a gully or a "turned out field," whereas in my Southern homeland I could never travel far without having some galled piece of land stir in me the same sense of poignancy that had caused Sidney Lanier to write:

> Yon old deserted Georgian hill
> Bares to the sun his piteous aged crest
> 　　And seamy breast
> By restless-hearted children left to lie
> Untended there beneath the heedless sky
> As barbarous folk expose their old to die.

Truly it seemed to me the French farmers were "artists working on a canvas of earth." The French, like the English, had been cultivating their land for centuries without wearing it out. And yet we Southerners constantly exhausted our fields and cleared "new ground." In a way it had been a curse to America that our land has been so plentiful as to make us wasteful.

One reason for the good care of land was that neither in France nor in England would any landowner have thought for a moment of renting a piece of land to an ignorant tenant to butcher or maltreat in such fashion as was common in the South. French tenants usually leased for fifty years or more and were given credit at the end of that time for whatever improvements they had made—an idea I commended to Southern landowners.

Women worked much in the fields: I saw numbers of them doing all sorts of work, not in any half-hearted or humdrum fashion, but strong, healthy, intelligent-looking women who worked earnestly and cheerily, simply because on these small farms everyone must work if the family is to prosper.

The main secret of the French farmer's success I found was a combination of crops and cattle. French farmers had two products—livestock and crops—and the combination was good for them and good for the land. For another thing, I had long mourned our lack in the South of good, strong work horses, and when I reached Belgium and Holland, the Dutch and Belgian Percherons seemed almost as big as Barnum's elephants! These kingly horses, bearing themselves as if conscious of royal blood, hauled gigantic loads on wagons that when empty would have made good loads for an average Southern mule. And I never saw a horse's (or cow's) ribs while I was in Europe.

In Germany, Belgium, and Holland I found that all things and all people worked: women, children, cows, and dogs. Even the breezes that passed over the country were caught and put to work to turn windmills to grind wheat, cut wood, and drain land. In Germany even the king and the king's son learned a trade, and the secret of the prosperity of all these crowded, overflowing countries, in my opinion, lay in two things. In the first place, Europe's nations had intelligent populations, with every person's natural intelligence trained and sharpened by education. In the second place, no man or woman thought of any task that came to hand as being "beneath" his or her station. Time and again on this trip I saw hotel proprietors or managers, men of education and refinement, come into kitchen or dining room in case of a rush and help wait on the table as if it were the most natural thing in the world.

To do work badly degrades it. I wondered if this was not a major trouble with us in the South. Our old slave-holding aristocracy set the ignorant newly captured Africans to work for them, and they worked so badly that this encouraged the too-widely-held feeling that all physical labor was "beneath" our upper classes. As I wrote from Europe:

"There is no task under heaven which an intelligent man cannot do better and more cheaply than an unintelligent man; there is no work under heaven which cannot be done better and more cheaply by educated labor than by uneducated. There is no other way given among men whereby a nation can achieve greatness than by training, developing, and educating its people, its common people." This has been one of my favorite themes, and the force of the idea was thrust upon me over and over again in Germany, France, and England in 1908.

The Germans especially stressed the training of young people for actual life and work. If German educators had been in charge of Southern education, I said, we should have had splendidly equipped agricultural high schools in every county or Congressional district, and the elements of agriculture and home economics would have been taught in every rural school, whether elementary school or academy.

To me it had been positively heart-sickening to see boys who were going to be farmers in academies in our country districts in the South studying subjects they would never use, such as "latitude and longitude" and "the metric system of weights and measures," while learning nothing whatever about how to compound a feeding ration for their livestock or a fertilizer formula for their crops.

Also in Germany I saw that forest owners regarded timber as a *crop* just as definitely as corn or wheat. It was interesting to go through the meticulously handled woodlands and to see how the trees of the right size had been marked, cut, and hauled out with not one-tenth as much damage to other timber as an average American lumberman would have inflicted.

Finally my tour of Eurpoe was ended and I sailed for home aboard the *S.S. Cretic.* The trip had made me gladder than ever that I was an American, much as it had taught me of the superior farming and educational methods of many European peoples. If we learned to care for our resources as well as Europe cared for hers and to educate our people as well as Germany educated hers, the time would come when the United States would stand the acknowledged leader among the countries of the world. My ambition was that we of the South, before this achievement was consummated, should make our section the foremost section of the United States and therefore the foremost section of what must become the foremost nation of the world.

After making my trip through Europe at age twenty-seven I next set up for myself three goals to reach by age thirty: to go around the world; to carry *Progressive Farmer* circulation past the 100,000 mark; and to get married. I do not list these objectives in the order of their importance but only as they developed chronologically!

So in August, 1910, five months before reaching age thirty, I left Raleigh on my round-the-world trip that was to end in March, 1911. On January 10, 1911, the day I was thirty, I was looking out on the Ganges River in India when I received word that *The Progressive Farmer* circulation had passed the 100,000 mark. And my marriage occurred one year after I returned home. I was almost running on schedule!

While going around the world now gives one no particular distinction, this was not so in 1910. At that time there were in Raleigh only three persons who had circumnavigated the globe. Nowadays a man in New York may almost order hardboiled eggs for lunch in London and get there by the time they are taken out of the kettle. But when I bought tickets from Thomas Cook & Son in 1910 for a trip "over the world and under the world and back again to you" it took sixteen days to cross the Pacific, broken only by a one-day stop in Honolulu. On all the other days we were entirely out of touch with all other human beings. With no radio or TV, the whole of America might have been sunk by some continental earthquake and we would have known nothing of it until we reached Yokohama!

I had prepared myself well for the trip both by extensive reading and by having letters of introduction to very important persons from British Ambassador Bryce, the governor of my home state, Walter Page of *The World's Work*, Theodore Roosevelt, along with letters from Dr. Seaman A. Knapp, who had dealt with important agricultural leaders in the Orient.

It was especially gratifying to learn, soon after landing in Japan, that farming in that country was considered the most honorable of all occupations. And the affection of the people for their farms was so great that they had a special term of contempt for any man who sold his ancestral lands. Their philosophy was that the men who actually produce wealth deserve more honor than men who trade or barter in the products of other men's labor.

What skillful farmers the Japanese were is shown by this fact: their little handkerchief-sized farms were cultivated so intensively, fertilized so painstakingly, and kept so continuously producing that the Japanese fed at that time 2,277 people from a square mile! How I wished that our Southern farmers could see how much they produced with so little to work with! Any neglect of the soil was considered a crime.

I wished, too, that our people might develop the Japanese love of the beautiful in nature. No matter how small and cramped the yard about a tiny Japanese home, you were sure to find the beauty of shrub and tree and neatly trimmed hedge. The most keenly anticipated nationally celebrated events of the year were the wisteria blooming season in earliest spring, the cherry blossom season in April, lotustime in midsummer, and the chrysanthemum shows in the fall. Who in America would have proposed four such events for national observance? Another utilization of the beautiful in nature is found in the twenty-five-mile-long avenue of giant cryptomerias, many nearly 200 feet high, leading to the tomb of Iyeyasu at Nikko. To me not even the tomb of Napoleon in Paris seemed half as impressive and beautiful a memorial. Why should not some American or Southern town or city honor its heroes in some such fashion?

As I wrote in articles sent back to *The Progressive Farmer:* "We in America should feel highly blessed in that we have such magnificent resources and yet feel humiliated that we are doing so little with them."

In Japan one incident especially amazed and impressed me. In Tokyo I went to the headquarters of the national education department and asked the average length of school term. The officer answered, "Ten months."

"That is very good," I said, "but what is the average length of term for your *country boys and girls?*" His answer almost took me off my feet—the rural school term was indeed ten months! Furthermore he showed me that, thanks to their compulsory attendance law, the average enrollment of children of school age had increased year by year until it was then 98 per cent of all the children of school age in the whole empire of Japan!

You may well imagine that I did not tell these pagan Japanese that in our Christian, enlightened Southern states in America we were then giving our country boys and girls not ten months of school but five months! Nor did I tell them that at that time we Southerners sacrificed all compulsory attendance laws on the altar of "personal liberty," thereby saying that it was fitting and proper to let any careless, indifferent parent bind his child for life in the bondage of ignorance.

Nowhere else have I ever seen as many babies to the square inch as in Japan. I saw legions of women, who hardly seemed more than children themselves, carrying babies strapped on their backs. With almost literal accuracy Kipling had said, "In Japan a four-foot child walks with a three-foot child, who is holding the hand of a two-foot child, who carries on her back a one-foot child!" I soon came to remark that it looked almost as unnatural to see a woman between twenty and forty without a baby on her back as to see a camel without a hump!

Among the truly great men of Asia I was delighted to interview was the venerable Count Okuma, once premier of Japan, who said to me, "I look for international arbitration to come not as a matter of sentiment but as a matter of cold financial necessity. Nations have labored for centuries to build up the civilization of today; it is unthinkable that its advantages must be largely sacrificed for the support of enormous non-productive armies and navies. That would be simply *the suicide of civilization.*"

A similar attitude was expressed by Dr. Timothy Richard, one of the most distinguished Englishmen in China: "The world is going to be one before you die, sir," he said. "We are living in the days of anarchy. Unite the ten leading nations; let all their armaments be united into one to enforce the decrees of the Supreme Court of the World. And since it will then be the refusal of recalcitrant nations to accept arbitration that will make necessary the maintenance of large armaments by these united nations, let them protect themselves by levying discriminatory tariff duties against the countries that would perpetuate present conditions."

In Japan I found a different world from that which I had

known, but a world in which East and West were strangely mingled. In Korea, my next stop, nothing was familiar. At that time it was almost untouched by Western influences— dirty, squalid, unprogressive, and yet with a fascination all its own. Great bare mountains looked down on its capital city, the old city-wall climbing their steep sides. The thatched or tiled roofs of the houses were but little higher than one's head. Most American merchants would have expected to make more in a day than the average easygoing Seoul merchants had in stock, but they smoked their long-stemmed pipes in peaceful contemplation of the world and did not worry. Certainly there was little in Korean farm life that would not have looked familiar to Moses or Abraham. Only oxen were used—no horses. The plows were wooden, made by hand from nearby trees with only a primitive point of steel, and there were no two-handled plows as we have, but only one handle and that little better than a stick of firewood.

Seoul was picturesque with its weird, white-robed figures moving in the dimly lighted streets. There were no electric lights except in a few shops, only lanterns, lamps, candles, and the light of the moon.

Never have I appreciated my American citizenship more than in Korea, for there the people were cursed by an utterly corrupt government. Property was freely confiscated, lives were taken upon the whim of the government, and the energetic and industrious were mercilessly taxed. Naturally, or at least understandably, the Koreans became disinclined to labor.

No country I visited surprised me more than Manchuria. I was amazed at its size, at the fertility of its land, and by the fact that it was not very heavily populated. By 1910, however, it had come under the domination of Japan. I wrote at the time, "If the Great Powers realize the serious-

ness of the situation and adequately warn Japan, there may
be no trouble. But a continued policy of ignorance, indifference, or inactivity by other nations means that Japan will
probably go so far that she cannot retreat without a struggle." Bitterly resenting Japanese domination and unfairness,
one Chinese of rank said to me in Manchuria, "If a Chinaman is killed by a Japanese bullet, the fault is not that of
the man who fired the bullet: the Chinaman is to blame for
getting in its way!"

Going next to China, I was struck by the fact that everywhere, in that exciting year 1910-11, people were athrill
with a new life. They were beginning to instigate reforms
in their educational system, their industry, and their government. And how had this great change come about? It was
the result of "a comparative view of the world," according to an eminent religious and educational leader there.
"Twenty years ago," Dr. Timothy Richard told me, "the
Chinese did not know how their country ranked with other
countries in the elements of national greatness. They had
been told they were the greatest, wisest, and most powerful
people on earth, and they hadn't cared to know what other
countries were doing. Since then, however, they have studied books, have sent their sons to foreign colleges and universities, and have found out in what particulars China has
fallen behind other nations. So they have set out to remedy
these defects. A comparative view of the world—this is what
is bringing about the remaking of China."

The old education in China taught nothing of science,
nothing of history or geography outside of China, nothing of
mathematics in its higher branches. Its main object was to
enable the scholar to write a learned essay or a faultless
poem, helping him by these means to get an office. The old
education enabled the pupil to frame exquisite sentences;
the new gave him a working knowledge of the world. The

old looked inward to China and backward to her past; the new looked outward to other countries and forward to China's future.

No doubt the men who brought the people this "comparative view of the world" were criticized for presuming to suggest that any other way might be better than China's— just as I have often been criticized for pointing out the South's defects—but they kept to their work, and they won. Dr. Richard's reiterated emphasis on "a comparative view of the world" influenced me in all my later efforts to make our Southern states see where we stood in agriculture, education, industrial progress, and culture as compared with other states and countries.

One small incident that occurred in China impressed me at the time as a significant revelation of the arrogance of the white man's rule over the native Asian people. I saw an Englishman angrily kick a Chinese who was handling his baggage not quite as the Engishman wanted. I think it also significant that this gesture did not seem to strike the bystanders as anything unusual. I reflected that in all my thirty years of living among white people and colored people in the South I had never once seen such a gesture of contempt for a Negro. Furthermore, while the English officials were generally courteous, the only time I remember being outrageously angry on my whole trip was when one British official "clothed with a little brief authority" showed not only arrogance but also broke a promise made the day before.

Few incidents of my trip to Asia were more memorable than my visit to the Governor-General of Hong Kong, Sir Frederick Lugard, K.C.M.G., C.B., D.S.O., etc., and Lady Lugard. In Hong Kong the Governor-General was regarded almost as a monarch and no title was omitted that might add to the awe with which the natives should regard him. When I presented my letter of introduction from British Ambassador James Bryce, an appointment was ceremoniously set up for me. In the official bulletin, which had something of the aspects of a "court circular" it was announced: "Tomorrow Mr. Clarence Poe, an American journalist touring Asia, will be a guest of the Governor-General at dinner."

Two things about this visit I shall always remember. One was the fact that this almost royal palace, high on "The Peak" overlooking Hong Kong, had been built of stones carried high up the mountain slope on the backs of poor Chinese women! The other was an intriguing remark made to me by Lady Lugard. She expressed one of the great "might-have-beens" of history when she said, "I have often wondered if it might not have been better for mankind if our English colonists had not broken their ties with the Mother Country. If they had not, the seat of the British government might well have been transferred from our tiny little island to the center of your vast new North American continent—'all British' from Mexico to the Pole." With Lady Lugard's sentence in mind any reader might well take a look at a map of the world—and ask himself, "With broader vision on the part of a British King in 1775 might not Lady Lugard's dream possibly have become a reality?"

In Rangoon, Burma, I was even more captivated by the elephants than by the people. The elephants were not so numerous as the camels in Peking, but those I saw displayed an intelligence and human-like quality that made them fascinating. One morning I went to a lumber yard to watch the trained elephants handle the heavy saw-logs that were being moved from place to place. It was very clear that the elephant, like most other beings in the Tropics, didn't entirely approve of work. What he did that morning he did with much deliberation, and he stopped frequently to rest between tugs. Also when an enormous log, thirty or forty feet long and two or three feet thick, was given him to pull through the mire, he would roar mightily at each hard place, getting down on his knees sometimes to use his strength to better advantage, and one could hardly escape the conclusion that he "cussed" in violent elephantese!

For stacking lumber the elephant is especially useful, I learned. Any ordinary sized log, tree, or piece of lumber he would pick up as if it were a piece of stovewood, and in piling heavy planks he was remarkably careful about matching. Eyeing the pile at a distance, he would look to see if it was uneven or any piece out of place, in which case he was quick to make it right. A young lady in our party was much amused when the trainer called out, "Salaam to memsahib" ("Salute the lady"), and his lordship bowed and made his salutation as gracefully as his enormous head and forelegs would permit!

Returning from the Orient, I stopped to see Columbus' birthplace in Genoa, got a sprig of ivy from Virgil's tomb, and saw again the art treasures of Paris. But most important of all, in London I visited the House of Commons where I was fortunate enough to hear Winston Churchill, Lloyd George, Asquith, Austen Chamberlain, and other great Britishers in lively debate. Such is my reverence for Winston Churchill now that I should rather have missed seeing the Matterhorn or Fujiyama than to have missed seeing him. Then in his thirties, he was probably the most eloquent speaker I have ever heard. At that time he was a member of the Liberal party and I bought a copy of his new book *Liberalism and the Social Problem.* One paragraph I remember ran like this: "We are going ahead and do what we can to improve the condition of the people—and we shall not be stopped if some old granny does come along and call it socialistic!"

When I came to publish in book form a collection of the

more important articles about Asia I had written for *The Progressive Farmer* and several national magazines, I could think of no more significant title than this—*Where Half the World Is Waking Up*. For this is precisely what I had found all the way from Yokohama to Peking, Hankow, Hong Kong, Manila, Singapore, Bombay, Delhi, and points between. The Japanese feared America and were steadily moving in on China. The Koreans hated their Japanese conquerors, as did the Chinese in Manchuria. After seeing the Chinese Parliament seething with revolt, I wrote in a magazine article, "Within nine months China will have a republic or a revolution." A nationally famous expert answered, "China has never done anything in nine months and never will." But she did. In the Philippines numerous leaders were battling for complete independence from America which was ultimately to become a reality. In India the nonviolent philosophy of Gandhi was slowly and almost silently undercutting the power of Great Britain, whose navy and armies were supposed to make it the one truly invincible nation on earth. The world's greatest continent, whose people had been for uncounted centuries subservient to royal masters, either native or foreign, was beginning to express that continent-wide demand for revolution that still poses one of the major problems of our world today.

I have now made three trips abroad. On my first European trip I enjoyed the company of two charming Southern girls. My trip around the world I made alone. For about four months I found enough excitement and pleasure in meeting new people, seeing new places, and learning new facts. But after that although I kept busy I was somewhat homesick. To prevent this on my third trip, I decided it would be an excellent idea to marry the woman of my choice and take her along with me. About her I tell more in other chapters;

here it is enough to say that she unanimously approved the suggestion and found ways to be helpful from the beginning. We planned of course to see London, Paris, and other such famous places, but for the most part we both agreed it would be well to visit two countries in which excitingly successful agricultural leaders and movements were attracting world-wide attention, Ireland and Denmark. Furthermore, she suggested that since she had taken a secretarial course and had served as secretary to Dr. R. D. W. Connor of the State Historical Commission, she would not only make my trips with me but take down in shorthand the reports I planned to send back to *The Progressive Farmer*. This part of the program was also unanimously approved by me—and with very happy results.

In London we saw most of the historic sights I had previously seen, visited Parliament, and had lunch with a member of the House of Commons, but we gave most of our attention to the art galleries and Kew Gardens, whose beauty has been perpetuated in the lovely song "Come Down to Kew in Lilac Time."

We next moved on to Ireland where the Irish Agricultural Organization Society, an internationally famous Irish movement for rural progress and cooperation, was making sensational progress under Sir Horace Plunkett and George W. Russell. Russell was later a guest in my home, having then become internationally famous as "A.E."—poet, editor, philosopher, and artist. With both men I had become familiar through *The Irish Homestead*, the official organ of I.A.O.S. and perhaps the most scholarly publication ever printed for farm people. They greeted me with typical Irish heartiness and we had long, satisfying talks about the Irish cooperative movement and its motto—"Better Farming, Better Business, Better Living." As Sir Horace said, "The problem of remaking rural life is threefold, technical, commercial, and social;

but the clearest and surest avenue of achievement is through
the commercial feature. First, make the farmer a better
businessman and all these other things will be added unto
him." Sir Horace also stressed the fact that Irish farmers
were suffering not only because the middlemen's tolls and
the "gombeen men's" charges for credit were excessive but
because lack of organization prevented farmers from giving
consumers uniform, high-quality products, thus expressing
a view I have often urged on Southern farmers. As he said,
"We must furnish one good kind of butter—not many sam-
ples of bad and good kinds; a uniformly fresh egg—not a
dozen stale ones of different shapes and sizes, with occasional fresh ones rubbing shells with their dingy neighbors; and farmers must furnish customers regular supplies
promptly at regular intervals—not three long weeks of famine
and then a week of surfeit." All these things I reported to
Southern farmers as handicaps they must also avoid. Persistence was one of Sir Horace's outstanding qualities and it was
persistence that led to his being knighted. He told me that
after holding fifty meetings he got the first local Irish cooperative started in 1889, and 1890 ended without another one
being added to this lonesome first-born! But in 1891 the
number jumped to 17, and when I was there in 1912 there
were more than 800 such societies. One of their important features was lending money to individual members,
but strictly "for production purposes," meaning that a loan
should be so used as to help produce benefits to liquidate it.
However, Sir Horace laughingly told me of Patrick O'Hagan
who applied for (but was denied) money to enable him to
marry Molly Murphy and protested, "If that's not for a
production purpose, I don't know what is!"

After leaving Ireland we returned to England and studied
its national program for breaking up the great estates and
selling them to small farmers in lots of fifty acres or less—

one-fifth of the purchase price to be paid in cash and the
rest in semi-annual installments running not over fifty years.
I also learned that most applicants for land preferred to rent
from government authorities rather than to buy. The farmer
who rented from the state was almost as much his own
master as if he were landlord; he knew that if he treated
the land well he could rent it as long as he liked and that
when leaving, if he should do so at all, he would get credit
for any permanent improvements he had made. This principle of compensation for improvements made by tenants is
yet too little regarded in our Southern states.

We went next to France, of which I wrote, "There is
hardly a prettier farming country in the world." France and
particularly Paris have always had a strong appeal for me,
not only because of the beauty of the country and the
Frenchman's love of life, but also because my mother's ancestors were French. Alice and I were thrilled by the charm
of Paris, its artistic and architectural treasures, especially
those at the Louvre, and the gaiety of the sidewalk cafes.

Of all countries we visited in Europe, however, the one
that we found of most delight was Denmark. In Copenhagen
we looked up the United States Minister, Mr. Egan, to whom
I had a letter of introduction. When we got down to serious
discussion about conditions in Denmark as compared with
those of our Southland, he told me, "There is nobody in
Denmark over seven years old, unless he is an idiot, who
cannot read and write." I also learned from him that nine
acres out of every ten were cultivated by the men who
owned them.

Alice and I were especially interested in learning about
Denmark's system of "folk high schools." Later when I was
asked to speak at one, the Danish farmer who introduced
me used a phrase I have never forgotten. "Denmark," he
said, "is *a little land full of happy people*"—and ever since

then I have often asked, "Is not this the highest or noblest claim that can be made for any country?" The Danish "folk high schools" were attended by thousands and thousands of young men and women from eighteen to twenty-five years of age. Differing greatly from our American high schools, which primarily aimed at preparing a boy or girl for college, the Danish "folk high schools" aimed at preparing for life, industry, or citizenship. To provide a broader culture for the great masses of the people; to get them to read, think, and love their country and their fellows; and to promote a spirit of good fellowship and to bind the neighborhood together in industrial, intellectual, and cultural activities—all this I found was their supremely noble purpose.

At one typical high school I visited at København I found that it offered eleven-day courses in such subjects as dairying, livestock feeding, poultry raising, and special crops. Eighteen of these courses were given each year. Since I had never seen such a sight in America it was both surprising and inspiring to see the older men and women who had come for these courses, gray-haired men smoking their crooked pipes walking across the campus alongside their gray-haired wives who had come to find out how science could also help them in their work! "We have had one pupil enrolled who was seventy-six, and at another time we had two pupils past seventy!" I was told.

But for all the good order, the high standards of civilized living, and the outer happiness of the Europe we saw, there were forewarnings of darker days to come. Looking back on it now, I think one of the most significant incidents of the whole trip had to do with an interesting German friend, Dr. Arthur Mez. A graduate of Heidelberg, he had the traditional sabre cut across his left cheek. Having written him early in 1912 of my impending wedding trip, I received a most cordial invitation to visit him and his family in Freiburg. He did indeed receive us with great cordiality—but then had to confess that he had just been called to another city for military drill the following day. It was an ominous forecast of World War I in which I feel sure Mez lost his life. The last letter I had from him was just after the Verdun battle and not a word since that time. I also recall the atmosphere of military preparedness when I registered as a guest at the Freiburg Hotel. In no other country had I been subjected to such inquiry about my past record and plans for my stay in the city. In the four years since my previous 1908 visit to Germany it indeed seemed to have become a police state. Two years later the lights were out all over Europe.

Concluding here some highlights of all my three visits to the Old World, I would reiterate my feeling that through them the education of Clarence Poe was tremendously broadened and enriched. I had indeed "studied abroad" and had brought back to a legion of readers not only many thought-provoking new facts but many action-promoting facts and ideas, useful to me and my readers in all the fifty years since I last saw London and the Great Wall of China. Perhaps most important of all, the trips had brought a broadening of my heart's sympathies. Certainly no one could witness "the huddled masses of the world's poor" in places like India and China without feeling that he must if possible show in some definite way that he has heard their cry, or without remembering the wisdom of the Jewish *Talmud,* "The truest charity is that which helps a man help himself so he will no longer need charity."

CHAPTER TWELVE

A Lifelong Crusade for Better Health

FROM 1944 TO 1952 I GAVE A LARGE PART OF MY TIME AND thought to state and national programs aimed at remedying health perils in the South—perils that then weakened bodies, shortened lives, and reduced work and cut productivity. And to make the general situation clearer two or three personal short stories and some pertinent official data might be helpful.

First here are three short sentences in which my Aunt Alice Poe Brown reported the distressing health perils in my old home community about the time I was born:

"Joe Elkins had four children; all died of diphtheria. Hath Gilmore lost four boys in two weeks from diphtheria. A man named Malone lost seven grown children the same fall from typhoid fever."

How very narrowly I myself escaped being among the fatalities caused by another children's disease, whooping cough, I have already reported in another chapter. The greatest difference between old-time cemeteries and present-day cemeteries is that the old-time cemeteries have a pathetically larger proportion of "short graves"—graves of little children whose lives were snuffed out by diseases of infancy now largely under control.

Just a few days ago as I write this a long time friend, J. E. Atkins, told me this incident illustrating how serious were the ravages of hookworm around 1900. Said he: "Just before the anti-hookworm campaign I had a brother eighteen years old just skin and bones. He weighed only eighty-two pounds, could do little or no work, and his skin was as yellow as tallow. After a few weeks of hookworm treatment he was as ruddy and healthy as the rest of us."

Because of background knowledge and personal observation I was ready to help improve health conditions as soon as I became editor of *The Progressive Farmer* in 1899. But the fight I had against greatest odds and severest condemnation was in connection with the Rockefeller campaign against hookworm in the South. It was one of the most important events of my life. Apparently it all began in 1902 when a New York reporter wrote a story about the hookworm headlined "Germ of Laziness Found." As Stewart Robertson has written:

"Overnight the hookworm became our most talked-about joke. Cartoonists drew pictures of it. Rhymesters wrote jingles. All the nation laughed—except the South. The physical and mental anemia that was sapping thousands in the South was no joke. Many thought its symptoms were caused by a form of malaria. Children especially were stunted by it, became backward in school, the easy victims of TB and other maladies. The blight extended over eleven states, from Virginia to Texas."

Then something happened. One day Walter Hines Page was riding with Dr. Charles W. Stiles who pointed out a listless, yellowishly pale, scrawny wreck of a man lounging on a railroad platform:

"He's a hookworm victim," said Stiles, as he had told countless others. "Fifty cents' worth of drugs would make a useful man in a few weeks. A few million dollars in the right hands could rid the whole South of a terrible curse."

Page interviewed and aroused the interest of John D. Rockefeller and Dr. Simon Flexner, head of the Rockefeller Institute of Medical Research. Then when the American Country Life Commission came through the South in 1908 Dr. Stiles came with them, indicting the hookworm as being a major cause of Southern backwardness.

Early reports covering the examination of 4,380 persons in North Carolina showed 43 per cent infected—forty-three persons out of every hundred in the survey! Nevertheless a Charlotte daily denounced Stiles and the Commission members as "a body of fanatics" and the Raleigh *News and Observer* at first shared this view, agreeing with Bishop Candler of Georgia who had said, "The Southern people will not be taken in by Mr. Rockefeller's vermifuge fund and hookworm commission." But as Mr. Daniels adds, "Towards the end of the campaign the *News and Observer* shifted to the side of the Commission."

No one now can ever say to what extent the inertia or so-called laziness of Southern people was due to hookworm disease. It was certainly prevalent enough to have caused a story attributed to Woodrow Wilson, speaking of certain Southern regions: "If you see two distant objects in a field but can't tell which is a man and which is a stump, just wait a minute. The one that moves is a stump!"

Hookworm was caused by a tiny parasitic germ that flourished on the ground surface wherever no sanitary sewage control existed. The germ first entered the skin of bare-footed people causing a slight trouble called "ground itch." From that point it entered the blood stream, then the lungs, then the intestines where it became a blood-sucking vampire destroying the strength and consequently the will to work of the unhappy victim. Treatment for the disease consisted mainly of sanitary sewage disposal, wearing shoes in summer, and a few simple and inexpensive drugs.

Authorities tell us that a female hookworm could lay 6,000 to 15,000 eggs a day which the Southern heavy rainfall scattered over wide areas. Dr. Stiles gave me a ready answer for those who insisted he and I were slandering the South but saying nothing about the North. His answer was, "Your warm Southern climate is favorable to all forms of life, good and bad. Hookworm is about the worst of the bad forms." I personally knew Dr. Stiles and vigorously defended him and the members of the Rockefeller Commission, both in *The Progressive Farmer* and in speeches to our farm people. One result was an unusually vitriolic controversy between Mayor Rhett of Charleston, South Carolina, and me. He insisted that Stiles and I were slanderers of the South, stirring up the people by unfounded charges. Mayor Rhett denounced us in letters to major Southern dailies, in North Carolina and South Carolina and I replied with equal vigor and conviction. Neither one of us convinced the other but the controversy did much to arouse interest in the subject involved.

Following is a quotation from a letter I published in the *Atlanta Constitution*, November 14, 1908, answering a statement by a prominent former governor of North Carolina criticizing Dr. Stiles and the Country Life Association. Editor Clark Howell printed the article conspicuously on the editorial page with his own hearty approval. I wrote:

"It is high time, anyhow, for the South to get over this morbid and babyish sensitiveness about the publication of every statistical fact that doesn't please our passing fancy.

"The true Southerner, the man we ought to honor and follow, is the man who looks an unpleasant fact squarely in the face and sets about getting a remedy. In heaven's name, let's have done with our quack, popularity-hunting doctors and leaders who tell us there is nothing the matter with us, that we are the greatest and happiest people on earth and that all we need to do is to keep on forever in our old ruts of illiteracy, undeveloped resources and out-of-date farming methods. Let us rather follow the doctor and the leader who loves the South with all his heart, but who loves her too well not to use the knife of criticism and reform upon the cancers upon her economic life and general well being."

In 1912 when I joined others in organizing the North Carolina Conference for Social Service, the improvement of health conditions in North Carolina was one of our chief objectives, and Dr. W. S. Rankin one of the foremost crusaders in this cause.

Only a few years later occurred the most dramatic and terrifying pestilence of my lifetime. It was the influenza epidemic in the fall of 1918. At that time a large number of World War I soldiers at Camp Polk near Raleigh fell victims to the disease. In Raleigh two popular young women, Lucy Page and Eliza Riddick, nursing the sick, caught influenza and died and many other young women served as nurses but escaped serious results. In North Carolina the brilliant young president of the University, Edward Kidder Graham, died of it and Dr. Marvin H. Stacy, quickly named as his successor, soon died of the same disease. In Raleigh, a relatively small town compared with its present population, there were sixteen deaths in one day. In many cases entire families were prostrated. In larger cities undertakers and burial forces could not keep up with their work and hundreds of coffins remained for days before the burial forces could inter them. For my own part I stayed away from public meetings and took the least frequented streets going to and from my office. In this way I escaped the disease until March, 1919, when the germ had lost its virulence and I recovered rather quickly.

In all my campaigns for better medical care for all our people I spoke in various parts of the South in addition to carrying on a continuous campaign in *The Progressive Farmer*. It was undoubtedly a result of my earlier interest in the cause of good health that led Governor Broughton in February, 1944 to call me into his office and tell me that he wanted me to accept a hard task, one which few men would undertake. This was the chairmanship (1944-45) and leadership of a commission to promote a program of which he said: "The ultimate aim of this program should be that no person in North Carolina shall lack adequate hospital care or medical treatment by reason of poverty or low income."

I immediately told Governor Broughton the proposal was so challenging that I could not reject it, especially since he promised me a free hand in making up the membership of what came to be called "The North Carolina Hospital and Medical Care Commission." Aggressive publicity followed and we soon had the aroused support of leaders in all parts of North Carolina. Sixty leading men and women accepted service on the commission, among them the following with whom I worked especially closely: Thomas J. Pearsall, Dr. James S. McKimmon, Harry B. Caldwell, Dr. Paul Whitaker, D. Hiden Ramsey, C. Horace Hamilton, Josephus Daniels, Dr. W. C. Davison, Mrs. R. J. Reynolds, John W. Umstead, Bishop Charles Purcell, Samuel J. Ervin, James A. Gray, Charles A. Cannon, Mrs. Julius Cone. All sixty members were assigned to subcommittees on the following subjects: hospital and medical care for our rural population; hospital and medical care for our industrial and urban population; special needs of our Negro population; four-year medical school at the University; mental hygiene and hospitalization; statistical studies; and hospital and medical care plans in other states.

"A program of great hope, of almost infinite promise, and of great practicability" was the opening phrase with which we presented the report of our commission, effectively documented and illustrated, to Governor Cherry and the General Assembly of 1945. I declared that this program should combine Emerson's declaration, "Hitch your wagon to a star," meaning that practical men should have ideals, and also Dr. Arthur Morgan's "Hitch your star to a wagon," meaning that ideals should be tied to earth and to everyday practicability. This program became the basis for a state-wide good health movement and led to the organization of a permanent state-supported Medical Care Commission by the General Assembly of 1945.

My interest in public health was further recognized when the American Hospital Association named me a member of the American Commission on Hospital Care in 1944. Head of the Commission was Dr. Thomas S. Gates, President of the University of Pennsylvania. In addition to the members appointed to represent American medicine, others named to represent the public included: Charles F. Kettering, Herbert Hoover, Sarah G. Blanding, Clinton S. Golden, William F. Ogburn, Edward L. Ryerson, and me. Conversations with Charles F. Kettering I found especially stimulating as this famous scientist talked of problems he was eager to help solve. I especially remember his anxious desire to find an answer to the question, "Why is nearly all foliage green in color?"

Perhaps the high point of my service on this commission came on March 12, 1945, when I appeared before the Senate Commission on Education and Labor and found my chief opponent to be Senator Robert A. Taft. I was ably supported by Senator Lister Hill of Alabama and Senator Claude Pepper of Florida. Senator Taft was a man with whom I disagreed on many things, but he always had the respect of those who differed with him. He was always courteous and I think really wanted to learn the truth. I was anxious both to convince him and to vindicate my friends from Alabama and Florida.

In the course of my speech I rehearsed nearly all the arguments I had used in my campaign to improve health conditions, both in the South and the nation as a whole. In beginning I said that every editor should be a one-man S.S.O.R.—"Society for the Suppression of Obvious Remarks," and I should try to omit unnecessary wordage in speaking as well as writing.

"From three standpoints," I continued "I am interested in Senate Bill 191." This was the bill to provide one hundred million dollars to help states and counties, especially rural areas, build more and better hospitals. Later Congressman Burton joined in its support and the final outcome may be seen today in the scores of hospitals aided by Hill-Burton funds. One of these now dominates a high hill directly in front of my home.

"Primarily," I said, "I have thought of this bill with three burial grounds in mind. One is about a hundred yards from where I was reared. Buried there is one of my uncles, a typhoid fever victim at age thirty-two. Another uncle died in the prime of life from a disease that need not have been fatal if a hospital had been reasonably near. My last aunt who was buried there died of childbirth complications; the doctor told me if he had reached her in time she need not have died. I think half the graves there are graves of children who died under fifteen years of age, and by the nearest squeak in the world I missed being among them, catching whooping cough when nine days old. I remember two other burial grounds where lie my most gifted male cousin who died of typhoid at age twenty-eight and my best-loved girl cousin who died at the age of fourteen leaving a mother broken-hearted for the rest of her life.

"Among which classes of our people is the need for better medical care most appalling? Among farmers. And among sections of America where is the need most appalling? It is in the South. American farm families with only 12 per cent of the nation's income must support 23 per cent of the nation's population, and must support, train, and educate 20 per cent of the nation's children."

At that point Senator Taft interrupted my appeal for federal aid to say, "Why should it be the federal government instead of the state? What are the reasons for that? After all, you people down south are strong for states' rights and responsibilities of the states."

I answered the Senator by pointing out that every American boy must be expected primarily to serve, not his state, but the nation, in case of an imperiled America, adding, "My boy, my youngest son, as the sons of many of the rest of you, is serving America now in the army. He is not serving North Carolina alone but he is serving all America, and we have got to think about our obligations to all America. And this may surprise you. When my boy was sent to camp with fifty-three other boys, thirty-five of them were turned down at Fort Bragg—only eighteen accepted."

I'm not sure whether Senator Taft had read the bill carefully but he answered, "Your whole argument seems to lead to the abolition of states' rights." Both Senator Hill and I pointed out that we were not asking the federal government to do the whole job but only part of the job, and that part only because of the great inequality of income between the rural states and the richer manufacturing states, saying, "In 1940 the per capita income of Ohio was $644, and in North Carolina $317, less than half."

A telling reply to the Ohio Senator was made by Senator

Pepper: "Under our federal constitution every citizen has a dual sovereignty, because he is a citizen of the state in which he resides and of the federal government. The federal government has citizens and the states have citizens and they are both interested in the welfare of those citizens. Whether you divide the money fifty-fifty or whether you should have a graduated scale is a matter about which you must exercise discretion, but certainly the theory is that it is the joint obligation to the citizens that the two sovereignties have."

In the next few minutes I had to leave my speech for a dialogue between Taft and Pepper.

TAFT: "I do not think it is part of the constitution to give the federal government power to regulate health."

PEPPER: "I haven't seen anything in the federal constitution about health being reserved to the states."

TAFT: "Everything is reserved to the states that is not given to the federal government, except the power to spend money."

PEPPER: "Under the national-defense provisions of the federal constitution, the federal government would have the power and right to provide for the health of the people so we would have soldiers and sailors."

TAFT: "I deny that, except under the general-welfare clause under which they could spend money for the thing. That theory, if extended, simply wipes the states out. There are no states left."

PEPPER: "That does not hold true at all."

TAFT: "Yes. If the two want to operate together the federal government will run everything."

To this last assertion I inserted something from my own experience in the federal government: "I think we have a very good illustration, Senator, of the relationship that I visualize here. I happen to be a member of the Federal Board for Vocational Education and there, of course, the federal government makes large appropriations, but the state also makes large appropriations, and the community also gives support. But the control of those operations is primarily in the state."

To this Senator Taft was generous and candid enough to answer, "Yes, I think as an example of the proper relationship it is a good example. I think the federal government contributes some aid but has not attempted to boss the job."

Next I pointed out that with the coming of the automobile age a great part of the income received by farmers had been diverted to states manufacturing automobiles, trucks, and tractors: "When I was a boy farmers used buggies and wagons. Buggies were made in Carthage and wagons in Wilson, about fifty miles in the other direction. Now it would be amazing to see what proportion of the whole income of the country is spent for automobiles and automobile tires, the money going mainly to Ohio and Michigan, and I think it is a good thing for Ohio and Michigan to help bring some of that money back to the poorer states, to help give our people equal opportunity in education and health."

"More Doctors, More Hospitals, More Insurance" had become the slogan of our North Carolina campaign. To further illustrate the need for doctors in rural areas I picked up six typical letters from *Progressive Farmer* subscribers with R.F.D. addresses in five rural states. One was from a doctor saying, "A beautiful little girl, three years of age, arms hanging limply, lips blue, eyes wide open. What will her father say when he returns from the South Pacific? How can I tell him that I, his doctor and his friend, was so busy that his child was dead the first time I saw her?"

From Leoma, Tennessee: "We live fourteen miles from town and there is only one doctor who will make country calls. A neighbor died two months ago because of lack of money and a way to get doctor and hospital help."

From McGehee, Arkansas: "My husband and I both had pneumonia last winter and no doctor would undertake the drive."

From Enid, Mississippi: "Our nearest doctor is fifteen miles away and will hardly come when we call him."

From Littleton, North Carolina: "Our farming people work the hardest of any class and have the least medical care. Lots of them die for lack of it."

From Monticello, Arkansas: "It is next to impossible to obtain a doctor where we live. We usually do not try."

Of all that I said on this occasion the one thing that made the greatest impression was a letter from Dr. I. G. Greer of the North Carolina Baptist Orphanage showing that whereas 58 per cent of the boys of North Carolina's general population were rejected for physical defects, in Dr. Greer's language, "We sent out from our orphanage 318 boys and had only three rejections by the army." I pointed out that the boys and girls in the orphanages were by no means luxuriously supported but did have good medical inspection, hospital and medical care, and sound nutrition.

From that point on Senator Taft, I must say to his credit and his honor, appeared to have been satisfied and made no further objection. I then concluded with an observation as pertinent now as it was in 1945: "And now one last word to everybody who is concerned about preserving free enterprise and 'the American way' here in America. If democracy is to prevail over communism here, then democracy must make the stronger appeal to the great masses of our plain people—industrial workers, farm tenants and laborers, small farmers. And one of the surest of all ways to do this is by providing equality of educational opportunity and equality of hospital and medical care."

I next served as vice-chairman of the state-supported Medical Care Commission while its program for establishing rural hospitals was being mapped and money allocated for the neediest sections of the state. Here my most important contribution was to insist on a scale of priorities whereby matching funds for hospital costs were provided on the basis of per capita wealth in the counties affected, the wealthiest counties paying a quite high percentage of the total hospital cost, and the poorer counties paying relatively less.

It was, I think, directly as a result of my work on the North Carolina Hospital and Medical Care Commission and the American Commission on Hospital Care that President Truman in 1951 appointed me to the Committee on Health Needs of the Nation where I served through 1952. Other members were: Dr. Paul B. Magnuson, Chester I. Barnard, Dr. Lester W. Burkett, Dr. Dean A. Clark, Dr. Donald M. Clark, Dr. Evarts A. Graham, Albert J. Hayes, Dr. Joseph C. Hinsey, Dr. Charles S. Johnson, Dr. Russell V. Lee, Elizabeth S. Magee, Dr. Lowell J. Reed, Walter P. Reuther, and Marion W. Sheahan. This commission accumulated much valuable information and made many important recommendations, including the establishment of a department of health to be headed by a member of the cabinet.

It is impossible in this volume to go into details regarding the Commission's activities and recommendations. I did most heartily agree with the Commission's major endorsements. One stressed insurance or "the prepayment principle" as the only method with which most individuals can meet hospital bills. The other stressed federal matching grants to states (upon the basis of relative wealth and needs) as the only effective way of insuring medical care for all people. Also I added a personal appeal of my own which I still feel of the utmost importance:

"To the men, women, and children in rural America I should be untrue if I did not add a sense of urgency and desperate need for prompt action. Among our rural people we have neither the wealth nor the insurance needed. Every day men, women, and children are dying needlessly for lack of proper medical and health facilities.

"And federal aid to states is justified. The patronage of the farmers in our rural states has helped the wealthier manufacturing states become rich and these richer states will be helped and not hurt by improving the health and education of their patrons in rural states. I hope that our report will lead more and more people to accept the principle I have so long proclaimed as follows:

"*Our democracy will never be complete until every person, rich or poor, high or low, urban or rural, white or black, has an equal right to adequate hospital and medical care whenever and wherever he makes the same grim battle against ever-menacing Death which sooner or later we must all make.*"

CHAPTER THIRTEEN

Poe for Governor

ONE SUMMER DAY IN 1914 NEAR GREENSBORO I UNOBTRUSIVELY
entered the back seat of a Southern Railway Pullman car,
feeling myself "at peace with the world, the flesh, and the
divil," as Mr. Dooley would say. Then I heard voices ahead
of me that I recognized as belonging to two prominent men
in state politics. Suddenly I heard one man say, *"The most
dangerous man in North Carolina—"* These seven words
were enough to pique my curiosity, but I was totally astonished to hear him add his concluding three words—*"is
Clarence Poe!"*

What he went on to elaborate was that we had a pre-
dominantly farming state and that nobody had a greater following of farmers than the ogre just mentioned. Hence what
more natural than that this ogre might run for governor,
build up a machine, and upset the whole political applecart
and the carefully devised plans of the chief priests and San-
hedrin of the party?

At that time the man with the political power to kill or
generate North Carolina politics was Senator Furnifold M.
Simmons. Simmons was not a corrupt political boss, but he
did love to build up power and the machinery necessary for
exercising power. His right-hand man in dispensing power

was A. D. Watts—"Aus Watts," as he was known all over the
state. Watts had once told me that I was regarded by his
organization as an up-and-coming gubernatorial possibility.
But I think he may have wished to encourage the inference
that although I need not fall down and worship the Machine,
I should at least keep on good terms with it—and this I had
made no effort to do. Actually I often differed with Senator
Simmons for the same basic reasons that had influenced
Governor Aycock, but after Aycock's death I supported Simmons for re-election to the Senate.

My friend J. W. Bailey once encouraged me to consider
the governorship by an indirect route. Having been himself
a candidate for this position, he knew just how much was
involved both in physical strength and in the expenditure
of money. "What I would advise," he said, "is that you first
run for lieutenant governor and use it as a tremendously
helpful steppingstone to the higher office. Usually the men
of highest prestige in the state do not get into the race for
lieutenant governor and no great expenditures of money
are necessary." But I never followed up his idea—which
later put Luther Hodges into the Governor's Mansion.

In 1912 my enthusiasm for the nomination of Woodrow
Wilson resulted in my receiving widespread credit for Wilson's support among the farmers of the South. After his election in November, numerous papers reported that I would
probably be appointed Secretary of Agriculture. After the
reprinting in North Carolina of a *Washington Times* story to
this effect, I wrote Josephus Daniels, who had of course
thrown all his influence behind Wilson, that I was in no
sense a candidate for Secretary of Agriculture but would do
everything in my power to help forward the movement
to put him in the Cabinet.

Repeating this statement in a letter to the *Charlotte Observer* in December, I said: "I should be both untruthful

and ungrateful if I did not say that I appreciate what my brethren of the press and others have been generous enough to say of me in this connection; but Mr. Wilson has no office that could tempt me away from the joy of having some share in the great constructive work of building up North Carolina and the South." My friends, however, still wished to see me in the top state office.

From this time on there were periodic suggestions that I should become a candidate for governor. In 1914 I discouraged a gubernatorial movement that had largely grown out of the fact that—along with J. W. Bailey, President H. Q. Alexander of the State Farmers' Union, and with the encouragement of Josephus Daniels and fifty other outstanding leaders—I had called a state-wide meeting of Democrats to consider proposals for more progressive policies than the party had previously been following. The response was surprisingly gratifying. We asked Governor Craig to preside and resolutions were adopted at this meeting favoring the following policies: a legalized state-wide primary for all state offices; a six months' public school term instead of the then required four months; a better rural credits system for farmers; increased support for public health; a modern penal system; fairer freight and insurance rates; advanced legislation for conservation; prohibition of employment of children in factories or women at night; more advanced temperance legislation; the establishment of a state highway commission.

Most of these planks were subsequently approved by the State Democratic Convention. My activity in inaugurating and promoting this movement led to much speculation that my friends would use it to promote my candidacy for governor.

It was very tempting to give in to the "Poe for Governor" movement, and I distinctly remember that I not only outlined a blueprint for state-wide progress but had rather fully developed the mechanics of the program by which I hoped to put this blueprint into effect. A short time before I had joined Dr. J. Y. Joyner, Edward K. Graham, the Governor, and other leaders in agriculture and education to promote the observance of a state-wide "Community Service Week." In this effort all such agencies joined to arouse the people in each county to do some constructive work toward better schools, better roads, public health, and the beautification of homes, churches, and highways. If elected governor I planned to go to about two counties a week until all one hundred counties had been reached to enlist all such agencies in a united program for progress in each particular county. I had also given considerable thought to having as my running mate a lieutenant governor from the western part of the state who would be fully in sympathy with such a movement and for this purpose considered Santford Martin, editor of the *Winston-Salem Journal.*

But in the end I decided against throwing my hat in the ring, and in letters to Howard A. Banks and others supporting me, I firmly declined. To this Mr. Banks replied: "We need a man in our highest state office today who will leave the beaten path; who will not drift in the old sluggish, miasmic legislative channels; who will take time to inform himself of how other states and other peoples are accomplishing reforms demanded by modern conditions; who does not care whether he ever steps up higher or not, and who therefore can serve the people without reference to his own future."

To my friends I stated, "If possible I should like to give a demonstration of how much a private citizen may do to advance the progress of the people without asking for or accepting public office."

I had been especially active in promoting the substitution of a legalized primary for the old system of choosing governors in conventions largely prearranged and predestined by "bosses" in the party organization. Not only had President Wilson sent a message through me to the people of the state supporting the legalized primary, but I followed it up by getting his support for a genuinely effective primary system. I had written him on March 25, 1914:

"I believe we have the enemy licked already by this preliminary skirmish, but our danger now is that men who are at heart opponents of the primary idea will profess to favor it so that they may work to get a half-hearted and ineffective measure.

"May I ask this favor therefore, that you will advise me (or advise Mr. Daniels) what state primary law you regard as best for us to model the North Carolina law after?"

Wilson recommended the system he had developed in New Jersey. After Governor Bickett had been chosen governor by the new primary system he told me, "I should not have risked running if you and others had not forced the adoption of the primary system."

Having made as many friends as I had made in supporting various progressive movements, every four years found many of them urging me to enter the gubernatorial race. And I must admit that it was a pleasant thing to meet so many friends in unexpected places who would say, "I want to see you governor of North Carolina."

Naturally my supporters came mostly from the farm people of a state then much more rural than now. It was in 1939 that I last seriously considered getting into the race. Among the most highly placed people who urged me to do so, I think especially of Cameron Morrison who had been governor, Clyde Hoey who was then governor, and W. Kerr Scott who was later to become governor. Most urgent of these was former Governor Morrison who kept up a continual effort by long distance phone and otherwise to get me to enter the race and to reiterate his confidence that I would win. Governor Hoey sent for me to say that while he could not use his office to try to name his successor, he had heard of so much support for me from various sources and areas that he felt I owed a duty to myself and the state to give the matter serious consideration.

Regarding the effort to project me into the gubernatorial race, Raleigh state news correspondent Henry Averill wrote:

"Your correspondent asked a rather acute political observer, interested in a different candidate, 'What elements of strength would Dr. Poe have if he did get into the race?' and received the rather surprising reply, 'Too many, I'm afraid.' Viewed objectively a Poe campaign presents more than a few interesting angles indicating that the suggestion of his candidacy is much more than a pipe dream.

"To begin with there probably isn't a man in the state of North Carolina better known to the farmers—and after all they form a tremendous proportion of the Tar Heel population—and it is very doubtful if there is any more favorably known to them. As editor of a powerful farm journal he has 'talked to' the people for many, many years and they have got to know him well.

"Then there is the probability that he would not be inacceptable to the business and industrial interests of the state. He is by no means a wild-eyed radical or capital-baiting 'farmer-labor' advocate."

Not a few friends outside North Carolina also expressed interest in the 1939 upsurgence in my behalf. For example, John Temple Graves of Alabama, whose syndicated columns appeared in morning dailies all over the South, said:

"In North Carolina they are talking Dr. Clarence Poe for governor. 'When the report first became general several months ago,' writes a political observer for *The Raleigh Times,* 'Dr. Poe waved aside the suggestion. Now he is doing no waving. He is not a candidate ... but he has reached the point ... of being prepared to discuss the issues of the campaign.' It may be improper for outsiders to pass judgment upon a North Carolina gubernatorial campaign but it is not improper for Southerners anywhere to salute the famous editor of *The Progressive Farmer* whenever his name appears in print. The South has had no more loyal and useful servant. If Clarence Poe should indeed become governor of North Carolina the gubernatorial tradition that would be nearest and dearest to him and most likely to inspire him would be the one established by his own father-in-law, Charles B. Aycock, who made his name in office another one for education."

On the other hand, there were various reasons why I should not have become a candidate. My fellow stockholders in *The Progressive Farmer,* while they did not bring pressure on me, did make clear their preference that I keep on building the organization to which I had given my major energies since 1899. In the second place, gubernatorial campaigns even then were very expensive and when it was suggested I would need to get funds from certain powerful financial interests with axes to grind, I could not welcome the idea of assuming any obligation that might handicap me in doing my fair and equal duty by all the people of the state.

These adverse considerations might have been overridden but for one important development that challenged me at the time as having potentialities for statesmanship and progress on a much wider and more challenging scale than even the office of governor might present. For two or three years I had been meeting and talking with governors from North Carolina to Texas at their Southern Governors' Conferences, developing plans for South-wide agricultural, industrial, and cultural progress. This finally took shape in late 1939 in the form of a proposed "Ten-Year Campaign For Balanced Prosperity in the South, 1940-50." This emphasized ten roads to a "balanced prosperity," including especially the following: balance money crops with "food, feed, and fertility crops"; balance farms with factories; balance crops with livestock; balance production progress with marketing progress; balance owner-prosperity with worker-prosperity; balance the gains in wealth with gains in regional beauty and culture.

A fully detailed ways and means statement proposing this South-wide ten-year campaign of progress was prepared by me with the help of the governors and was published and signed by the following governors then in office: E. D. Rivers of Georgia, chairman; Clyde R. Hoey of North Carolina; Burnet R. Maybank of South Carolina; Fred P. Cone of Florida; Frank M. Dixon of Alabama; Prentice Cooper of Tennessee; Carl E. Bailey of Arkansas; W. Lee O'Daniel of Texas; Leon C. Phillips of Oklahoma. At the same time it was announced that I would serve as "General Chairman on Behalf of Organizations of Citizens and Public Agencies" with able state chairmen including such men as Douglas S. Freeman in Virginia; Frank P. Graham in North Carolina; D. W. Watkins in South Carolina; Paul W. Chapman in Georgia; Donald Comer in Alabama; C. C. Flannery in Tennessee; Herbert T. Thatcher in Arkansas.

It was at a meeting of the Southern Governors' Conference in Atlanta (called especially to see the premiere showing of "Gone with the Wind") that this South-wide program of progress was enthusiastically approved and signed by all the Southern governors present. The Governor of Georgia declared, "The achievements of this ten-year period of progress may well be climaxed by a great Southern exposition in 1950—probably in Atlanta." The declaration issued over the signatures of nine governors attending the Atlanta meeting, with others expected to be added, quickly excited Southern

publicity and interest, and it was noted that I had with-
drawn from a personal contest for governor in order to promote the South-wide program.

When the governors not only promulgated this ten-year
program but designated me to head it up, I expressed my
positive and final decision about the governorship by saying
to Dr. Frank Graham who was in the hotel with me, *"This
means I shall not be a candidate for governor of North
Carolina."* To the North Carolina press I had given a date
when I would announce a final decision. On the previous
day the *News and Observer* said it was confidently expected
that I would announce my candidacy. Instead I said I would
seek to promote the progress not merely of North Carolina
but of the whole South through the proposed "Ten-Year
Campaign For Balanced Prosperity in the South, 1940-50."

Thus was auspiciously inaugurated a campaign I confidently thought would prove one of the shining landmarks
of Southern progress. And so it indeed might have proved
but for one overriding "if"—if World War II had not inter-
vened. By the time war ended almost the entire list of
governors had changed and the demoralization and public
weariness resulting from war, together with the increased
age of the earliest leaders in the movement, prevented a
formal, post-war revival of what had been a wisely planned
and drastically needed forward step. But like John Brown's
body its principle "kept marching on." It inspired educational, agricultural, and industrial progress all over the
South in some degree, but not in the degree that the fully
implemented "Ten-Year Campaign For Balanced Prosperity
in the South" would have achieved.

After making the decision not to become a candidate for
governor I later came to ask myself, "Which of three possible
honors, if I could have attained them, would have given me
the greatest personal happiness and satisfaction?" One was,

of course, my work on *The Progressive Farmer* with its almost limitless opportunities for service to farm people, including the South-wide Ten-Year Campaign For Balanced
Prosperity in the South. Another was the position of governor, a position anyone would prize not merely for its
power but as an expression of confidence and even affection
by a great body of voters. Another was the position of Secretary of Agriculture for which I had strong support in the
administrations of Woodrow Wilson and Franklin Roosevelt.
But even more than being governor or a cabinet officer I felt
that I should have been happiest of all if circumstances in
my youth had permitted me to win a Rhodes Scholarship,
with its three years of study and contacts in one of the
world's most famous seats of learning, before entering on a
later career. This would have been almost a case of "All This
and Heaven Too."

Now I know, however, that any other position would have
reduced the period of continuous service I first gave to some
thousands of farm people and later to some millions as editor-in-chief of *The Progressive Farmer*. Once when I had an
appointment with a newly-inaugurated governor, one of the
most prominent men in the state remarked, "Governors have
their influence, each four years at a time. But your service
on *The Progressive Farmer* is counted by generations."

A final paragraph concerning this matter might serve two
purposes. Written by former Judge L. A. Martin in the *Lex-
ington Dispatch*, January 2, 1963, it illustrates both the generosity of my friends during the period when my name was
actively in the news as a possible gubernatorial candidate
and the persistence with which this generosity was maintained through the succeeding two score years. Perhaps I
might even say that it represents what theologians call "the
perseverance of the saints." Anyhow, in January, 1963, Judge
Martin, who had himself been an important figure in the

politics of his section and an active supporter of mine, published this gracious comment:

"Here is a man who should have been governor of North
Carolina a long time ago. I do not know of a man who has
done more for his state and its people, and had he been
governor he would have done even more. Not even his distinguished father-in-law, Governor Charles B. Aycock—the
man who set in motion the educational renaissance in North
Carolina—would dissent from our appraisal of the work of
Clarence Poe. He has built for himself a monument that will
endure not only across all the fertile fields and valleys of
North Carolina, but one that will live and throb in the
hearts of our citizenship through all the years to come."

At this point it may be asked what doctrine I had been
preaching in *The Progressive Farmer* and in public addresses
all the way from Virginia to Texas that had brought to my
support such earnest friends. In answer to this I might first
refer to the various movements I have helped and then
quote from a Memphis, Tennessee, dispatch of April 25,
1908, to the *Charlotte Observer* which summarized an address I had made the previous day to the Southern Educational Conference. Here were my exact words:

"Every man whose earning power is above normal is an
asset to the community, a wealth-maker for every other man;
but every man whose earning power is below par is a burden
on the community. His poverty makes every other man
poorer. Suppose you are his fellow citizen. Then because of
his inefficiency, his poverty as a taxpayer and as a citizen, you will have poorer roads, poorer schools, a shabbier
church, lower priced lands; your teacher, your preacher,
your doctor will be more poorly paid (or give way to some
one less efficient); your newspaper will have smaller circulation, your town a poorer market, your railroad smaller

traffic, your merchant smaller trade, your bank smaller deposits, your manufacturer diminished patronage, and so forth.

"Inevitably and universally the prosperity of every trade, art, and industry in a community is measured by the prosperity of its average man, its common man.

"The South's greatest fallacy has been the belief that the farmer, the common laborer of every sort, needs no training; educate him and you spoil him; the poorer you keep him, the richer will be the upper classes.

"Hugging these vampire delusions, the Southern plantation owner has seen his land abandoned to broomsage and gullies, in spite of the fact that intelligent handling would have kept it productive a thousand years. Preaching this fatal doctrine, the merchant has sold Western meat and scooters and tobacco, when with prosperous patrons he might have quadrupled his profits by selling sulky plows and harvesters and carriages, and pianos. Still arguing that education and training would spoil the common laborer, our manufacturer has struggled with a small business when a prosperous average man would give us the great industries of the North and West.

"And so with men in every other vocation. Our men of talent—artist, sculptor, orator, poet—flee to other sections unshackled by these errors, or else lie with vision unfulfilled among a people untrained to appreciate their genius—when but for these things you might see statues of Southern leaders in every city, the work of Southern artists in the world's great galleries, the thought of the Southern poet the common heritage of mankind. It is not that we have had no mighty dreamers; it is that they sleep in neglected graves, victims of war and waste and error.

"Now, war and waste, thank God, are behind us. Let us also put error behind us.

"Of all errors our greatest has been the doctrine that having cheap, ignorant, untrained labor is a help instead of the curse that it is. And our second greatest error has been the belief that even if education does help the common man, we are too poor to furnish it. The truth is we are too poor not to furnish it. The fullest and freest training of the average man is the one and only substantial guarantee of Southern prosperity."

In sum, my supreme purpose has always been to help the man at the bottom and to proclaim that by so doing we not only help him but everybody else.

CHAPTER FOURTEEN

When the Great Depression Came

FEW YOUNGER PEOPLE TODAY HAVE ANY ADEQUATE IDEA EITHER of the depth or the expanse of the Great Depression period. The gathering storm began with the calamitous collapse of stock prices in 1929 and then went from bad to worse until a cold day in early March of 1933 when above the roar of the winter rainstorm I heard over the radio the voice of a man who had himself triumphed over great tribulation— *"We have nothing to fear except fear itself."*

Even then, however, the clogging chains of the Great Depression hindered progress for months and years before America could again move with anything like normal speed.

One incident of the gathering storm is vividly sketched in my memory against its dark background. I had not yet been forced to rent out (almost for a song) my lovely home overlooking the Neuse and Crabtree Valleys and move my family to a much smaller home I rented in Raleigh. But the Depression was deepening and on the dark nights of early winter, when I rode my horse home from the city, I kept repeating to myself these lines:

> I bring you naught for your comfort,
> Yea naught for your desire

Save that the night grows darker still
And the storm rises higher.

From these challenging words I found a fierce, masculine, primal summons to all that a man can have of fortitude and stamina which—in spite of its desperateness—was not wholly without comfort. If I could meet and survive the test of the hour I might somehow feel a kinship with some great oak, deeply rooted, that meets the long blasts of the hurricane and emerges at last, battered but not destroyed.

I had acquired several tracts of suburban land that I had consolidated into a seven-hundred-acre cotton, tobacco, and dairy farm but had by no means fully paid for. Banks were failing, businessmen going broke, and a chronic financial panic was at its height. Not only were material losses tragic in their depth but human losses were even greater. One North Carolina insurance company reported that 1932 was the only year in its history in which it had to pay out a greater amount of death losses because of suicides than from heart trouble!

In all this period my friends stood by me but thought for a time I could not survive financially. Mr. W. E. Henley, the president of our Birmingham bank, said to me, "The bankruptcy laws were made especially to enable men with a terrific debt burden like yours to clean the slate and start all over again." In this connection he gave me an illustration of the consuming power of interest, saying, "When Thomas Jefferson made the famous Louisiana Purchase, including the area now covered by nine states and parts of three others, everybody naturally assumes that he made a wonderful bargain. Yet some expert has figured it out that if this $15 million had been put out at interest compounded quarterly it would now buy every farm, home, business, factory, school, church, and other industry in the entire region!"

One day early in 1933 my attorney, Mr. J. M. Broughton, later to become governor, called me for a conference in his office. Joining us were my long-time business partner, John S. Pearson, who came up from Birmingham; my able brother-in-law, Major Lennox P. McLendon, who came over from Greensboro; and my banker and friend, Frank Page. After reviewing all my circumstances they unanimously told me they saw no way out except voluntary bankruptcy. My reply was, "I may have bankruptcy forced upon me but I shall never voluntarily take bankruptcy. I will fight it out to pay every debt I owe," and in this subsequent effort I had their cooperation. Frank Page told me, "We shall have to publicly sell at the courthouse door *The Progressive Farmer* stock you have pledged with us as collateral, but we will buy it in and hold it for you to recover after this depression passes and you find yourself able to pay off your notes." (Later this was done.)

About this time one impatient and covetous creditor, who had a reputation for picking up "distressed properties" at the bankruptcy value then prevailing with the expectation of realizing handsome profits later on, had the sheriff knock at my door with a notice of foreclosure on the mortgage I owed him. It was then that Broughton circumvented him by a device that I, not being a lawyer, might never have thought of. "This man," he said to me, "while not now living in Raleigh was in Raleigh when the note was made and the state laws required him to list it for taxation which I am sure he never did."

"But I can't swear he did not list it," I protested.

"You don't have to *say* that he did not do it," was the reply. "All we need to do is to *allege* that he did not, and it will be up to him to prove to the contrary."

This plan worked. If it had not, other creditors would have been forced to join this man in other foreclosure sales in order to get their just share of what my property would bring under panic conditions.

Going with me to the offices of the North Carolina Baptist Foundation which had lent me $20,000, Broughton discovered that through sheer inadvertence the word "seal" had not been added after my signature. This would have put the Foundation at a serious or complete disadvantage in any effort it might make to collect. Upon learning this I seized a pen and wrote in the needed word. Perhaps it was because of this action that the Foundation forgave all interest on the loan, when I later voluntarily repaid it.

The widespread character of the Depression might be illustrated by one other incident. Near my house was a small tract of virgin forest which W. R. Poole's will had required to be kept inviolate until after his last heir came of age. I coveted for State College and the state this unique tract of "forest primeval" and had induced three other trustees to join with me in forming "The North Carolina Forestry Foundation" and incidentally in giving notes for purchase of the "Poole Woods." All four of us thought ourselves well-to-do and expected to remain so. But then came the Depression and of the four men, one died, one took out bankruptcy, the third man reported he had no assets, and I was left alone to carry the note—and the amount of the note given to an insurance company was for a much larger amount than could possibly be realized by selling the collateral timber at prices then prevailing. Month after month I was hounded for payment when I could not even meet the interest. But Ernest Haywood, a Raleigh lawyer who had been attorney for Mr. Poole, gave me money enough to pay part of the interest, and the tract was later consolidated with an 86,000-acre pocosin tract that I had helped secure for the State College Forestry Foundation. Success in this respect was largely due to the cooperation of my long-time friend T. D. Warren of

New Bern. Later the timber on the virgin forest was cut (I remember seeing one stump whose markings went back to the 1750's.) Thus what might have been a unique beauty spot with its magnificent century-plus trees became simply another area of cutover land. Now I do not know where any area of true virgin forest remains in central North Carolina where the young people of today may see how magnificent was the tree growth that covered all North Carolina when our pioneer ancestors came here.

During the Depression years I reduced my farming activities but remember having to sell a large part of one tobacco crop at two cents a pound. Truman King, a farmer in an adjoining county, tells what he and other dirt farmers remember about those days:

"They remember the sweat of an entire crop year with nothing in hand at the end to show for their labors, walking everywhere they went because there was either no car or no gas; swapping eggs for the absolute necessities at a penny apiece; working (when any work was available) at five cents an hour, and getting paid in anything but money; and learning to live at home, leaving money almost entirely out of the picture."

One poignant memory of that period is that of seeing a strong man come to my office to get work on the relatively insignificant task of moving a small farm building and weeping like a child when he found that another man had already been engaged.

America is now so far advanced in its economic thinking that we realize a supreme need in 1932 was that everybody should have been encouraged to redouble buying by persons who had enough money to spare. Yet I remember hearing so able (and rather wealthy) a man as A. L. Brooks advise everybody to economize to the utmost limit and proclaim, "I never intend to buy a new suit of clothes until the situation changes."

Only the Negroes in Raleigh seemed happy. But with their restricted diets someone estimated that their total weight decreased about one million pounds during this period! At a time when a bank failure seemed to be occurring almost every day, I had my horse shod at a blacksmith shop where I found a group of Negroes laughing and talking, and I have never forgotten the significant explanation they gave me: "All the rich folks is having plenty of trouble," they said. "But a man that ain't got nothin', he ain't got nothin' to worry about!"

Especially hard was the lot of men and women among my friends who owned stock in national banks. To encourage safe banking in normal times the law had provided that in case of bank failure the owners of bank stock should be liable not only for the loss of the stock, but for an additional equal amount—double liability. A man with $50,000 worth of stock in a bankrupt bank was expected to pay $100,000 to recoup depositors.

Meanwhile our publishing company had been forced to make drastic cuts in salaries and wages, those of us at the top cutting our own salaries to the bone. In the worst month of the Depression it was agreed that every employee would go one month without either wages or salary—providing, indeed, a magnificent test of loyalty on the part of the group. (Of course this month's salary was repaid when times got better.)

Possibly only the survival of two banks enabled *The Progressive Farmer* also to survive. The bank in Birmingham where our central office was located was, I think, the only one there that did not go broke—and the Wachovia Bank of which I had been a director was also the only bank in Raleigh which failed to close its doors. I remember seeing mob-like numbers of people lined up to withdraw their deposits. When people began making such runs on banks, the president of one Raleigh bank declared, "Don't worry—this bank will stay open until hell freezes over." I do not yet know what may have happened to hell, but I do know that his bank went down with the others. Before that time I remember having urged federal government guarantee of bank deposits only to have my great friend Senator Carter Glass of Virginia—the father of the Federal Reserve System—write me that any such idea was a dangerous extension of government activity. Now who would favor doing without it? Not only did the Birmingham Bank & Trust Company help us in the conduct of our business during the war period but lent us $105,000 and encouraged us to put four-color covers on the magazine before the Depression had fully passed.

As an act of enlightened statesmanship after the Depression both Mr. Butler and I proposed we should divide the profits of our company on a 1-1-1 basis: one-third as a bonus to employees, one-third as dividends to stockholders, and one-third as a reserve that would enable the company to keep functioning in case of another crisis such as we had had in 1932-33.

For a long time during the Depression it seemed that Lawyer Jim Pou of Raleigh had been right when he made his memorable comment on the 1932 election: "This man Franklin Roosevelt thinks he's been elected president of the United States. And Blucher Ehringhaus thinks he's been elected governor of North Carolina. But what has really happened is this: Franklin Roosevelt has been appointed receiver for the United States and Blucher Ehringhaus receiver for the state of North Carolina."

All over the South men like myself who were in debt for land bought at prices far beyond what it would bring at Depression prices were saved by compromises worked out

by the Farm Debt Adjustment Organization, very compe-
tently headed in this state by my friend who later became
governor, W. Kerr Scott.

Even during the most harrowing days of the Depression
the universality of the disaster made it somewhat more bear-
able. Former Governor O. Max Gardner illustrated the situation by an apt story. "When I was a small boy," he said,
"some boy in school got the itch. He would slouch down
behind his desk, put up a big geography in front of him,
and scratch to his heart's content. Soon the itch spread
and the prettiest girl in school had to resort to the same
device. Then a little later when everybody in school had
the itch, all of us scratched together—happily, openly, and
unashamedly."

At long last, however, the tide turned and the whole
nation began singing that historic song of cheer, "Happy
Days Are Here Again." Especially happy was my son Charles
who had had to quit college to work in our Chicago office
in order to supplement the family income. Now with help
from the University loan fund on a note signed by my always helpful friend, Dr. B. W. Kilgore, he returned to school
in time to join the graduating class of 1935 when the commencement address was made by the wife of the President
who had brought new hope to America in its darkest hour.

One thing I lost in the Depression I could never recover.
Always one of the happiest days of the year had been the
day when the circus came to town and I would take the
entire family to see the clowns and the acts. It is a mark
of the depth of the Depression that when it held full sway
I did not feel justified in withholding from my creditors even
the small amount it would have taken to pay the once-a-
year price of a circus ticket.

To make any money during the depression was almost impossible. About the only exception was the man who was

able to buy up "distressed property" and hold it until it regained normal or nearly normal value. On the other hand, the great majority of people thought they were doing very well if they were able to say with Groucho Marx:

"When I came to Florida, I didn't have five cents; now I do have five cents."

CHAPTER FIFTEEN

Presidents I Knew

AT THE END OF MY FIRST YEAR OF LIFE ONE MIGHT WELL HAVE asked, "Is Clarence Poe going to specialize in Presidents?" For in the first nine months of my existence I had lived under three Presidents—during the last weeks of the Hayes administration, six months under the ill-fated Garfield, and the remaining months under an accidental president who seems to have done mighty little except popularize side-whiskers, Chester Alan Arthur.

I remember the high "Cleveland hat" my cousin Charlie Riddle wore when he came to visit us in the campaign of 1888. (This Cleveland hat, now forgotten, was then as famous as the "brown derby" that became the trademark of Al Smith's campaign.) But the first president I ever saw was Benjamin Harrison, not long after he left office, at Richard Mansfield's production of *Henry VIII* in New York City. And the first president I knew personally—and the most immediately captivating—was Theodore Roosevelt.

But the president for whose nomination I worked hardest and whose inaugural I first attended was Woodrow Wilson, so perhaps it might be well to recall first my contacts with him. None was more revealing than the reply he made early in 1911 when I told him of my hope that he would be our next president. His immediate comment was, "I am of course tremendously grateful to you and all my friends who have such confidence in me. But I can say in all sincerity that these messages do not bring me any sense of elation—but rather a sense of profound and sobering responsibility." Herbert Hoover, in his book *The Ordeal of Woodrow Wilson,* has further emphasized the all-compelling sense of duty which drove Wilson all through his years in the White House. In Browning's phrase Wilson often seemed to me "amidst a grove the very straightest tree." But unquestionably he should have made concessions to save the basic principles of the League of Nations instead of risking the loss of it all.

Returning from a trip around the world I wrote Mr. Wilson from shipboard just off Port Said on February 17, 1911. In part I said:

"I am just on my way home, having been in the Orient since last September; and it may interest you to know that among the Americans I have met abroad—tourists and temporary residents in foreign lands—there is no such enthusiasm for any other possible candidate for the next Democratic presidential nomination as there is for Governor Woodrow Wilson of New Jersey.... My letters from North Carolina also indicate a rapid crystallization of sentiment in your favor in the South ... and I think I shall be able to help along the Wilson boom when I get home next month— partly for your sake but more for the sake of the party and the nation."

Wilson's reply, dated March 13, 1911, indicated the same cautious approach to the presidential campaign which usually characterizes candidates a year before the nominating convention. In part he said:

"It was very delightful that you should think of me. I am both surprised and gratified at what you tell me of the widespread attention attracted outside the country as well as in it by my campaign. I am a bit daunted to have been brought so much into the public eye but I am trying to saw wood with diligence and close attention to the matters immediately at hand."

My admiration for Wilson was so great that a friend and I once made a horseback trip of thirty-three miles from Raleigh to Chapel Hill and back the next day to hear him speak—the longest horseback trip I have ever made.

Probably Wilson's supreme achievement as governor of New Jersey was securing the establishment of a state-wide primary law as a substitute for the old boss-controlled convention system. After becoming president he continued his interest in this reform on a national scale. On March 21, 1914, he sent me a message obviously intended to be a definite message to the whole Democratic party in North Carolina and which won front page priority in the newspapers. In this message he said:

"I have noticed with a great deal of interest the movement inaugurated by yourself and others to secure a law for state-wide primaries in North Carolina. I must admit that I was very much surprised to learn that so great and progressive a state was so far behind the procession in a matter of such capital importance to the people. May I not express my deep interest in your efforts to bring about the necessary legislation? I am sure it would cheer Democrats everywhere to see this done by North Carolina." This message has been credited with major influence in turning North Carolina from the convention system to the state-wide primary.

Because Wilson was willing to sacrifice—and probably did sacrifice—his own life for the sake of his ideal of world peace, it should never be assumed that he was without a saving sense of humor. Of course everybody remembers the rhyme he liked to quote about himself—

> For beauty I'm not a star
> There are others handsomer far;
> But my face I don't mind it
> For I stand behind it—
> It's those in front that I jar!

Having attended Davidson College, Princeton, Johns Hopkins, and the University of Virginia, he remarked after an introduction recalling these facts at the last named place, "It took so many colleges to educate me that I am sometimes reminded of the inscription on an Irish tombstone—'Here lies the body of Lucy O'Corrigan, who was the faithful and loving wife of the seven following gentlemen!'" Again speaking at Columbia, South Carolina, where so many people had known him as a young man as "Tommy" Wilson, I heard him say that, being among people who knew him so well, he felt much like a dear old lady attending a show where a magician suddenly appeared to be reading fine print through a one-inch plank. Immediately she arose and stalked out of the room exclaiming, "This ain't no place for me with these thin things on!"

Nor was Woodrow Wilson above resorting to the so-called lowest form of wit—the pun. Josephus Daniels told me of a time during World War I when a show he had gone with Wilson to see was found to consist largely of nearly unclad females. Next morning when someone asked Wilson if he had gotten some release from the strain of war and war subjects the night before, he replied with a smile, "No, I am afraid not—Joe took me to a navel parade!"

After his election, without any urging on my part, I was surprised to find numerous papers reporting that Wilson was considering me for Secretary of Agriculture. Of course I might not have been offered the position anyhow but I could not afford to leave my company and paper at that stage of their growth. So I wrote Wilson on December 18, 1912, as follows:

"While a score of papers have been generous enough to urge my appointment as Secretary of Agriculture, I do not wish the office myself but do wish most earnestly that you shall appoint a man of extraordinary vision and ability. There is a nation-wide awakening to the possibilities of rural cooperation and better marketing methods and you can win everlasting gratitude of American farmers by naming a man who will broaden the department and make it not only an agency for increasing crop production, but an agency for remaking country life and solving the pressing problems of rural cooperation, rural credit, and more economical distribution. After thoroughly canvassing all names suggested, I believe Walter H. Page, formerly of the Country Life Commission, could perform this epoch-making task while it may be that Dr. Liberty Hyde Bailey or President Henry J. Waters of Kansas Agricultural College would do equally well."

I have mentioned my contacts with Wilson first because of my having been for years his enthusiastic supporter, even before he became president. But the president I first knew personally and also admired very greatly, in spite of his being of a different political party, was that always colorful figure, rough-riding Theodore Roosevelt. In the period from Grant's presidency to McKinley's, America was a relatively placid and unexcited nation. But no sooner had Theodore Roosevelt become president after McKinley's assassination in 1901 than a new spirit of youthfulness swept the continent. He was the youngest president we had ever had and acted accordingly, and I was just one of a host of young American writers and editors to whom he gave recognition and stimulus.

He was not only young but vibrantly joyous. Before his time was there ever a picture of a president laughing—or even smiling? Teddy Roosevelt not only laughed, but in laughing he showed a gorgeous set of teeth that became the delight of every cartoonist. To all elements in America he brought the call for increased activity—"the strenuous life." If he did not actually discover the Ten Commandments, as some critics said he seemed to believe, he at least gave them a terrific shot in the arm! If he mainly preached the old-fashioned virtues lauded by Emerson, Poor Richard, and our greatest religious leaders, it must be said that under his enthusiastic presentation they acquired all the freshness of coins newly minted. I doubt whether in all his writings one could find a single paragraph that more characteristically summarized his often emphasized exhortations than the following letter he sent me (at my request) from Oyster Bay, December 14, 1915:

"Through you I send this brief message to the boys on Southern farms. I am glad of the fine record the farm boys of the South are making. They have the stuff in them to succeed if they choose to go about it in the right way. They must show the qualities of self-reliance, of independence, of power, of self-help. Yet they must remember that it is equally important to be able to cooperate with others and each to merge his individuality for the common end. Of course no man, whether as a farmer or a city-resident, can succeed unless he has the root qualities of honesty, of character, of common sense—unless he desires to do justice to others and at the same time to secure his rights."

Nothing was too sacred for "Terrible Teddy" to tackle if he thought he might make it better—and there were always plenty of things he thought he could improve. At one time he had Americans spelling phonetically—at least to a certain extent—a habit he hoped might become expansive and contagious. He looked at the words "In God We Trust" on our metal coins and decided that they were too sanctimonious or hypocritical and ought to go. And so they went.

The people were not prepared to follow him in these last two matters, but if he had to backtrack on these minor details his enthusiasm for change was only to break loose in some more important quarter. Well-to-do parents who did not bear enough children he denounced as committing "race suicide." The rich who were lacking in public spirit or in fairness to other classes he pilloried as "malefactors of great wealth." Army officers who had not ridden a horse in ten or twenty years were commanded to ride thirty miles a day! At one time he publicly advocated the recall of judicial decisions by popular vote but did not get very far with this especially alarming proposal. The nation, indeed, had a hard time keeping up with its fast-stepping president. But it was great fun—even if some wearied participants did say that "he kept America going night and day as if it were racing to a fire."

Personally, I first was captivated by T. R. at the Charleston Exposition in 1902. There in old South Carolina he and my future father-in-law, Governor Aycock, spoke from the same platform and spoke with such frankness and vigor that they liked each other ever after. Both men admired the courage of soldiers, both from the North and South, and Roosevelt was proud of the fact that he was the son of a Southern mother—a Georgian—and that two of his uncles had fought in the Confederate service. In this connection everybody who has not already done so should enjoy one of the most hilarious of all O. Henry stories, "The Rose of Dixie." Its wholly unreconstructed old editor would never contaminate the columns of his magazine with anything of recognizable Northern source but finally inserted something Roosevelt had written by giving it the credit line: "By T.

Roosevelt, a Member of the Distinguished Bulloch Family of Georgia."

My most intimate contact with T. R. came not long after February, 1904, when the *Atlantic Monthly* published an article of mine, "Lynching: A Southern View." Since this article not only won so much unexpected praise from Roosevelt and led to our lifelong friendship but especially because it dealt with the problem of lynching so long with us and of mob rule not yet extinct in the South, I shall include at this point some extracts from my *Atlantic Monthly* article:

"That lynching is an evil is denied by no one. Even Mr. John Temple Graves, who defended it in his recent Chautauqua address, had to admit that it is demoralizing and criminal, and that its logical consummation is anarchy.... We cannot encourage a hundred men to disregard law without encouraging the individual to disregard law; we cannot encourage law-breaking to gratify vengeance without encouraging law-breaking to gratify hate or greed or lust. The mob spirit breeds disrespect for all law....

"For yet other reasons is lynching to be dreaded and deplored.... Our judges, as a class, are men of high character and ability, and our juries are composed of fair-minded and intelligent men. But the mob may be recruited from the worst element of the community, men of bad character and low intelligence; its members may even have private grudges against the alleged criminal. The court, too, acts in the open, seen and scrutinized by all; the judge and the jurymen are known, and they know that their reputations will be injured if they act carelessly or unrighteously. But the mob has no such incentive to right action. It hides itself in the dark; it shrinks from the gaze of men; its members are not known to their fellow citizens; the fear of incurring individual condemnation does not restrain them from injustice. Moreover, the court considers evidence calmly and carefully.... But the mob works in the heat of passion and in great haste. Too often it hangs the man on incomplete circumstantial evidence, hangs the wrong man....

"We must excuse lynching under no conditions, for as certainly as a fire, fanned to a fury in one room, will sweep on to other rooms, so certainly will the mob, if generally encouraged to punish one crime, sweep irresistibly on to supplant the court at all points. Instead of excusing it where the crime is horrible and the guilt of the criminal undoubted, we must teach that in such cases mob law is the more indefensible—because of the increased certainty and speed of legal punishment.

"It is not the criminal's rights, but the court's rights, that we need to emphasize.... We need to teach that if Satan himself should commit a crime we should try him in legal form—not for Satan's sake but for the sake of law and order and civilization; not that he would have the right to a court trial but that our courts alone would have the right to try him; and that trial by any other body is, and will ever be, usurpation and minority rule, un-American, undemocratic, and unendurable.

"... Fraught with much meaning is the fact that the crime against white women was practically unknown in slavery; that not one of the hundreds of graduates who have gone out from Hampton and Tuskegee has ever been guilty of it; and that of those who commit this crime today few are able to read, have steady employment, or own homes. Ignorance, idleness, thriftlessness—out of these does crime come, and against these must our warfare be waged if we would destroy the spirit that breeds crime.... I look then to right industrial, educational, and religious training as our chief safeguard against Negro crime."

A few months after this article appeared I was both surprised and even excited to receive a letter of hearty appro-
bation from T. R. in the White House. Later at a reception
given him in the Senate Chamber in Raleigh, when I was
introduced to him I thanked him in just a word for his letter. But with his usual unpredictable enthusiasm for any
subject he had become interested in, he held up the receiving line to ask me several questions and then asked that I
remain and talk further with him immediately after the
reception. Our Southern race problem was still his major
interest. He rebuked those holding extremist positions on
both sides and said: "What I wish to do is not to force views
of my own on the South but to follow the lead of your liberal and broad-gauged Southerners—men like Bishop Strange
of North Carolina and Judge Jones of Alabama. . . . I have
never seen a white man North or South since Reconstruction
who favored intermarriage and amalgamation of the races."
As for the Negro he said his policy was, "Help him if he
stumbles, but if he lies down, let him stay."

Later, in 1912, I was to see T. R. back in Raleigh on his
Bull Moose campaign—his rumpled clothes attesting how
strenuously he had been campaigning—when he exclaimed
about the Panama Canal, "While others kept talking about
a canal to join the two oceans, I got it!"

Herbert Hoover's spirit of internationalism was first made
evident in his work for the Red Cross on Belgian Relief.
Again as Food Administrator he fought a magnificent one-
man battle after the Armistice in an effort, only partly successful, to make our allies accept food already aboard ship
on which they wished to cancel contracts; to delay a re-
moval of wartime farm price supports at home; and to get
surplus food (at any price or none) to starving peoples of

Europe and Russia—not only to those who had been on our side in World War I, but to some who had been our enemies. So monumental had been his success in these fields and so far removed from politics that—along with Democratic Governor Bickett of North Carolina and many others—I unsuccessfully tried to encourage Mr. Hoover to say that he would accept the Democratic nomination for president in 1920.

Under his shy and often gloomy manner and bearing, Hoover was at heart really "The Great Humanitarian" his party declared him to be in their campaign slogans. And this is a designation that could not be wiped away by cheap taunts concerning "The Great Engineer" at the close of his presidency in the Great Depression.

Hoover was gracious enough to ask my counsel about a number of matters. Once he wired me to come to Washington when he was in the midst of difficulties as Food Administrator here and abroad. Later I saw him in the White House during the initial postwar struggle to cope with unsalable food surpluses through his Federal Farm Board. That proved an abortive effort, but so, in varying degree, have been all like efforts since. His Federal Farm Board was plainly a forerunner of F. D. R.'s AAA and later farm programs.

When I saw him Hoover appeared, not without cause, to regard himself as being blamed for forces beyond his control. I regard him as a man who paid in his own person for the sins of our entire nation—for the nation-wide greed, the immoral get-rich-quick hysteria to which our nation had succumbed even in the years just before he came into office. In those years America sowed the wind and later reaped the whirlwind—the cyclonic stock market collapse of 1929 and the general bankruptcy of 1932. True, he had none of the political experience or daring needed to get effective legislation and action, but to throw on him the major blame for the so-called "Hoover Depression" is to do him woeful wrong.

If Herbert Hoover had little genius for politics, his successor had it in superabundance. Franklin D. Roosevelt's slow but final triumph over a shattering physical disaster gave him the courage to meet the disasters that later came to our people as a whole. Who now of middle years or older does not recall some part of his First Inaugural? In memory I can still hear above the monotonous drone of a dreary winter rain a voice on the air, clear, bold and confident, that lifted our hearts and reassured us.

While he was in the White House I saw him fairly frequently. Once he wired me to come to see him when the opposition to his Standard Wage and Hour Bill was going strong here in the South. Among his most potent Southern opponents was the late Gene Talmadge, father of the much more able and highly regarded present Senator from Georgia. The Gene Talmadge of that day was a rabble-rouser of the first water. He usually became so vehement when speaking that he would take off his coat, partly, it would seem, to display a pair of startlingly red or scarlet suspenders which soon became his trademark. Roosevelt said to me, "If the opposition proposes to play the demagogue and stir up the people against me—well, I can beat them at their own game —and I shan't have to wear red suspenders to do it!"

One extraordinary trait of F. D. R., which has been too little noted, was his intuitive and sharply realistic sense of geography, world-wide, immediately local, and extending to both land and sea. In fact his love of the sea amounted to a passion. Every time I visited him his desk was literally cluttered with ship models. During World War II my friend Senator J. W. Bailey went to see him about some matters relating to the harbor at Morehead City, North Carolina. "I was almost stunned," Bailey told me, "when I found that Roosevelt seemed to know more about the harbor, the ocean depth, and all that sort of thing than I did!" In like manner, Roosevelt's published personal observations concerning the essential unity of soil restoration and water conservation, forestry, and tillage, based on experiences both on his family holdings at Hyde Park in the North and his piney-woodlands around "The Little White House" in Georgia, provide an amazingly illuminating document that should be much more generally read by students of these problems. Roosevelt often laughed about his father's financially costly experiences as an importer of Alderney (now called Guernsey) cattle. He also reminded me that Southern farmers were losing a great deal by not using more attractive and modern methods of grading and packaging their fruits and vegetables. "The best-tasting apples I have ever eaten," he said, "come from your Southern mountain and Piedmont areas but I can never find them on the markets here or anywhere in the North or even at my Little White House in Georgia." My service on Roosevelt's Commission on Farm Tenancy, as agricultural member of his Federal Board for Vocational Education, and numerous personal conversations made me realize his deep concern about farm matters—and his especial interest in "tree farming," as he called forestry.

He died at war but there can be no doubt in the minds of those who worked most closely with him, such as his press secretary Jonathan Daniels of Raleigh, that he hated war. Long before World War II I heard Rex Tugwell, one of his closest associates, say, "The only time I ever see a look of distress on his otherwise constantly cheerful face is when the possibility of another war is mentioned." And Tugwell believes that his years of healing and helping heal others of polio at Warm Springs brought him so intimately in touch, for the first time in his life, with the goodness and valor of plain, ordinary people that he became a real democrat with a small "d."

Most of his war policies I supported but with one I heartily disagreed. I felt that his demand for the "unconditional surrender" of Germany was a tragic mistake, unnecessarily prolonging a war that might have ended sooner and with less unsatisfactory results.

As for the two most recent presidents that I have personally known—Truman and Eisenhower—they have been so extensively appraised by everybody in America I shall now say little by way of my own appraisal except that I have found them both personally charming, able, courageous alike in peace and war, and sincerely dedicated to the welfare of the nation as they see it—no matter how many of us may sometimes question some of their methods or choices of friends. (This I think is equally true of Mr. Kennedy.) I do wish, however, to report here (in verbatim form that both men read and approved) two remarkable interviews I secured first with Eisenhower and later with Truman. In these interviews they talked with me not only in more intimate detail than I have found anywhere else about the difficulties they had to encounter on their way to the presidency but also their views on many of the most important issues and problems both young people and older ones have to consider today.

Dwight D. Eisenhower I once interviewed at length when he was president of Columbia University and to my question, "What was the greatest difficulty you had to overcome as a boy?" he answered, "Well, there were so many I hardly know where to begin. But like nearly every normal boy, I had a great desire to succeed in athletics—football, basketball, and boxing—and yet I was not of a size to succeed in them. I weighed only 106 pounds when 15 years old, so you can guess the terrific punishment I had to take to make the high school football team. I had to work like a dog. But it was good for me. Then, because there were six of us brothers in a poor family, how to get a college education presented a tremendous difficulty. An older brother and I were ready for college at the same time. I helped him go for his first two years, then he helped me."

Next, about the selection of a life work, General Eisenhower offered counsel of interest to all boys and especially farm boys.

"All my life," he continued, "I have had work in which I could have fun. There should be joy each day in tackling some problem and doing something about it—confidently and cheerfully. We should not merely believe that 'Life is real, life is earnest,' but that we should get pleasure from it every day. If a boy has an ambition to have the nicest farm in the community or county, for example, he can have fun every hour he lives, working toward that ambition. And so with any other worthwhile purpose. Not to have such real pleasure and satisfaction every day—this is one of the greatest tragedies of life."

About world peace General Eisenhower had counsel as pertinent today as then: "To begin with, if we are to preserve world peace, we must cooperate with other nations through the United Nations and all other agencies working to prevent war. But we cannot cooperate with them successfully unless we are strong. By strength I do not mean merely tanks and armies. We must be economically strong. We must also be morally strong—not only fair and decent, but even more, we must be altruistic. And the people must value and defend their democracy and their freedoms—freedom such as we have here today where we may criticize our President, no matter who he is, and anybody else—without fear."

As for the qualities one must have or cultivate in order to be a leader among his fellows, General Eisenhower answered:

"In order to be a leader, a man must have followers; to have followers, a leader must have their confidence. Hence the supreme quality for a leader is unquestionably *integrity*. Without it no real success is possible, no matter whether it is on a section gang, or a football field, in an army, or in an office. If a man's associates find him guilty of phoniness, if they find that he lacks forthright integrity, he will fail. His teachings and actions must square with each other. The first great need therefore is integrity and high purpose.

"Next I would name *optimism*. Nothing defeats one so quickly as lack of faith—that means a readiness to be defeated.

"The third great quality needed by any leader is *love of people*. Nobody should enter any occupation where he must deal daily with people unless he loves people. A leader must get others to do things he asks of them because they like him and wish to help him, and find pleasure in helping him."

Not to have my interview deal only with serious problems, General Eisenhower was next asked the question—"General, what are your favorite hobbies?"

Golf and fishing, he mentioned—fresh-water fishing for trout and bass—and bridge as his favorite game. Then he added: "I cannot dignify it by calling it painting," he insisted, "but I enjoy dabbling with colors—sometimes a portrait, sometimes a landscape." In his reading, history and biography have long been his favorite subjects. Washington and Lincoln are his two favorite American heroes, while he regards General Lee as one of the greatest soldiers of all time.

In sports, he still thinks the Indian Jimmy Thorpe about

the best America has produced. He also tremendously admired Babe Ruth. "Why?" I asked and his answer was significant. "Because he started from nowhere as a poor orphan, and after slipping later in life, then got hold of himself and so gave America an object lesson in self-mastery."

Finally, General Eisenhower who had a Southern mother is still Southern enough to like hominy grits. "But please don't ask any of your subscribers to send me any," he warned. "Once during the war, Bing Crosby asked me what I should like to have while away off from home, and I casually mentioned hominy grits. He reported it over radio, and friends sent me nearly two tons! I gave them to our hospitals. There the boys from Dixie lapped them up, but the Northern boys never showed any enthusiasm!"

For farm readers President Truman had some especially memorable remarks to make when I saw him just before he left office in 1953.

We were sitting in the White House, and the man who spoke I knew was a former farm boy who had become the chosen head of the most powerful nation this world has ever known. Significantly enough the chief ornament on his desk was a gold-plated 4-H club emblem such as I had on my own desk at home.

"I believe, Mr. President," I said, "that you not only can speak as a farm boy but as a once-poor farm boy encouraging poor farm boys today. In fact, I believe that, like me, you grew up working long hours to help a farmer-father pay off indebtedness. Nevertheless, you have said that the years you spent farming were the happiest of your life. Why?"

"Simply because there is something about a farmer's life—its independence, the constant variety of activities, the opportunity to be your own boss and make your own deci-

sions, the wholesome and exhilarating life in the open air
—all these things made farming a happy vocation for me,"
he answered. "Then, too, I enjoyed the usual country social pleasures—the family, church, school, and Sunday school
get-togethers, the parties, picnics, box suppers, political meetings, and so on.

"But the thing that gave me the greatest satisfaction and
happiness of all—especially after I began farming for myself—was something else. It was bringing up an old, eroded,
half 'wornout' farm by rotation, legumes, stable manure—
manure not only from our own animals, but hauled in from
the town stables. I recall now one fifty-five-acre field where
we soon brought up the corn yield from eighteen bushels
to fifty, and wheat yield from eight to twenty bushels. An
achievement like that—something you do with your own
hand and head and can see with your own eyes—that gave
me a downright satisfaction as great as I have since received
from doing many a job that made big headlines in the dailies."

Following up one of his suggested rules for success, "To
every job you undertake always aim to do it better than you
are expected to," Mr. Truman reminisced about his own
farm experiences. "My mother," he said, "used to brag on me
and cheer me on by saying that whenever I sowed a field
of wheat or oats or planted a field of corn, nobody could see
a place skipped or skimped when the wheat or oats came
up, and the corn rows were straight as if laid by a ruler.

"I have never claimed any genius, and if it will encourage
any farm boy to have me say so, you may say that if I
have gotten anywhere, it has only been by downright hard
work and a determination to give every job the best that
was in me. It was that habit I learned between the corn
rows on a Missouri farm that enabled me to do my work
better than the public expected of me as chairman of the

Truman Committee investigating war contracts. And the surprise I gave the country by doing this sort of usual job unusually well—that's the real reason I was made vice president in 1944—and so became president in 1945."

"Did you have trouble learning to be a good speaker?" I next asked.

Mr. Truman answered this one with emphasis. "I had a veritable heck of a time—and you can make that stronger if you want to," he answered. "Why, the first time I was ever scheduled to make a political speech I was so scared I could not say a word! It's amazing that they elected me anyhow—but my stubbornness kept me trying until I learned that to be a good speaker, only two things are needed: you just need to have something worthwhile you believe in and then say it in plain cornfield language anybody can understand."

One paragraph from my interview with Mr. Truman may very appropriately sum up his basic message to all young people: "Learn all you can about each job you tackle. Any success I have achieved as president is largely due to the fact that I have all my life been an enthusiastic student of history and biography—a student of all that history could teach me about men and governments, ancient and modern. Tell the boys who can't go to college that they can go a long, long way toward educating themselves if they will read enough and purposefully enough."

As a member of the International Development Advisory Board headed by Nelson Rockefeller, I had frequent contacts with Mr. Truman. Once when I suggested to him that maybe he had never had to buck up against any such discouragements as most of us run into, he answered: "Haven't I though? Haven't I though? Just listen: I wanted to be a musician and worked at it so hard I'd get up at five o'clock in the morning and practice two hours on a stretch without anybody making me—and yet in the end I had to own up that I couldn't make the grade as a musician. Then because financial conditions wouldn't let me go to a regular college, I tried to get into West Point and then into Annapolis, but my weak eyes kept me out of both. Then I tried a haberdashery business and the Depression ruined my business (as it did nearly everybody else's at that time). I wouldn't take bankruptcy, but we went broke and it took every spare cent I could make for fifteen years to settle the debts I preferred to shoulder rather than to dodge."

In concluding this interview with President Truman in the White House I said, "I wonder if you would be willing to list a half dozen rules you would suggest that every ambitious farm boy might well consider in order to be a success as a man, a farmer, and a citizen?" In reply he offered these six rules: to every job you undertake—no matter how big or how little—always give everything that is in you. Always aim to do it better than you are expected to; always resolve to learn every important thing there is to learn about any job you have to do—no matter how big or little—and also how to get people who work with you to do their best; never let discouragement get you down; keep fighting all your life for some great cause outside yourself—some movement or program not yet popular or not yet generally understood or accepted; have a personal ideal of life and conduct by which you will measure yourself every day and come back to it continuously and persistently—even though you sometimes trip, sometimes stumble, perhaps sometimes fall. And as soon as you are old enough, find a fine, smart girl you like, stick right to her till you get her—and then keep on sticking to her forever after!"

To illustrate his fourth rule the President declared that all his life he had made it a major hope and purpose to help end war and promote world peace. With this always in mind he said he has carried in his pocket for more than thirty years these lines from Tennyson:

Till the war-drum throbb'd no longer, and the battle-flags
    were furl'd
In the Parliament of Man, the Federation of the world.

There the common sense of most shall hold a fretful realm
    in awe,
And the kindly earth shall slumber, lapt in universal law.

CHAPTER SIXTEEN

About Myself

"NO MAN HAS REALLY LIVED UNTIL HE HAS BUILT A HOUSE, planted a tree, written a book, and gotten a child," says an ancient proverb. But if its author had been older and wiser, he would have added, "and until he has experienced a great love and endured a great sorrow." This book is not a formal autobiography, but it is proper in concluding it to talk of some of life's deeper experiences and the ideals I have sought to follow over the years.

Returning to North Carolina from our European wedding trip in 1912, Alice and I found a warm welcome from our many Raleigh friends. These included my faithful saddle horse "Sunny Jim" who had, however, misbehaved one time during my absence by running away in front of the Governor's Mansion when my sister-in-law, Mary Aycock, was trying to drive him to a buggy. He may have thought his social status impaired by having to pull a buggy instead of being ridden under a saddle!

After we had bought a neat, two-story house on Peace Street at what now seems like a ridiculous price of $4,000 and added a sleeping porch such as doctors at that time recommended that people endure even in the coldest winters, we settled down to homemaking, housekeeping, and preparation for the arrival of the first of the three children who were to provide us life's greatest happiness. Not long after we had settled on Peace Street, we began to plan for a home in the country. For me country life not only had all its normal appeals, but I also wished to put into actual practice all the best methods of crop production, animal production, and marketing we were advocating in our magazine.

Since horseback riding was my favorite daily exercise and means of transportation, it was almost literally true that in my efforts to find a beautiful building site Sunny Jim and I learned every pigpath within seven miles of Raleigh. Always looking for the high places affording widest panoramic views, I finally decided that no other place equaled a high hill overlooking the Neuse River on the east and Crabtree Creek on the north. To this original purchase of ninety acres I gradually added about a dozen smaller tracts until I had a complete unit of about seven hundred acres, where I regularly grew cotton, tobacco, and truck crops and established an excellent herd of purebred Jerseys—activities that led to my becoming president of the State Dairymen's Association in 1929-30 and president of the Jersey Cattle Club. I still think that the head of a purebred Jersey is one of the most beautiful of all forms of animal life. Not only did I plant many trees and flowering shrubs but made it a rule to cut no dogwoods, redbuds, or deciduous holly in my woodlands, and to let the largest trees grow to still ampler proportions. A neighbor once remarked, "Them trees ought to thank God they belong to Dr. Poe. But for that some saw-mill man would have had 'em long ago." My custom of horseback riding also enabled me to watch the progress of crops, cattle, and woodlands. My standard rule was to ride horseback every day unless the thermometer dropped below 18° and to "park" Sunny Jim a few blocks from my office.

Eventually a considerable part of my land came into demand for residential purposes. To this end I organized Longview Gardens, Inc., with the aim of developing "Raleigh's Most Beautiful Subdivision."

Alice and I enjoyed our children and enjoyed having them and their many friends at our spacious twelve-room home built of native stone in 1925, and we brought them to maturity with nothing but pleasure. Before we knew it they were old enough to go to college, choose careers, and to marry.

The older of my two sons, Charles Aycock Poe, preferred to take up the profession of his maternal grandfather, Governor Aycock. After completing his studies at Chapel Hill he began the practice of law in Raleigh, first as an assistant of Governor J. C. B. Ehringhaus. Before the outbreak of World War II he had associated himself with the FBI and was asked to continue in that service until the war's end. As a member of the FBI Charles's duties carried him to several important Eastern cities and involved adventures of which he could tell us little or nothing until after the war's end. One of the stories that especially interested me was this: He was located in a city in which a number of important plants were working day and night turning out munitions for shipment to the Allies. Everybody at that time was on the lookout for spies and at one particular plant a new worker fell under strong suspicion. The wastebaskets containing correspondence with the firm, or at least some carbons of correspondence, were carried out daily to a place not far away for burning—and this new individual was discovered to be frequently going to this place about nightfall and searching with eager interest through whatever he found there. So concerned did the plant officials become that they began to fake letters for the special purpose of misleading Mr. Suspect. They would write letters reporting operations and conditions exactly in reverse of the fact and let carbons of these letters be carried out in the wastebaskets for the special purpose of misinforming the enemy. The FBI continued its investigation for a time, then pounced upon the suspect— only to find that he had long been known by close friends in a former city as a stamp collector and had merely been looking for stamps from foreign countries.

My younger son, William Dismukes Poe, studied for three years at State College, majoring in agricultural economics, and then two years at Chapel Hill, majoring in journalism. First a member of our advertising staff, he transferred to editorial work and then volunteered for regular army service in World War II. I remember a morning when he and his wife joined in saying to me, "When so many others are going we both feel it is his duty to go with them and you *must not* stand in the way of his doing so." After preliminary training at Fort Bragg he served in several other places and was apparently scheduled to join in the massive assault on Japan when the dropping of bombs on Hiroshima ended the war.

Before the outbreak of World War II, Charles had married Miss Betty Shigley of Lansing, Michigan, and William, Miss Rosalie Richardson of New Bern. My daughter, Jean Shepperd, after attending Peace and St. Mary's, took her final two years of college work at Mary Baldwin College. Then after taking a commercial course and doing some secretarial work, she married Gordon Smith, Jr., of Raleigh in 1941. Having graduated in engineering at N. C. State College, he served in the army first in the Pentagon and later in Puerto Rico, and was retired as a lieutenant colonel. Since the war he has been in business in Raleigh. And to have Jean's family and those of Charles and William (seven grandchildren in all) so near us has been a constant delight and satisfaction.

All during World War II, I found some relief from its strain by meetings of the Watauga Club (of which I was president) every other Tuesday night and the Sandwich Club every other Friday night. Nearly every member had some son or near kinsman in the struggle. It was a happy time when all the boys could come marching home—my own boys and the sons of my associates.

An old friend of mine, Currin Keeble, used to say, "People are fools about their children and damn fools about their grandchildren," and I have found this practically true in my own case. But the arrival of my first grandchild presented a problem in semantics. Much as I liked and loved every grandchild, the word "grandfather" suggested an image I strongly disliked. The average grandfather today is younger than when I grew up. The phrase then suggested some venerable citizen "whose beard descending swept his aged breast." I accordingly had my grandchildren call me not "Grandfather" but "Bah-bah." And about the happiest time of our lives came when each summer we took a seaside cottage at Atlantic Beach and conducted what was called "Bah-Bah's Seaside University—With Courses in Astronomy, Gastronomy, Piscatology, Canasta, and Velleity." (That last word may send many to the dictionary but mainly I think it is a disinclination for any kind of work.) All these courses proved enjoyable and at the end of each session I put on one of the colorful academic robes—cap and gown—I had received from one of the five colleges and universities that had then given me honorary doctorates, and with great dignity handed out to each grandchild a certificate duly signed, sealed, and delivered much in the form of a college degree!

At home we had enjoyed having each child and grandchild for supper on his or her birthday with all the rest of the family as fellow guests. For a long time Alice or I provided numerous verses for the occasion. This function has now

largely been taken over by the children and grandchildren.
Some of these verses have been of the traditional kind but
others have illustrated the camaraderie of our group such as
this couplet from Charles:

> So in conclusion I say to my parents
> Thank you so much for not naming me Clarence!

On the anniversary of our golden wedding we gave a party
and I remarked to our guests, "Alice and I have been married fifty years and she has never tried to shoot me but
once." Instantly of course the astonished guests wanted
fuller details and she insisted on my supplying them. What
had happened was this: Just after we had moved to our
house in the country with no houses nearby, I left one night
for a meeting in Raleigh, saying I would get back home
about ten o'clock. Alice is the world's champion locker-up
and I often tell her, "If you should get to heaven first and
I later I know your first question will be, 'Did you get
everything in the house well locked up before you left?' "
So after telling her to expect me about ten o'clock, I went
to Raleigh and she immediately locked herself and our small
children in an upstairs bedroom, taking my revolver with
her and making sure all downstairs doors were locked. But
the meeting I was to attend was cancelled and I reached home
a couple of hours earlier than she had expected. After shak-
ing and knocking every door and ringing every bell I finally
somehow managed to get inside through the furnace room
and had started up the stair-steps when she called through
the door, "Who is it? Who is it?" "It is I—Clarence," I replied. But by that time she was so excited she wouldn't trust
my voice and answered, "No, it isn't! *No, it isn't!* It doesn't
sound like him and I am going to shoot." I then said, "Don't
shoot—I'm the man you married on May 29, 1912!" That
identification proved so satisfying that she threw down her

pistol, broke into tears, and has never tried to shoot me since.

On January 10, 1958, when I reached age seventy-seven, I confidently looked forward to seeing my younger son William share with me in ever-increasing degree all my activities as farm editor and farm leader and to continue till my life's end as my comrade and daily companion in our work. But at daybreak a few weeks later Charles and Jean awakened Alice and me and when I asked, "Where is William?" received the whispered answer, "He has gone to God."

Seemingly in the very glow and prime of health and vigor he had only the previous afternoon delivered in Birmingham what his hearers called "an electrifying speech." It was an inspiring speech that he had asked the privilege of making to cheer all his fellow workers in the very gloomiest day of the 1958 recession when their salaries had just been severely cut and the whole American business outlook was alarmingly dark. After speaking and then hurriedly catching a plane, he had been carried off by a heart attack in his sleep on the homeward-bound night trip to Raleigh.

A further word about William is necessary here if the full degree of my loss is to be understood. Returning to Raleigh after World War II, he had become my associate editor and served so well that in 1956 he was made vice president and editor-in-chief of our Carolinas-Virginia edition, while I served as senior editor and board chairman (as I am still doing). Finding himself also in almost constant demand as a speaker, William accepted many invitations and made constant advancement both by voice and pen as a spokesman for our farm people. As Chancellor Bostian of State College said of his untimely death, "It was a great loss to his state and the nation; at an early age he had emerged to become one of America's key figures in agricultural journalism."

For the superior or princely man merely to do "the right

thing" is not enough; certainly it was not enough for William Poe. He approved Thomas Davidson's test for any situation, "Ask yourself what does nobility command?" Not merely to do the right thing, but the helpful, gracious, and if possible the inspiring thing—this was his constant purpose. To illustrate the feeling our farm people had for him nothing could be more revealing than the resolution adopted by the 1958 meeting of the North Carolina Master Farm Families' Association:

"Now and for always, his name stands immortal in the hearts and minds of the farm people. We who stand on the shore will often in memory envision him as we recall those things he said and did to make our lives richer, better, and happier. What shall we say of one who loved us and our way of life, whose heart burned with our problems, whose mind worked for our good, whose voice spoke always in our behalf and whose fingers wrote of our needs and problems, whose handshake inspired our hands to nobler work, whose smile encouraged us in our darkest hour, and whose life inspired us to higher, nobler living?"

Of William himself perhaps I have spoken adequately. Now, however, my best opportunity for service to my readers may be to mention some of the things that helped me endure the shock of his passing and that may therefore help others who have suffered—or may yet suffer—a similar loss. Speaking from my own heart two years later I sought to carry a message to all those who, having lost loved ones, had found it hard to make the severest readjustment of their lives. As I said:

"The first thing to do is this: *Try to put your experience in proper perspective.* You have had a great sorrow. But would you not agree with what Tennyson wrote after the death of his beloved young friend, Arthur Hallam—

'Tis better to have loved and lost
Than never to have loved at all.

"Suppose you have lost a child. Yet would you not agree
with that poignant sentiment in one of James Whitcomb
Riley's poems in which a woman who has no children seeks
to comfort a bereaved mother—

But ah! so sadder than yourselves am I,
Who have no child to die.

"Or if, having lost one child, you think you have known
the ultimate in sorrow, may you not well think of the far
greater tragedies fifty to one hundred years ago when such
things happened as in my old home neighborhood where
one man lost seven children from typhoid fever and two
other families lost four boys each from diphtheria?

"Work is the one supreme antidote for sorrow that earth
can offer and you must change futile sorrow into fruitful
service. We even have a modern phrase for it, 'You must
sublimate your sorrow' by love and service to other people.
Be happy by helping others be happy. The wisest and most
Christian attitude is not to fruitlessly lament that a loved one
is no longer with us but to thank God that for so long we
were blessed by that loved one's radiant presence."

Of all the things I have ever written I think William
probably liked most the concluding paragraph of an address
I had made to our North Carolina Press Association. I say
this not only because it expressed the *spirit* in which we had
constantly worked together but also because it suggested the
wide range of betterment we sought to bring about in Southern life in general and in farm life in particular:

"It matters little whether men tomorrow will remember
or forget the mere combination of consonants and vowels
which make our names. It matters little whether men to-

morrow will treasure in painting or sculpture or utterly forget the form of our bodies and the mould of our features.
But what does matter mightily is that in the hearts and
hopes and spirits of men there shall live on and gleam on
some flame that we have kindled. To live on in some consolidated school which insures a larger opportunity for childhood; in the lightened labors of some housewife to whom
home demonstration work has brought more of leisure and
recreation; in the happy smile of some boy or girl to whom
improved health facilities have meant joy and strength; in
some public library which immeasurably widens the intellectual horizon of the community; in some new and larger
appreciation of beauty in art or nature, or in some passion for
justice which sweetens law and life—this is our high privilege.
To win such a simple but genuine immortality is better than
to have the empty glory of any career, however dazzling,
which burnt itself out in serving the ends of self. May every
one of us get such a vision of his possibilities for service and
strive for their fulfillment, finding while he lives the happiness of constructive activity and dying—

> . . . . Join the choir invisible
> Of those immortal dead who live again
> In minds made better by their presence. . . .
> Whose music is the gladness of the world."

About denominational differences or creeds, I have always had little interest. Rather I have felt that the essence
of Christianity is expressed in the two great Commandments, to love God and to love your neighbor as yourself.
I have also felt that these principles are exemplified in the
Parable of the Last Judgment. There the supreme question
is not "What was your creed or denomination or profession?" Rather it is, "What did you do or fail to do in service
to others—the needy, the hungry, the sick, the poorly clad,

the prisoner, and the stranger (the stranger being anyone separated from us by distance, creed, color, education, or poverty)?" Always, too, I have felt that this parable implies the duty not only of meeting the physical needs of others but also the duty of helping enrich life for all classes. Many of our wealthiest people are sorely in need of an enrichment of life. Hence more frequently than almost any other sentence I have quoted a remark the poet Edwin Markham once made to me, "Man's supreme needs are represented by three B's: Bread, Beauty, and Brotherhood."

Starting then with these three texts from the Christian religion—the two great Commandments and the Last Judgment—I would next mention three wonderful texts that for many years I kept framed and hung in my office:

First, a quotation from Confucius written in Chinese for me by a descendant of Confucius of the seventy-fifth generation.

Second, an autographed copy of an extract from a stirring message to young men by Rudyard Kipling entitled "The Man to Watch."

Third, a quotation from a remarkable statement, "The Secret of Influence," autographed for me by my constant friend, Ambassador James Bryce, afterward Lord Bryce.

The quotation from Confucius I obtained in Peking when I became acquainted with a promising young Chinese university student, young Mr. Kung Hsiang Koh (Kung is the family name of Confucius, the Chinese always putting the family name first). I merely asked if he would write for me in Chinese characters one of my favorite texts from his illustrious ancestor. Instead he sent me a handsomely executed scroll about three feet long accompanied by a quaint volume about which he added in awkward English, "I believe you favour Confucius's words and therefore I want to present to you a book of Confucian Analects. The seal which

put on the scroll in center has following—the 75th descendant of Confucius." The saying from Confucius reads as
follows:

"Szema-New asked about the Superior Man. The Master
said, 'The superior man is without anxiety or fear.'

" 'Being without anxiety or fear,' said New, 'does this
constitute what we should call the superior man?'

"The Master replied, 'Yes, when a man looks inward and
finds no guilt there, why should he grieve? Or of what
should he be afraid?' "

The quotation that Rudyard Kipling autographed at my
request was accompanied by a letter dated "Burwash, Sus-
sex, 9th Dec., 1909." What he autographed for me was a
passage from an address Kipling had recently delivered in
McGill University. It is a superb illustration both of Kipling's powerful masculine style and of his deep moral conviction. Almost like a passage from some flaming Old Testa-
ment prophet thundering the anathemas of God against the
sins of his age, it reads as follows:

"Sooner or later you will see some man to whom the idea
of wealth as mere wealth does not appeal, whom the methods of amassing that wealth do not interest, and who will not
accept money if you offer it to him at a certain price. At first
you will be inclined to laugh at this man, and to think that
he is not smart in his ideas. I suggest that you watch him
closely, for he will presently demonstrate to you that money
dominates everybody except the man who does not want
money. You may meet the man on your farm, in your village,
or in your legislature. But be sure that, whenever or wherever you meet him, as soon as it comes to a direct issue
between you, his little finger will be thicker than your
loins. You will go in fear of him; he will not go in fear of
you. You will do what he wants; he will not do what you
want. You will find that you have no weapon in your armory

with which you can attack him; no argument with which you can appeal to him. Whatever you gain he will gain more.

"I would like you to study that man. I would like you better to be that man, because from the lower point of view it doesn't pay to be obsessed by the desire of wealth for wealth's sake. If more wealth is necessary to you, for purposes not your own, use your left hand to acquire it, but keep your right for your proper work in life. If you employ both arms in that game you will be in danger of stooping; in danger also of losing your soul."

In my quotation from Lord Bryce he mentions four elements, "two or more of which," he said, "will be found to be always present in whoever leads, or is trusted by, or inspires, those among whom his lot is cast" as follows:

"1. *Initiative*—the power of thinking for oneself instead of borrowing thoughts from others, and of deciding on a course instead of having to ask for and follow others.

"2. *Tenacity of Purpose*—Whoever, lacking this, lets himself be blown about by every wind of doctrine or every pressure of menace or persuasion may be a very acute man or a very adroit man, but will never impress himself on others as a person to be followed.

"3. *Sound Judgment*—The man who sees several moves ahead and whose forecast is usually verified by the event, soon grows to be the man whose advice is sought and taken. . . ."

For myself I have always been most impressed by the fourth of the secrets of influence listed by Lord Bryce:

"4. *Sympathy*—That is the possession of a capacity for entering into the thoughts of others and of evoking their feelings by showing that he can share them. The power of sympathy is so far an affair of the emotions that it may exist in persons of no exceptional abilities. Yet it is a precious gift, which often palliates errors and wins affection in spite of faults and weaknesses. It is a key to unlock men's hearts."

So far I have quoted from the rich thoughts of other men: Confucius from the Orient, Lord Bryce and Rudyard Kipling from England. Some ideals that came directly from my own heart were included in A Morning Prayer: Ideals for a Working Day, which I wrote on my twentieth birthday and which may well conclude this book:

"O Thou Eternal God, Master of All Good Workmen, for this new day with its new tasks and its new opportunities for faithful effort, I thank Thee.

"With the fled past and the uncertain future, I can now do nothing; today alone Thou givest me to shape and mould while yet I can, into an epitome of that complete life to which I aspire. Worthy and noble therefore, O God, make my ideals for this day.

"Not great tasks, but tasks greatly done make Thou my first high aim, teaching me that it is better to till a garden skilfully than to rule a kingdom wretchedly, and that the approval of one's own conscience is rather to be chosen than the plaudits of the multitude.

"Diligent in business let me be, falling below the best that is in me in no task, large or small, that I undertake. And making sure of this, let no seeming failure shake my courage or ruffle my spirit. Any evil that can be remedied, let me remedy, losing no time in worrying; any evil that cannot be remedied let me not make doubly evil by unmanly repining.

"Nor let me sacrifice, O Lord, in any toilsome quest of wealth or power, Thy greater glories nearer at hand. Whether or not the beauty of mansions be mine, let me look gratefully on the beauties of Nature—fruitful lands and restless seas and starry heavens. Whether or not ease and luxury be within reach, let me know the physical pleasure of vigorous health and of honest toil and wholesome play. And however far removed from any measure of fame or greatness, let me rejoice that for me is the common happiness that comes through love and friendship, and for me the spiritual delight of striving, even in our clumsy and blundering fashion, toward the Ideal that Thou givest us to dream of. So may I this day, working strenuously and yet with cheerfulness and serenity, make a record a little more worthy than yesterday's and—

> Earn for myself the evening rest,
> And an increase of good for man.
> Amen."